Five Dimensions of Quality

The Jossey-Bass Higher and Adult Education Series

Five Dimensions of Quality

A COMMON SENSE GUIDE TO ACCREDITATION AND ACCOUNTABILITY

Linda Suskie

Foreword by Stanley O. Ikenberry
Professor and President Emeritus, University of Illinois, and
Co-Principal Investigator, National Institute for Learning
Outcomes Assessment

JB JOSSEY-BASS™
A Wiley Brand

Cover design by Wiley

Published by Jossey-Bass
A Wiley Brand
One Montgomery Street, Suite 1200, San Francisco, CA 94104-4594—
www.josseybass.com/highereducation

Jossey-Bass books and products are available through most bookstores. To contact Jossey-Bass
directly call our Customer Care Department within the U.S. at 800-956-7739, outside the U.S.
at 317-572-3986, or fax 317-572-4002.

Wiley publishes in a variety of print and electronic formats and by print-on-demand. Some
material included with standard print versions of this book may not be included in e-books or
in print-on-demand. If this book refers to media such as a CD or DVD that is not included in
the version you purchased, you may download this material at http://booksupport.wiley.com.
For more information about Wiley products, visit www.wiley.com.

**Library of Congress Cataloging-in-Publication Data has been applied for and is on file with
the Library of Congress.**

ISBN 978-1-118-76157-1 (hbk); ISBN 978-1-118-76150-2(ebk); ISBN 978-1-118-76140-3

Printed in the United States of America
FIRST EDITION
HB Printing   10 9 8 7 6 5 4 3 2 1

To my husband Steve and our children Melissa and Michael

To everyone whose passion is helping students get the best possible education

And in memory of Petey

● CONTENTS

LIST OF TABLES AND EXHIBITS   ix
LIST OF JARGON ALERTS   xi
LIST OF ACRONYMS   xv
FOREWORD   xix
PREFACE   xxv
ACKNOWLEDGMENTS   xxxi
ABOUT THE AUTHOR   xxxiii

INTRODUCTION:
Today's Quality Context   1
   1. Why Is American Higher Education Under Fire?   3
   2. Understanding American Accreditation   11
   3. Quality: Committing to Excellence   25
   4. Why Is This So Hard?   35

DIMENSION I:
A Culture of Relevance   49
   5. Integrity: Doing the Right Thing   51
   6. Stewardship: Ensuring and Deploying Resources
     Responsibly   59

DIMENSION II:

A Culture of Community 75

7. A Community of People 77

8. Leadership Capacity and Commitment 89

DIMENSION III:

A Culture of Focus and Aspiration 97

9. Purpose: Who Are You? Why Do You Exist? 99

10. Goals and Plans: Where Are You Going? How Will You Get There? 107

11. Who Is a Successful Student? 119

12. Helping Students Learn and Succeed 129

DIMENSION IV:

A Culture of Evidence 145

13. Gauging Success 147

14. Good Evidence Is Useful 161

15. Setting and Justifying Targets for Success 167

16. Transparency: Sharing Evidence Clearly and Readily 177

DIMENSION V:

A Culture of Betterment 189

17. Using Evidence to Ensure and Advance Quality and Effectiveness 191

18. Sustaining a Culture of Betterment 197

CONCLUSION:

Integrating and Advancing the Five Dimensions of Quality 209

19. Demonstrating Quality to Accreditors 211

20. Program Reviews: Drilling Down into Programs and Services 229

21. Where Do We Go from Here? A Six-Point Agenda for Ensuring and Advancing Quality 239

REFERENCES 249

INDEX 265

LIST OF TABLES AND EXHIBITS

Table 12.1 Strategies That Help Students Learn 130

Exhibit 12.1 Curriculum Map for a Hypothetical
Four-Course Certificate Program 135

Exhibit 12.2 Template for a Curriculum Map for a Course
Syllabus 136

Table 13.1 Examples of Dashboard Indicators for Some
Hypothetical College Goals 151

Exhibit 15.1 Rubric Results for a Hypothetical Assessment
of Written Communication Skills 168

Exhibit 16.1 A Dashboard for a Hypothetical College
Strategic Goal 182

Exhibit 18.1 Sample Template for Documenting Nascent
Student Learning Assessment Processes 204

Exhibit 18.2 Rubric to Appraise a College's Culture
of Evidence and Betterment 207

Table 19.1   Comparison of Research Reports and
             Accreditation Reports   219

Table 19.2   Examples of Assertions with Suitable
             Evidence in Accreditation Reports   221

Table 20.1   Questions to Consider in Proposals for
             New Initiatives and in Academic Program
             Reviews   233

● LIST OF JARGON ALERTS

In lieu of a traditional glossary, this book has "Jargon Alert!" sidebars sprinkled throughout that explain some of the jargon used in the worlds of higher education, accreditation, and accountability.

Academic freedom	44
Accountability	58
Accreditation standards, criteria, and requirements	211
Action steps	113
Assessment	152
Attrition	133
Backwards curriculum design	136
Balanced scorecards	181
Bloom's taxonomy	122
Brightline	183
Capstones	131
Carnegie classification	171

Chief executive officer   90

Closing the loop   191

Competency-based   72

Completion   133

Continuous improvement and continuous quality
    improvement   191

Critical thinking   126

Curriculum alignment and curriculum maps   135

Dashboard indicators   147

Dashboards   181

Data   180

Direct evidence of student learning   157

Environmental scan   110

Financial ratio analysis   61

Flipped classrooms   140

General education   138

Improvement   30

Indirect evidence of student learning   157

Infographics   181

Information   180

Information literacy   123

Institution   4

Institutional assessment   148

Institutional effectiveness   52

Institutional governance   86

Key performance indicators   147

Learning-centered   132

Learning outcomes, learning goals, learning objectives,
    and learning competencies   123

Liberal arts   138

Massive open online courses (MOOCs)   72

Metrics   147

Mission   101

Mission creep   102

Objectives   113

Operational plans   113

Peer review   16

Performance indicators and performance measures   147

Persistence   133

Quality assurance   11

Reliability   164

Retention   133

Scaffolding   131

Scholarship of teaching   68

Stakeholders   51

Strategic goals, strategic directions, and
    strategic aims   107

Student-centered   133

Swirl   9

SWOT analysis   110

Tactical plans   113

Teaching-learning center   83

Title IV gatekeepers   16

Transparency   58

Validity   163

LIST OF ACRONYMS

AAC&U	Association of American Colleges & Universities
AACC	American Association of Community Colleges
AACSB	Association to Advance Collegiate Schools of Business
AASCU	American Association of State Colleges and Universities
AAUP	American Association of University Professors
ACBSP	Accreditation Council for Business Schools and Programs
ACCJC	Western Association of Schools and Colleges (WASC) Accrediting Commission for Community and Junior Colleges
ACCSC	Accrediting Commission of Career Schools and Colleges
ACE	American Council on Education
ACS	American Chemical Society
ACTFL	American Council of Teachers of Foreign Languages
AGB	Association of Governing Boards
AIR	Association for Institutional Research
APLU	Association of Public and Land Grant Universities
ASA	American Sociological Association

ATS	Association of Theological Schools
CCSSE	Community College Survey of Student Engagement
CHEA	Commission on Higher Education Accreditation
CIRP	Cooperative Institutional Research Program
CLA	Collegiate Learning Assessment
C-RAC	Council of Regional Accrediting Commissions
CSWE	Council on Social Work Education
DQP	Degree Qualifications Profile
ED	U.S. Department of Education
FSSE	Faculty Survey of Student Engagement
HEA	Higher Education Act
HEOA	Higher Education Opportunity Act
HLC	Higher Learning Commission of the North Central Association of Colleges and Schools
IACBE	International Assembly for Collegiate Business Education
LEAP	Liberal Education & America's Promise
MFTs	Major Field Tests
MOOCs	Massive open online courses
MSCHE	Middle States Commission on Higher Education
NACIQI	National Advisory Committee on Institutional Quality and Integrity
NACUBO	National Association of College and University Business Officers
NAICU	National Association of Independent Colleges and Universities
NCLEX	National Council Licensure Examination
NEASC	New England Association of Colleges and Schools, Commission on Institutions of Higher Education
NILOA	National Institute on Learning Outcomes Assessment

NLASLA	New Leadership Alliance for Student Learning and Accountability
NSSE	National Survey of Student Engagement
NWCCU	Northwest Commission on Colleges and Universities
OECD	Organisation for Economic Co-operation and Development
P&T	Promotion and Tenure
PP	Proficiency Profile
SACS-COC	Southern Association of Colleges and Schools Commission on Colleges
SCUP	Society for College & University Planning
U-CAN	University and College Accountability Network
USED	U.S. Department of Education
VALUE	Valid Assessment of Learning in Undergraduate Education
VFA	Voluntary Framework for Accountability
VSA	Voluntary System of Accountability
WASC Senior	Western Association of Schools and Colleges Accrediting Commission for Senior Colleges and Universities
YFCY	Your First College Year

● FOREWORD

Accreditation of colleges and universities in the United States may be the linchpin that holds our highly decentralized and incredibly diverse academic enterprise together, but it is also one of the most poorly understood and controversial features of American higher education. Even for many academics, accreditation remains a mystery. Most faculty members and many academic administrators have had little or no direct involvement with the purposes and processes of accreditation and see it as a mysterious external force, intrusive and demanding, unnecessarily burdensome and distracting.

Critics from outside the academy tend to be even more skeptical, but for quite different reasons. Some policymakers, for example, see accreditation as self-serving, an affinity group of insiders in which academics scratch one another's backs. Grievances are often contradictory: accreditors are too lax and indecisive—or—too harsh, uncaring, and precipitous.

Just what does "accreditation" really mean? On what grounds are decisions made to grant or withdraw accreditation? Why have the standards and expectations of the seven regional accrediting groups come under scrutiny?

Answers to these and similar questions have evolved and changed over time. In the beginning, accreditation was created by colleges and universities themselves to serve the needs of the academy. Which academic institutions were legitimate colleges and what academic work should be accepted for transfer? Status as an accredited college or university helped answer these practical questions.

Over time, however, the functions of accreditation expanded. Oversight and assurance of academic quality and student success remains paramount, but the list of users of accreditation has grown to include members of the general public, employers and—particularly relevant to this book—the federal government. With literally thousands of institutions offering academic programs and degrees, which institutions are reputable? Which should be eligible to receive federal funds for student aid and research? The federal government relies on accreditation to inform these and other national policies.

While the functions and uses of accreditation by governments, employers, academic institutions, and the general public are many, they signal a fundamental truth: the quality of American higher education matters more than ever before. For today's college graduates who will live and work in a dynamic global society and economy, what they know and can do will shape their lives and define their place in the world. For those who pay for college—students, parents, governments, donors, and others—concerns for value escalate along with price. The success of businesses that recruit college graduates will turn on quality—what those new employees know and can do. The quality of life and economic competitiveness of communities and regions are tied to the strength of the academic institutions that serve them. Virtually everyone has a huge stake in the learning outcomes that flow from college and, as a result, accreditation is in the spotlight as never before. The key questions become: Who will assess academic quality and institutional integrity? What standards will be applied? and What evidence will inform accreditation decisions?

In most other nations, academic quality assurance is a governmental function. That a non-governmental agency such as a regional accreditation commission would play such a role would be—to say the least—novel. It would be especially difficult to understand why colleges and universities themselves—as is the case in the United States—would be allowed to perform such tasks, which raises the question: Why is it that this quite different approach to quality assurance—accreditation—has evolved in the United States?

In retrospect, the answer appears obvious. Unlike most other nations, the United States has no Ministry of Education and no direct governance control over the higher education enterprise. While federal policies shape higher education in myriad ways, direct oversight and governance are diffused among the fifty states and thousands of independent governing boards. The result is an incredibly diverse array of academic institutions with quite different histories, missions, and academic programs serving students with widely varying expectations and capacities. For this country, regional accreditation played a crucial role in enabling the "system" to work, to evolve, and to flourish in response to changing needs in the society and the academy.

What has been the result? To the extent higher education in the United States is recognized as among the best in the world, some credit is due to the flexible, evolving system of "voluntary accreditation" that began over a century ago. It placed public and private institutions, large and small, under a large common tent. In many practical respects, regional accreditation has served the nation well, preserving academic freedom and protecting institutional autonomy and integrity, while also enabling innovation and experimentation to flourish in ways a governmental bureaucracy might well have resisted.

Even so, the stakes today are higher. Expectations for accreditation are higher, and the critics are more vocal. What began as a "voluntary" commitment by like-minded academic institutions to uphold compatible academic standards is not really "voluntary" any longer for institutions. And as national interests and student aid and research funding have grown more prominent in higher education, the relationship between accreditation and the federal government has become increasingly contentious.

Is there a better way? Might the fifty states take on the quality assurance responsibility? Should a new federal agency be formed to create the capacity for the federal government to make decisions on academic quality and integrity? Is it desirable to create an independent not-for-profit agency totally independent from government and the academic world to make these high-stakes judgments?

Such questions have been debated by academics and policy wonks for decades. Time and again, the consensual view has favored an approach to academic quality assurance that relies on the existing system of regional accreditation that has evolved over many decades—while at the same time pressing for reforms to make accreditation more effective.

The most important and needed step to strengthen accreditation is to increase the amount and quality of the evidence used to support accreditation actions. The central challenge is to define and assemble a range of evidence to confirm that students have learned what institutions and society consider to be important and can transfer this learning to the unscripted problems and circumstances they will face after college. Documenting what students have learned and are able to do and using that information to improve student and institutional performance has moved much higher on the agenda of colleges and universities. Assessment of student learning will continue to be the defining priority for regional accreditation. Issues of institutional capacity and the processes of teaching and learning remain important, but attention has shifted to evidence of results—the outcomes of student learning, student success, and the use of assessment to improve institutional performance.

To preserve the freedom of the academy to define and oversee the quality of higher education, accreditation must be strengthened, and colleges and universities themselves will be indispensible in that challenge. There is no more respected and knowledgeable voice on accreditation in American higher education than Linda Suskie. Drawing on her rich academic experience, she is a highly respected thought leader in accreditation and the assessment of student learning. She helped guide a regional accrediting commission and understands accreditation and the challenges of academic quality and public accountability from a campus perspective. She has shared her many talents and rich experiences as an internationally recognized consultant, speaker, and writer on assessment and accreditation in higher education. She places regional accreditation of institutions in the context of the accreditation of specialized, professional, and disciplinary accreditation.

Most important, Linda Suskie provides in this book a framework to help us think clearly and deeply about questions of quality: what matters to creating a culture of excellence and high aspiration, defining and achieving relevance, and building a learning environment informed by evidence and committed to improvement in a well-functioning academic community.

Ultimately, the quality of American higher education will be defined by the students, faculties, and institutions that create venues to facilitate teaching and learning. The National Institute for Learning Outcomes Assessment recently completed its second national institutional survey of learning outcome assessment on the nation's campuses. Findings confirm continued progress across the nation in gauging student learning and using that evidence to improve decisions and policies that lead to student success. Results also confirm that accreditation remains the prime driver of institutional efforts to assess student learning.

It is important to bring these two worlds of accreditation and quality assessment together, and the pages that follow do precisely that. This book deserves to be read by an exceptionally broad and diverse audience—not just those working with accreditation, but faculty members and college presidents, trustees and government policymakers, foundation heads, and other "thought leaders" inside and outside academe. The quality of American higher education matters immensely, more now than ever before, and all of us must play a role in meeting the challenges and capitalizing on the opportunities that lie ahead.

Stanley O. Ikenberry
April 3, 2014

● PREFACE

For years I have joked about writing my tell-all exposé, relating all that I have seen and heard during my years working for a regional accreditor and as a consultant on assessment and accreditation. I can never do that, of course—my work is confidential. But for a long time, I have been thinking about sharing some of the inspiring work of today's colleges and the advice I have found myself giving frequently on accreditation and accountability. This seems to be the right time to share these things, as conversations and initiatives on higher education quality, accountability, and accreditation multiply by the day.

Opinions and ideas on what is right, what is wrong, and how to fix things in higher education understandably vary, but some enduring, pervasive truths emerge. Everyone cares about higher education more than ever. Everyone recognizes that higher education is more important than ever to the ongoing success of every country on the planet and its people. Everyone wants students to receive the best possible education.

But these simple statements raise powerful questions:

- What *is* the best possible education?
- What is a quality college?

- What is an effective college?
- How can colleges ensure that their students are receiving the best possible education?
- How can colleges demonstrate their quality and effectiveness to accreditors, government policymakers, students, and others?

This book answers those questions by providing straightforward guidance on understanding and meeting calls for ensuring and advancing quality, including responding to calls from accreditors and from others asking for greater accountability.

A Simple Model of Five Dimensions of Quality

I define quality as having five dimensions: *relevance, community, focus and aspiration, evidence*, and *betterment*. They are really cultures of quality, because quality today must be pervasive and enduring, not practices implemented in a few spots before an accreditation review and then forgotten.

A Common Sense Approach to Accreditation and Accountability

I take a practical, common sense approach to my work, and that is what you will find in this book. It offers plenty of sensible tips on how to establish, ensure, and demonstrate the five dimensions of quality. Everything here is based on my experiences working with thousands of people in all higher education sectors and roles in the United States and abroad. This is not theory; this is practice.

How Will This Book Help You?

If you are looking for help with any of the following, you have come to the right place!

We want to improve our college's quality, but the prospect is overwhelming. The fundamental purpose of this book is to help you understand the traits of a quality college in the 21st century through a simple, accessible model designed to work for any college, including those without U.S. accreditation. This book discusses practical issues that should be addressed in order to thrive in these challenging times. It will help you figure out, in a very pragmatic way, what you need to do to improve your college's quality and thereby its sustainability.

We do not understand what our accreditors are looking for. Of course, each accreditor has its own requirements, guidelines, publications, and events, and this book does not supplant those important resources. But many accreditors understandably focus on conveying thoroughly *what* must be done more than on *why* those things must be done.

We know from research (see Chapter 12) that many people find it easier to learn something if they understand why the concept is important and relevant to them. This book provides that understanding of accreditation and accountability with simple, straightforward explanations of the underlying principles behind what accreditors are looking for. Those principles focus on ensuring, rather than reporting, quality and effectiveness, a focus that can help lead you to a successful accreditation experience.

Regional accreditors accredit colleges with a wide range of missions and apply their requirements within the context of those missions. These accreditors are therefore generally not prescriptive about how to comply with their requirements. This book is not prescriptive either, but it gives more concrete suggestions than a regional accreditor might be able to. It points out, for example, that rubrics are often the easiest and fastest tool for assessing student learning.

People sometimes question the quality of our college or ask us to "demonstrate accountability." This book will help any college, including those without U.S. accreditation, identify ways to demonstrate its quality to its stakeholders.

We do not understand all the jargon being thrown around.
It certainly is confusing! The jargon surrounding quality in higher
education can make simple concepts come across as complicated.
What is a mission statement? What is institutional effectiveness?
Top the jargon with the seeming complexity of accreditation
requirements, which can run dozens of pages, and the prospect of
ensuring quality seems overwhelming.

This book explains the concept of higher education quality in everyday terms, using plainspoken language and a simple,
straightforward model for understanding and meeting accreditors' requirements and calls for accountability. (While the
principles in this book are universal, this book focuses on U.S.
regional accreditation.) You will see "Jargon Alerts!" sprinkled
throughout the book to help you deal with confusing vocabu-
lary. Overall, this is designed to be an easy read, quickly digested
even if you are new to higher education or are overwhelmed or
confused by talk of accreditation, assessment, or accountability.

We want to help improve the quality of higher education.
With its forthright approach, simple model, and practical ideas,
this book can help higher education leaders and policymakers,
both in the United States and elsewhere, develop appropriate
strategies and policies for ensuring and advancing the quality of
higher education. The last chapter summarizes my key ideas.

Overview of the Book

This book is divided into seven sections. The first section,
"Today's Quality Context," begins with two chapters designed to
orient you to the current higher education environment: "Why
Is American Higher Education Under Fire?" and "Understanding
American Accreditation." Chapter 3 introduces the five dimensions or cultures of quality using an analogy comparing your college's
journey to a road trip. Chapter 4, "Why Is This So Hard?," explains
many of the reasons why implementing the five cultures of quality

remains so difficult at many colleges. Addressing these challenges is, of course, the focus of the rest of the book.

The next five sections of the book explain the five cultures of quality: relevance, community, focus and aspiration, evidence, and betterment.

The section on the first dimension of quality, "A Culture of Relevance," includes chapters on integrity and stewardship. The section on the second dimension of quality, "A Culture of Community," includes chapters on community and leadership. The next section on the third dimension of quality, "A Culture of Focus and Aspiration," includes chapters on purpose, goals and plans, defining student success, and helping students learn and succeed. The section on the fourth dimension of quality, "A Culture of Evidence," includes chapters on gauging success, characteristics of good quality evidence, setting and justifying targets for success, and sharing evidence. The section on the fifth dimension of quality, "A Culture of Betterment," has chapters on using evidence to ensure and advance quality and effectiveness and sustaining a pervasive culture of betterment.

The final section of the book, "Integrating and Advancing the Five Dimensions of Quality," includes chapters on demonstrating quality through accreditation reviews and program reviews. The final chapter, "Where Do We Go from Here?," lays out a six-point agenda for colleges and higher education leaders who seek to advance quality and effectiveness and closes with additional ideas for accreditors.

Using This Book

If you are looking for a broad overview of what quality means in higher education and the relation of quality to accreditation and accountability, this book is designed to be an easy cover-to-cover read. If you or your accreditor is concerned about a particular dimension or aspect of quality, this book has many short chapters to help you find quickly whatever will help you most. Feel free to jump straight to relevant chapters. Every chapter has plenty of subheadings to help you find what you are looking for.

This book is a relatively brief overview of quality in higher education and does not provide in-depth treatment of any topic. Most chapters end with a "For More Information" section providing seminal readings and key organizations, websites, events, examples, and models.

● ACKNOWLEDGMENTS

I have had the privilege to work with people at hundreds of public and private colleges of all shapes and sizes across the United States and throughout the world. These experiences have given me an incredibly broad overview of higher education. I have met and worked with thousands of faculty and administrators who have offered me insight through anonymous written comments and brief conversations. Many of their thoughts and ideas are reflected in this book, and I only wish I had their names so I could acknowledge them all individually.

My cited sources in this book include personal communications from individuals with whom I have worked or interacted and who shared with me their insight and successes. I want to offer deepest thanks to the very special colleagues and experts who were willing to do this or who otherwise contributed ideas, inspiration, and feedback: Catherine Andersen, Trudy Banta, Alexis Collier, Mark Curchack, August Delbert, Judith Eaton, Douglas Eder, Tami Eggleston, Rose Mary Healy, Elizabeth Jones, George Kuh, Patricia O'Brien, Mary Ellen Petrisko, Lynn Priddy, Jose Jaime Rivera, Jennie Robertson, Ephraim Schechter, Donna Sundre, Lewis Thayne, Belle Wheelan, Elizabeth Ann Whiteman, Ralph Wolff, and Barbara Wright. Special bouquets of gratitude go to Virginia Anderson, John Erickson, Patricia Francis, and Joseph Hoey, all friends as well as experts, who read the entire manuscript and offered wonderful, thoughtful feedback and suggestions. Finally, I am incredibly grateful to Stanley O. Ikenberry for his thoughtful and enlightening foreword.

● ABOUT THE AUTHOR

Linda Suskie is an internationally recognized consultant, writer, speaker, and educator on a broad variety of higher education accreditation and assessment topics. Her book *Assessing Student Learning: A Common Sense Guide* (2009) is one of the best-selling books on assessment in higher education. Her other publications include books, chapters, and articles on assessment, accountability, and survey research.

Linda is now a full-time freelance consultant on assessment and accreditation. Her experience includes serving as a vice president at the Middle States Commission on Higher Education, associate vice president for assessment and institutional research at Towson University, and director of the American Association for Higher Education's Assessment Forum. Her nearly forty years of experience in college and university administration include work in accreditation, assessment, institutional research, strategic planning, and quality management, and she has been active in numerous professional organizations.

Linda has taught graduate courses in assessment and educational research methods and undergraduate courses in writing, statistics, and developmental mathematics. She holds a bachelor's degree in quantitative studies from Johns Hopkins University and a master's degree in educational measurement and statistics from the University of Iowa.

Five Dimensions of Quality

INTRODUCTION:
Today's Quality Context

CHAPTER 1

WHY IS AMERICAN HIGHER EDUCATION UNDER FIRE?

A generation or two ago, accreditation was typically a gentle, collegial affair. Once every few years, a college wrote a report, a team visited and offered some advice, and that was pretty much it. The concept of accountability was not on many folks' radar screens. Government policymakers and the general public seemed to accept that, if a college was accredited, its quality was fine—end of story.

What a different world we live in today! Almost every day seems to bring some new report or statement on the perceived shortcomings and failures of U.S. higher education. Accreditation processes have become more onerous and the aftereffects—an additional report, visit, or public censure—more serious and more numerous, affecting as many as two-thirds of colleges undergoing review.

What on earth has happened? Simply put, there is a growing perception—and evidence—that *U.S. colleges are no longer meeting the United States' needs effectively*. And this concern is broad-based, with four particularly prominent voices:

Jargon Alert!

Institution

Institutions of higher education go by many different names: college, university, institute, school, seminary, and academy, among others. Most people in higher education, including many accreditors, use the generic term *institution* to refer to them all. I have always found that term a bit off-putting. Students in the United States do not "go to institution"; they "go to college." So in this book I use *college* as a generic term to refer to a two- or four-year college, university, and any other institution of higher education.

- Government policymakers, both state and federal
- Private foundations such as Lumina and Gates that are increasingly driving higher education reform (Marcus, 2013)
- Employers
- Students, both currently enrolled and prospective, and their families

There are many other voices, of course, including research organizations such as the National Institute on Learning Outcomes Assessment, higher education associations such as the Association of American Colleges and Universities (AAC&U), and think tanks such as *The Hechinger Report*. But the four voices I have listed—especially government policymakers and private foundations—seem to be driving much of the conversation.

Each of these groups has somewhat different concerns, but there is a good deal of overlap. Government policymakers, for example, want to address the perceived concerns of their constituents, who include employers and students, and students want educations that meet employers' needs.

In what ways do these groups believe that U.S. colleges are no longer meeting U.S. needs effectively? There is a constant ebb and flow of issues raised in op-eds, white papers, and Congressional hearings, of course. But Paul LeBlanc has summed up the major concerns: "Cost, access, quality, productivity, and relevance problems . . . are reaching crisis proportions in higher education" (2013, para. 6). The federal government expresses similar concerns when it defines higher education quality as "compliance with federal law and regulation in relation to *employment, graduation, consumer protection, transparency, and affordability*" (Eaton, 2013, para. 3, emphasis added). Altogether, three general issues have been pervasive over the last decade and show no signs of going away:

- Economic development
- Return on investment
- The changing college student

A fourth key issue, higher education's historic culture of isolation and reticence, is discussed in Chapter 4.

Economic Development

Higher education is under a microscope because it is fast becoming a necessity for economic development, rather than "a luxury or a privilege reserved for the elite" (Duncan, 2013, para. 17). As the Council on Foreign Relations has explained, "Human capital is perhaps the single most important long-term driver of an economy. Smarter workers are more productive and innovative. It is an economist's rule that an increase of one year in a country's average schooling corresponds to an increase of 3 to 4 percent in long-term economic growth. Most of the value added in the modern global economy is now knowledge-based. Education, especially at the college level, will therefore likely become even more important for a nation's economy and an individual's income" (2013, p. 1).

Research confirms this. "Going back to the 1970s, all net job growth has been in jobs that require at least a bachelor's degree"

(Council on Foreign Relations, 2013, p. 5) and, "by 2020, 65 percent of all jobs will require postsecondary education and training, up from 28 percent in 1973" (Carnevale, Smith, & Strohl, 2013, p. 15).

But current U.S. college completion rates raise doubts about whether U.S. colleges can meet these needs (Morrill, 2013). In a competitive global marketplace, "other countries are lifting their high school and college attainment, while the United States is not" (Council on Foreign Relations, 2013, p. 1). The United States no longer leads the world in the rate of college completion; it now ranks twelfth among thirty-six countries in the higher education attainment of 25-34-year-olds (Organisation for Economic Co-operation and Development [OECD], 2013). The United States is now one of only five OECD countries in which the proportion of 25-to-34-year-old men with post-secondary education is *less* than the proportion of 55-to-64-year-old men with post-secondary education.

Higher education needs to be not only available but effective in graduating students with the college-level skills and competencies that employers—and the economy—need. Those skills and competencies are discussed in Chapter 11.

Return on Investment

A generation or two ago, someone with a high school education had a good prospect of making a decent living. But in 2011 the median annual earnings of those in the U.S. holding only a high school diploma was under $24,000 (U.S. Census Bureau, n.d.). This makes postsecondary education an economic imperative for individuals as well as for society. While there are many benefits to a college education, as discussed in Chapter 5, college tuition and fees—and the time students spend in college—are viewed fundamentally as an individual economic investment leading to a better standard of living. Today, about 75 percent of entering full-time first-time students say that a very important reason they are going to college is to make more money, and over 80 percent say an essential or very important goal is to be very well off financially. These percentages are up dramatically from about 45 percent and 33 percent, respectively, forty years ago (Eagan, Lozano, Hurtado, & Case, 2014; Pryor, Hurtado, Saenz, Santos, & Korn, 2007).

At the same time that the need for a college education has been growing, the costs of higher education have been persistently growing faster than the general cost of living (Evans, 2013). Today, the average tuition charged by *public* colleges in the United States is second highest among OECD countries (OECD, 2013), although it is offset to a degree by a federal investment in postsecondary financial aid reaching nearly $180 billion in 2011 (American Council on Education [ACE], 2012).

Why is college so expensive in the United States? A major reason is that it is traditionally a labor-intensive endeavor (Carnevale, Smith, & Strohl, 2013), and many of the costs associated with that model, such as health insurance, facilities upkeep, energy costs, and regulatory compliance, have been spiraling up. Another reason is that state support for public colleges has seen years of decline (Lederman, 2012), pushing more of the cost of public college onto students and their families.

Despite rising costs, an investment in higher education continues to pay off. U.S. citizens with more education are more likely to be employed, are more likely to be working full-time, and earn more on average over their lifetimes (Berger & Fisher, 2013; Council on Foreign Relations, 2013; Looney & Greenstone, 2012; OECD, 2013; Regnier, 2013), with lifetime earnings outstripping their investment. From the 1970s to 2012, the "college wage premium" doubled from 40 percent to 80 percent (Schramm, Aldeman, Rotherham, Brown, & Cross, 2013).

Of course, average earnings are not guarantees. Everyone knows someone with a college degree who is struggling to get by. Earnings of college graduates vary by job: musicians, video producers, preschool teachers, probation officers, social workers, and others in public service and the arts may earn less than accountants, chemists, and engineers. Some employers require college degrees for positions that may not pay well and for which a degree is not essential to job performance. The head of Enterprise Rent-a-Car has said, for example, that Enterprise hires people who are "college educated" simply because it is "a sign to use that they've accomplished something" ("Enterprise asks," 2006, p. 6B).

The variability in earnings of college graduates has led to calls to provide consumer information comparing tuition against starting salaries as a crude measure of return on investment. It has also led to increasing questions across the United States about the value of spending time and tuition on courses such as those in the liberal arts that do not appear to relate directly to a better-paying career. I talk more about the liberal arts and general education in Chapter 12.

The Changing College Student

Anyone who works at a U.S. college today knows that today's students are very different from the college students of a couple of generations ago.

Changing demographics. More people in the United States than ever before are going to college, and they are from increasingly diverse backgrounds. Today, for example, 43 percent of undergraduates are over 24 years old (National Center for Education Statistics [NCES], 2012).

Fewer with the resources to pay for college. The percent of 25-year-olds with student loan debt has increased from 25 percent to 43 percent in less than a decade, and the average student loan balance has nearly doubled in the same time (Brown & Caldwell, 2013).

Weaker preparation for success in college (ACE, 2012). Some of today's college students are those for whom learning does not come easily and who have always struggled a bit in school. Lectures and homework assignments are not enough to help them succeed in college; they need research-informed teaching and support, as discussed in Chapter 12.

Fewer following the traditional college pathway, in which high school graduates immediately go on to college as full-time students and remain at one college until they graduate. Today, only one-quarter of U.S. college students are attending college full-time at residential colleges (Complete College America, 2011). As they increasingly try to balance college classes with a job and family responsibilities, today's students are more likely to "stop out"—stop attending college for a semester or more, and then return—and "swirl" among colleges and programs as their needs, career paths, and lifestyle change and evolve (Kelly & Hess, 2013).

Jargon Alert!

Swirl

Student *swirl* (Adelman, 2006) refers to students moving back and forth among multiple colleges, such as between community and four-year colleges. Students who swirl may not transfer formally from one college to another.

Initiatives to Address These Concerns

In recent years there has been an explosion of efforts attempting to address these concerns, including:

- Research and ventures on improving student learning and student success, discussed in Chapter 12
- Challenges to the traditional higher education model of full-time face-to-face study of credit-bearing courses, discussed in Chapter 6
- The rise of national accountability movements, discussed in Chapter 16

- Advancements and improvements in the assessment of student learning, discussed in Chapter 13
- Calls for accreditation reform, discussed in Chapter 2

For More Information

The two go-to resources for breaking developments in the world of higher education are *The Chronicle of Higher Education* (www .chronicle.com) and *Inside Higher Ed* (www.insidehighered.com). Both deliver daily e-mails with links to the day's news.

Another great resource for cutting-edge information on the forces affecting higher education is the Lumina Foundation's daily e-mail, *Higher Ed News*. It consists of links to news stories and newly released studies, white papers, and the like.

Jeffrey Selingo's *College (Un)Bound: The Future of Higher Education and What It Means for Students* (2013) is an excellent review and analysis of the challenges currently facing U.S. higher education.

CHAPTER 2

UNDERSTANDING AMERICAN ACCREDITATION

In most countries, higher education quality is ensured by a government agency, often called a quality assurance agency. In the United States, quality assurance is the shared responsibility of a "triad" of entities (National Advisory Committee on Institutional Quality and Integrity [NACIQI], 2012):

Jargon Alert!

Quality Assurance

Quality assurance is the term used around the world to describe the systems and processes to ensure higher education quality.

- State agencies that license or otherwise authorize colleges to operate
- Several dozen accreditors, each serving the needs of a different sector of America's incredibly diverse higher education enterprise

- The U.S. Department of Education (ED or USED), which regulates and reviews accreditors and colleges according to the provisions of the Higher Education Opportunity Act (HEOA), as discussed later in this chapter

Members of this triad interact, but not as a seamless, consistent system. Some state agencies, for example, have extensive criteria and processes for review of licensed colleges, while others rely more heavily on accreditors and accreditation reviews.

Accreditors are "owned and operated" by member colleges under the leadership of boards that are elected by the members and composed of individuals from those colleges and members of the public. Requirements, policies, and procedures are approved by the membership or board and enforced by the board.

Accreditors fall into three broad groups.

Regional accreditors accredit entire colleges. They are among the oldest accreditors and collectively accredit the majority of U.S. colleges. They accredit a vast array of colleges, from huge land grant universities to small private seminaries and art schools. Their standards are therefore relatively imprecise, more sets of principles than prescriptive requirements, that are applied in the context of each college's mission.

Specialized or disciplinary accreditors accredit specific programs. Examples include the Council on Social Work Education (CSWE), the Association of Theological Schools (ATS), and ABET (formerly the Accreditation Board for Engineering and Technology). Some specialized accreditors, such as ATS, may accredit entire colleges. The requirements of some specialized accreditors can be quite prescriptive—and for good reason. If graduates of a nursing program have not mastered a particular competency, patients could conceivably die. If graduates of an engineering program have not mastered a particular competency, they could go on to design a bridge that might collapse.

National accreditors, like regional accreditors, accredit entire colleges. Examples include the Accrediting Commission of

Career Schools and Colleges (ACCSC) and the Council on Occupational Education. They typically accredit colleges or post-secondary schools that are not eligible for regional accreditation, such as career schools that do not offer degree programs or colleges that do not require students to complete a liberal arts core.

Regional Accreditors:
The Cornerstone of U.S. Accreditation

The beginnings of regional accreditation go back over a century, when liberal arts colleges and universities began collaborating on standardizing admissions requirements and, ultimately, facilitating student transfer from one such college to another. The idea was that, if students wanted to transfer to your college, your college would accept their credits only if their college was accredited. In those days, students rarely transferred from one part of the country to another, so these groups recognized colleges in discrete geographic regions of the United States. Today there are seven regional accreditors:

- Higher Learning Commission (HLC) of the North Central Association of Colleges and Schools
- Middle States Commission on Higher Education (MSCHE)
- New England Association of Schools and Colleges (NEASC) Commission on Institutions of Higher Education
- Northwest Commission on Colleges and Universities (NWCCU)
- Southern Association of Colleges and Schools Commission on Colleges (SACS-COC)
- Western Association of Schools and Colleges Accrediting Commission for Community and Junior Colleges (ACCJC)
- Western Association of Schools and Colleges Accrediting Commission for Senior Colleges and Universities (WASC Senior)

Accreditors have been described as private clubs (Associated Press, 2013) and, for decades, the analogy was apt. Private clubs are by definition exclusive, and in order to thrive they must maintain a reputation of exclusivity, limiting membership to those they consider appropriate. Private club membership is voluntary; peer pressure notwithstanding, there is no law requiring anyone to join. Private clubs keep an eye on their members' behavior, because one member whose behavior is embarrassing can diminish the reputation of other members and the club itself. ("So and so is a member? But he's a mess! The other members must be a mess, too; they must hide it better. I wouldn't want to join a club with people like that.") Private clubs try to address troublesome members collegially and quietly, through private conversations. If those conversations do the trick, the problem is resolved without any public embarrassment to the club or the member. If not, the club puts the wheels in motion to kick out the member who has become a liability, an action that can become public knowledge.

For generations, regional accreditors followed this general model of exclusivity. Colleges initially "approved" by MSCHE in 1921, for example, included Bryn Mawr College, Georgetown University, Lehigh University, New York University, and the University of Pennsylvania, among others (Middle States Commission on Higher Education [MSCHE], 2009). Regional accreditors defined quality by the strengths of their (prestigious) members, which were largely what I call inputs into the educational process: attributes such as faculty credentials, incoming students' qualifications, library collection, facilities, and money in the bank. The regional accreditors also required—and continue to require—a commitment to the traditional values of higher education, including:

- Study of the liberal arts and sciences
- Shared collegial governance
- Faculty research and scholarship

- Ongoing improvement beyond the minimum required for accreditation
- Collegiality within and across colleges

Actual student learning did not factor much into this equation; the assumption was that if a college had all these inputs, well, of course learning was bound to happen.

Also, for generations regional accreditation was purely voluntary; many colleges operated successfully without accreditation, with quality assurance provided only through state licensure.

And regional accreditors, just like private clubs, have always kept a quiet eye on their members, because continuing to accredit a college of poor quality can damage the reputation of the accreditor and its other member colleges. The accreditors' traditional approach has been to work with troubled member colleges collegially and quietly, giving the college a chance to improve without damaging its public reputation. Only in the rare instances when it has become clear that a college does not have the capacity to bring its quality to an appropriate level has the accreditor traditionally taken steps to remove accreditation and make its action public.

Accreditation as a Process of Collegial Peer Review

Today the foundation of the accreditation process remains peer review. The American Council on Education (ACE) National Task Force on Institutional Accreditation has explained the benefits of peer review: "As in medicine and scientific research, peer review is the foundation of professional integrity and largely defines what it means to be a profession. . . . Peer review also promotes the dissemination and exchange of best practices as faculty and administrators visit other institutions and provide advice designed to improve performance" (2012, p. 12).

Jargon Alert!

Peer Review

Peer review is an accreditation process in which faculty members and/or administrators from peer colleges review evidence from the college under review. They may visit the college to confirm the evidence firsthand.

The Higher Education Act and Title IV

Things began to change in 1965 with passage of the first Higher Education Act (HEA). Title IV of the 1965 HEA established a number of federal postsecondary financial assistance programs, including Pell grants and federally guaranteed student loans. To be eligible for these programs, students must attend a college accredited by an accreditor that is recognized by the U.S. Department of Education as a Title IV gatekeeper.

Jargon Alert!

Title IV Gatekeepers

Accreditors recognized by the U.S. Department of Education as making a college's students eligible to receive Title IV funds are called *Title IV gatekeepers*. Specialized accreditors that do not want or need Title IV gatekeeper status, as well as some Title IV gatekeepers, often seek recognition from the Commission on Higher Education Accreditation (CHEA) (www.chea.org).

After the 1965 HEA was signed into law, colleges that wanted their students to have access to Title IV financial aid programs—and that would be just about every U.S. college—saw accreditation no longer as an option but as a necessity. Hundreds of colleges that had not been accredited sought and earned regional accreditation in the 1960s and 1970s, including most community colleges.

Other accreditation organizations sought Title IV gatekeeper status to meet the needs of colleges that did not meet regional accreditation requirements. The Accrediting Commission of Career Schools and Colleges (ACCSC), for example, was founded in 1965 (n.d., "History of ACCSC," para. 1).

HEA is reauthorized or amended every few years, and each reauthorization brings more requirements for accreditors in order to maintain their federal recognition. Further complexity is added by regulations developed by the U.S. Department of Education (ED) to implement each HEA reauthorization or amendment. For example, if HEA requires colleges or accreditors to report on something, ED regulations explain what to submit, how, and when. (While HEA/Title IV requirements are part of the U.S. accountability picture, this book does not discuss them in any detail, because they are subject to frequent and dramatic change.)

While accreditors are still private membership organizations, accreditors recognized as Title IV gatekeepers are now subject to so many federal regulations that some people (incorrectly) refer to them as quasi-government agencies. If an accreditation policy or requirement does not make sense to you, it may well flow from a federal regulation, with the accreditor no happier about it than you are. SACS-COC lists its requirements flowing from HEA and ED regulations separately from its other requirements and standards (Southern Association of Colleges and Schools Commission on Colleges [SACS], 2012). Even if your college is not accredited by SACS-COC, its separate list is a good way to identify those accreditation requirements that flow directly from federal regulations.

A Focus on Evidence of Outcomes

By the late 1980s, HEA was requiring Title IV gatekeeper accreditors to require the colleges they accredit to demonstrate that they are achieving their missions. Because the fundamental mission of virtually every college is education, this was essentially a requirement to demonstrate that each college's intended student learning outcomes were being achieved by its students.

The 1998 HEA strengthened this language, requiring Title IV gatekeeper accreditors to require colleges they accredit to demonstrate "success with respect to student achievement in relation to the institution's mission, including, as appropriate, consideration of course completion, state licensing examinations, and job placement rates" (1998 Amendments to the Higher Education Act of 1965, Title IV, Part H, Sect. 492(b)(4)(E)). This language has remained largely in place through subsequent amendments and acts. The examples in this statement imply that the federal government defines student achievement as a combination of student learning, course and degree completion, and job placement. After the 1998 HEA, many accreditors rewrote their standards to require more directly and explicitly the assessment of student learning outcomes and other aspects of college mission.

The Spellings Commission and Its Aftermath of Criticisms

In 2006 the Commission on the Future of Higher Education appointed by U.S. Secretary of Education Margaret Spellings (and commonly referred to as the Spellings Commission) issued a report that was highly critical of U.S. higher education, including accreditors. As Judith Eaton has explained, "Accreditation was called upon to provide more robust public accountability, to strengthen the rigor and thoroughness of its reviews, to take responsibility for what were characterized as higher education's limitations in serving students, and serve as a catalyst, not a barrier (as alleged in the report) to educational innovation" (2013, para. 5).

While the Spellings Commission report led to greater federal regulation of accreditors through the 2008 enactment of the Higher Education Opportunity Act (HEOA), criticisms of U.S. accreditation from both within and outside the higher education community have not abated (ACE, 2012; NACIQI, 2012).

Perceptions, whether true or not, include the following. (In Chapter 21, I suggest some ways that accreditors might address some of these perceptions.)

Accreditation is perceived as insufficiently rigorous. Some assert that, because accreditation is a collegial affair, reviewers are loath to create problems for colleagues at the colleges they are reviewing, so shortcomings and failures are swept under the rug.

Accreditation is perceived as inconsistent and unreliable. Some assert that two colleges with similar levels of quality and effectiveness may receive very different accreditation actions, partly because a degree of subjectivity is unavoidable—colleges are complex human enterprises, and many accreditors use volunteer peer reviewers with limited training—and partly because of inconsistency in requirements and procedures across accreditors. A regionally accredited college on the east shore of Lake Champlain in Vermont, for example, must require 40 credits of general education for a bachelor's degree, but one on the west shore in New York can require less. These kinds of disparities can encourage "accreditation shopping" by colleges that operate locations in more than one accreditation region or are located outside the United States and are seeking regional accreditation. Such colleges may try to identify the regional accreditor whose requirements appear easiest to comply with and locate the university's "main" campus in that region.

Accreditors are perceived as slow to remove the accreditation of subpar colleges, although accreditors' hands are tied by federal regulations that require due process before accreditation is removed (ACE, 2012).

Accreditation is perceived as not putting enough emphasis on meeting stakeholder needs, especially relevance and stewardship (Chapters 5 and 6). At this writing, only two of the seven regional accreditors explicitly mention serving the "public good" in their requirements (Higher Learning Commission [HLC], 2013; Western Association of Schools and Colleges Accrediting Commission for Senior Colleges and Universities [WASC Senior],

2013). As noted in Chapter 1, ED defines quality as "compliance with federal law and regulation in relation to employment, graduation, consumer protection, transparency, and affordability" (Eaton, 2013, para. 3), but some of these aspects of quality, such as affordability, have not been consistently areas of accreditation focus.

Colleges are perceived as too complex for accreditors to ensure across-the-board quality. U.S. colleges may offer dozens, if not hundreds, of incredibly diverse programs of study, and there is no simple, cost-effective way to review and validate every single one thoroughly. Some regional accreditors require an ongoing system of program reviews (Chapter 20) but, as with college-wide accreditation reviews, such reviews remain subjective, imprecise processes.

Accreditation findings are not perceived to be communicated transparently. Because of the complexity of most U.S. colleges, their quality and effectiveness cannot be summed into a simple report card or checklist; employment, graduation, and affordability measures do not tell their full story.

Accreditation is pass/fail; excellence is not recognized. The best possible action of many accreditors is simply to reaccredit a college; there is no public action that helps the public separate excellent colleges from the merely adequate. The National Advisory Committee on Institutional Quality and Integrity (NACIQI) has urged the federal government to "afford accreditors greater opportunity to offer more gradations in their accreditation decisions" (2012, p. 6).

The reputation of regional accreditation may be pushing some square pegs into round holes. Because the regional accreditors accredit America's most prestigious colleges, they have the strongest reputations. Today, some employers require job applicants to hold a degree not just from an accredited college but from a regionally accredited college. This has led more and more colleges to seek regional accreditation, even though they may not be a good fit with regional accreditors' traditional values of the liberal arts, shared governance, and academic freedom or with some regional accreditation requirements, such as faculty credentials.

Accreditation is perceived as taking too much time. Colleges can find accreditation work incredibly time-consuming. Some colleges have full-time administrators who work year-round solely on compiling documentation needed for a specialized accreditor. Many colleges have multiple specialized accreditations, and those accreditors have diverse and sometimes conflicting requirements.

Does U.S. Accreditation Work?

While some of the criticisms of America's somewhat messy "system" of quality assurance have merit, the system is not irreparably broken.

Accreditation remains a well-regarded seal of approval on college quality. "Accreditors are the most experienced source of information about academic quality" (NACIQI, 2012, p. 2). U.S. higher education and its accreditors continue to enjoy a good reputation at home and internationally; one indicator of this is the number of requests that U.S. accreditors regularly receive from colleges abroad to apply for U.S. accreditation. Despite recent criticisms, the general public still accepts accreditation as evidence of a college's quality. Indeed, as you might imagine, after years of working for an accreditor, I routinely hear questions from friends and family members along the lines of: "So and so is thinking about applying to X College. Is it any good?" The first three questions I look into are these:

- Is the college accredited?
- Is its accreditor recognized by the U.S. Department of Education or CHEA? Just as there are diploma mill colleges, there are what I call "diploma mill accreditors." An unaccredited college or one accredited by an unrecognized accreditor may be legitimate, but enrolling there is risky, as credits and

degrees earned there may not be accepted by other colleges or by employers.

- Is the college experiencing any difficulties with its accreditor and, if so, what are they? Some concerns, such as an outdated faculty handbook, can be promptly addressed, but sometimes the concerns are so great that the institution's viability or legitimacy is called into question.

Accreditation weeds out the deadwood. Accreditation actions leading to a college's closure are relatively rare, because colleges with the capacity to improve do so. But over the last decade, actions by regional accreditors led to more college closures than actions by the U.S. Department of Education (ACE, 2012). "Negative" accreditation actions, such as warnings, sanctions, or orders to show cause why accreditation should not be removed, increased about 50 percent from 2009 to 2011 and 2012 (Krupnick, 2013).

Accreditation respects and facilitates the diversity and complexity of U.S. colleges, which is the greatest attribute of U.S. higher education (ACE, 2012; Baker, Baldwin, & Makker, 2012) and makes it unique in the world. No matter what students want to learn, no matter how they want to learn it, there is a college in the United States that meets their needs, and that is thanks in large part to an accreditation system that lets that happen. A diverse network of accreditors, each with requirements appropriate to its member colleges, offers a comprehensive, balanced approach to quality and effectiveness that examines all five dimensions of quality discussed in this book. The U.S. accreditation system recognizes that most colleges aim to accomplish a lot more than simply prepare students for jobs. It allows a theology seminary, a research university, and a technology institute to address what is vital to each and to deemphasize what is irrelevant to each.

Accreditation can have high impact, forcing necessary improvements. Ralph Wolff has called accreditation "the most incredible process for institutional transformation that exists" (personal communication, July 17, 2013). Accreditation processes are community-building exercises (Mark Curchack, personal communication, July 11, 2013) that generate useful introspection and ideas, yield helpful recommendations from the review team, and force colleges to address issues that would otherwise be swept under the rug. Lebanon Valley College, for example, used a request for an accreditation report as an opportunity for study and introspection, leading to several "Eureka!" insights that led to tangible improvements (Damiano & Dodson, 2014).

Accreditation is a relatively low-cost system of quality assurance. While accreditation work takes considerable time, the reviews are often conducted by volunteers from peer colleges. This is far less expensive—both to colleges and to taxpayers—than paying government employees to do this work.

For More Information

Your go-to source for accreditation information is, of course, your college's accreditor. Every accreditor has helpful resources on its requirements and procedures. CHEA (www.chea.org) is another important resource.

Paul Gaston's *Higher Education Accreditation: How It's Changing, Why It Must* (2013) offers a comprehensive overview of U.S. accreditation and the issues facing it, and Marylin Newell's three-part series, "The Pursuit of Credibility" (2012a, 2012b, 2012c), offers a succinct history of U.S. accreditation from the perspective of the proprietary sector.

CHAPTER 3

QUALITY
Committing to Excellence

A quality college aims for excellence in all that it does, across five dimensions of quality that are reflected in the requirements of all seven regional accreditors and discussed in this chapter:

- Relevance
- Community
- Focus and aspiration
- Evidence
- Betterment

A Commitment to a Pervasive, Enduring Culture of Excellence

At a quality college, excellence across the five dimensions does not come and go based on an accreditation cycle or the latest accountability kerfuffle. Excellence does not happen in some parts of a college and not others. The commitment to excellence is enduring and pervasive. The dimensions of quality are thus *cultures* of quality, and that is how I refer to them throughout this book.

In the fast-changing world of higher education in the 21st century, a quality college is not static but going on a journey. The five cultures of quality can thus be explained by using the analogy of taking a road trip.

A Culture of Relevance (Chapters 5–6)

If you are taking a road trip on your own, paying for it with your own money, with no one waiting for you at your destination, it may not matter what route you take, when you reach your destination, how you spend your money along the way, or indeed whether you reach your destination at all.

But sometimes the resources for a road trip are not entirely your own. You may be using a borrowed car and money from your grandmother. Both the car owner and your grandmother expect you to use their resources wisely to travel to the destination you have described to them. The car owner expects you to keep the car clean and maintained. Your grandmother probably wants you to enjoy the journey but not dawdle unnecessarily nor spend her money on endless surf and turf dinners. In short, both want you to be prudent stewards of the resources they have entrusted to you.

Just like this underwritten road trip, your college runs on other people's money—tuition and fees from students and their families, grants from government agencies and foundations, contributions from alumni and other donors and investors, endowments funded by money contributed by others—and it has similar responsibilities to them. It keeps its promises to them (Chapter 5), and it is a prudent steward of the resources they have entrusted to it (Chapter 6).

A Culture of Community (Chapters 7–8)

The road trip analogy fails in one respect in defining a quality college. It is possible, with sufficient preparation, to take a road trip alone. But a quality college cannot function without many people—faculty, administrators and staff, governing board members, students, alumni, donors, community leaders—working together to take the college on its journey. A quality college thus has a culture of community characterized by respect, communication, collaboration, and collegiality, among other traits.

A Culture of Focus and Aspiration (Chapters 9–12)

Planning a road trip begins by knowing your starting point and your destination. You can then use a GPS or a paper map to choose the best route to your destination.

A map, whether digital or paper, lets you visualize your route in broad terms and identify key points and choices en route, such as where there are populated areas likely to have good choices for hotels and restaurants. You can also use a map to explain your general route to your grandmother and the car owner.

A list of specific step-by-step, turn-by-turn directions, laying out exactly where you need to drive, may be more useful once your road trip is underway. A friend making the road trip with you in another car may want those turn-by-turn directions to help you both stay together.

A quality college similarly begins its journey knowing where and what it is (Chapter 9) and where it is going (Chapter 10). It also knows who its students are and where they are going (Chapter 11). It then decides how it and its students will reach their destinations (Chapters 10 and 12). It can visualize its destinations and routes in both broad terms, like a map, that are engaging and compelling to its stakeholders and in specific terms, like step-by-step directions, that provide concrete guidance to the college community.

A Culture of Evidence (Chapters 13–16)

If you have to reach a specific street address by a specific time and within your budget, you will likely judge your road trip a success if:

- You reach your destination.
- You reach your destination on time, or at least not so far behind schedule that the delay creates problems. You would not want to arrive so late that you miss a wedding, for example.
- You reach your destination without spending significantly more money than you had anticipated.

You might have other measures for determining whether or not the road trip is successful, such as how many historic sites you visit along the way. You might also have some "sub-measures," such as spending no more than a certain amount on meals. And, of course, you want to arrive safely, so you will keep an eye on things like engine temperature and tire pressure.

But the three measures I have listed above—distance, time, and money—are probably your most important indicators of success. Your odometer showing miles elapsed, your clock showing the current time, and your wallet showing how much money you have left are your "dashboard indicators" of your trip's success (even though they are not all located on your car's dashboard). You may have targets for these measures, deeming the trip a success if, perhaps:

- You drive the full 277 miles to your destination, reaching the specific address you entered into your GPS.
- You complete the drive in no more than seven hours, including stops for meals and breaks.
- You spend no more than $130 on gas, food, tolls, and other expenses en route.

Once your road trip is under way, you keep an eye on these dashboard indicators of your progress toward your destination. You watch your car's odometer to monitor how close you are to your destination. You keep an eye on the clock to see whether you are getting there on time. And you keep an eye on your wallet to make sure you stay within your budget. For example, after three and a half hours, you should probably have driven at least 140 miles and spent no more than $65.

And you may want to share some of this information with the car owner and your grandmother. The car owner might appreciate quick e-mails or texts on your expenditures to keep the car in good working order. Your grandmother might most appreciate time-stamped photos of yourself at your destination, along with a summary of how you have spent her money along the way. Keeping them apprised is not only thoughtful but prudent; showing that you are using their resources responsibly could convince them to underwrite future trips.

Similarly, a quality college continually gauges its progress toward its goals with a set of measures or dashboard indicators (Chapter 13), choosing measures that will be useful (Chapter 14). It continually compares those measures against targets of where it needs to be at various points in its journey, to ensure that it will arrive at its destination safely and on time (Chapter 15). It keeps key stakeholders apprised of its quality and effectiveness, giving each information relevant to his or her key interests and needs in clear, useful forms (Chapter 16). A college that is accountable, demonstrating these things publicly and clearly, can convince additional stakeholders—students, government policymakers, foundations, and donors—to invest in and support it.

A Culture of Betterment (Chapters 17–18)

Keeping an eye on your clock, odometer, GPS, and wallet, comparing time, distance, and expenditures against each other and your targets, is not a moot exercise when you take a road trip; you use what you learn from those measures to make adjustments in your travels:

- If you find that you are behind schedule, you may decide to take shorter breaks for the rest of the trip.

Jargon Alert!

Improvement

Improvement does not sound like jargon, but it is used so frequently in the worlds of higher education accreditation and accountability that it has taken on a life of its own. Many people interpret *improvement* to mean *enhancement*, so they respond to calls to use evidence for improvement by enhancing what they are doing, often with minor tweaks around the edges. Evidence can be used in bigger ways than enhancements, such as deciding to make major changes or introducing new initiatives. To encourage this broader conception of improvement, in this book I use the term *betterment* instead of *improvement*.

- If you have spent less money than you planned, you may stop at a nicer restaurant . . . or buy a gift for your grandmother.

- If there is a serious unexpected delay, such as a snowstorm that slows traffic to a crawl, you may need to stop somewhere for the night until the roads are cleared, arriving later and spending more along the way. In other words, you will need to adjust your targets for your arrival time and your expenditures.

And then there is the worst-case scenario: a blizzard so bad that roads are closed for a day or more, and you simply cannot arrive in time for the wedding. In this situation, you may decide to change the destination, thinking, "I've got a week off, but I can't get to Grandmom's and I don't want to spend the time at home. I'll head south and spend the week at a beach." (Well, maybe this is not a worst-case scenario.) In other words, you will change the overall goals of the road trip and therefore the trip itself. But you can do this only if you monitor time, mileage, and expenditures routinely, compare them against your targets, and make prompt adjustments. Otherwise, you may find that you are out of money or you have lost so much time that, even if you make it to the beach, you will have no time there before having to head home.

Even if your road trip progresses smoothly and you do not need to make any adjustments en route, few people take only one trip during their entire lifetimes. You may reflect on your experience and use it to plan the next trip, perhaps adjusting your route, budget, or schedule. Or you may adjust the destination: having seen Seattle, you may now decide to move on to Vancouver. These are examples of using evidence—time, distance, and expenditures—to inform decisions, including modifying plans, expenditures, and goals.

A quality college is never satisfied with the status quo. It cannot be. In today's rapidly changing world, a college that is static quickly falls behind and loses relevance and appeal. This makes the culture of betterment—continual improvement and advancement—the foundation of the other four cultures of quality. A quality college uses evidence of its progress, quality, and effectiveness to inform decisions and modify plans, expenditures, and goals (Chapter 17), and it ensures pervasive, sustained use of evidence (Chapter 18).

Interrelations Among the Five Cultures

Just as accreditation requirements are interrelated (New England Association of Colleges and Schools, Commission on Institutions of Higher Education [NEASC], 2011), so are the five cultures of quality. A quality college not only ensures and advances all five cultures of quality but appropriately interrelates them. Regional accreditors are unanimous, for example, in believing that a quality college links goals, plans, evidence, and resource deployment decisions. Goals inform assessment strategies and resource allocations, while evidence informs goals, plans, and resource allocations. In other words, the culture of focus and aspiration (goals) affects the culture of evidence (assessment) and the culture of better-ment (resource allocation). The culture of evidence, meanwhile, informs the culture of focus and aspiration (goals and plans) and the culture of betterment (resource allocation).

Defining Program Excellence Through the Five Cultures

The five cultures define the quality of a college's individual pro-grams and services as well as its overall quality. Program review, a tool to examine and improve program quality and effectiveness, is discussed in Chapter 20.

Defining Teaching Excellence Through the Five Cultures

The five cultures define not only the quality of a college and its programs, but also the quality of the education it provides to its students. A quality college's definition of teaching excellence incorporates all five cultures of quality. A quality college views teaching as not solely a faculty responsibility; it expects compa-rable quality in the work of student development and student sup-port professionals as they help students learn, grow, and develop.

A *culture of focus and aspiration.* At a quality college, faculty articulate learning outcomes for their students and develop cur-ricula and teaching methods that help students achieve those outcomes.

A *culture of relevance.* At a quality college, faculty look out for the best interests of their students, treating them fairly and consis-tently. They ensure that what and how they teach meets students' and society's needs. They look upon stated learning outcomes as promises they are making to students, employers, and society: if you pass this course or complete this requirement, you will be able to do these things. Faculty work to keep these promises effectively, appropriately, and efficiently.

A *culture of evidence.* At a quality college, faculty verify that their students are indeed learning what they want them to learn through systematic, compelling evidence. They have clear, justifiably rigorous expectations for student work.

A *culture of betterment.* A few years ago, I led a discussion of the characteristics of great teaching and one participant had a wonderful, simple response: "A great teacher is always improving." At a quality college, faculty continually try to improve their teaching, using evidence of what students are and are not learning and applying research on effective teaching.

A *culture of community.* At a quality college, faculty work collaboratively as well as individually to articulate learning outcomes, develop curricula and teaching methods, assess learning, and use evidence and research to improve teaching.

CHAPTER 4

WHY IS THIS SO HARD?

The movement to define quality according to the five cultures summarized in Chapter 3 has been the backbone of regional accreditation standards for decades, and accreditors have been emphasizing the culture of evidence since at least the turn of the 21st century. Why, then, do some of the cultures remain a struggle? Why is assessment still sometimes likened to a returning plague of locusts (Dunn, McCarthy, Baker, & Halonen, 2011)? These are important questions because, in order to break through obstacles, we need to understand what those obstacles are and why they exist.

Unfortunately, there is no one simple answer. The reasons why some of the cultures of quality remain a challenge are as diverse as U.S. colleges and universities themselves. In this chapter, I review the reasons I encounter most often. I offer strategies to address these challenges throughout the rest of this book.

Quality Continues to Be Defined by Reputation, Not Effectiveness

Many sectors of the public continue to define quality by reputation, rather than by the five cultures. *U.S. News & World Report*, for example, gives about 23 to 25 percent of its college ranking weight to "undergraduate academic reputation" from its peer assessment survey and high school counselors' ratings (Morse, 2012, 2013), and today 18 percent of entering full-time first-year students say rankings in national magazines like *U.S. News* were a very important influence on their decision to attend their college, up from 10 percent in 1995 (Eagan, Lozano, Hurtado, & Case, 2014; Pryor, Hurtado, Saenz, Santos, & Korn, 2007). Margaret Fiester acknowledges that "a lot of [hiring] decisions are made based on name recognition and reputation" (Webley, 2012, para. 4).

Reputation is, in turn, largely defined by the obsolete accreditation model of inputs discussed in Chapter 2—the college's age and resources, and credentials of its students and faculty—rather than the current model of outcomes or effectiveness. *U.S. News*, for example, gives roughly another 13 percent of its college ranking weight to "student selectivity" (acceptance rate, high school class rank, and SAT/ACT scores) and 10 percent to "financial resources" (per student).

As a result, some college leaders focus on building reputation according to this outdated model of inputs, rather than on the five cultures of quality. They deploy resources to things like increasing the number of student applications or hiring faculty with doctorates from prestigious universities, even though these inputs may have little if anything to do with quality as defined by the five cultures. Research by George Kuh and Ernest Pascarella found, for example, that "selectivity and educational quality are, for all practical purposes, unrelated" (Kuh & Pascarella, 2004, p. 54).

Many of America's oldest, wealthiest, and most influential colleges are well served by the obsolete input model of quality. Some nonetheless eagerly embrace purposeful, evidence-informed innovation and improvement. Some faculty at the Universities of Chicago and Illinois, for example, have used their involvement in the Illinois Initiative on Transparency in Learning and Teaching to research and implement practices that enhance students' metacognition skills (Winkelmes, 2013). But some prestigious colleges see no reason to engage in, say, the systematic assessment of student learning outcomes (Ewell, 2012) and are less likely to do so than other colleges (Kuh, Jankowski, Ikenberry, & Kinzie, 2014). As Margaret Miller has explained, "universities and colleges already assumed to be among the best . . . already have the reputation for educating students well, so they can only lose" (Marcus, 2014, paras. 15–16). When the presidents of these colleges talk, people listen. Longstanding reputation, no matter how irrelevant to quality, still matters, and it is not going to go away.

The Money Is Not There

When I hear complaints from faculty that their college president is not actively supporting assessment or teaching improvement, my response is pretty blunt: "Why should she? There's no money in it." Most college presidents today need to focus on bringing in revenue. While some foundations such as Teagle focus on improving student learning, today the big money is by and large addressing other things. (Do you know of an endowed college center to support faculty teaching improvement, for example? They do exist, but they are very rare.) Most foundations like to support research; most donors like to support facilities and scholarships; and most government policymakers like to focus on efficiency, especially supporting efforts to help students earn degrees and other credentials at a lower cost and more quickly. There is simply not a lot of external financial support for many aspects of the five cultures of quality.

A Culture of Isolation

While many U.S. colleges are actively engaging in adopting research-based teaching and learning practices and in designing relevant programs and services, too many colleges continue to:

- Offer courses and programs based on what faculty want to teach, rather than on evidence of the skills and competencies most needed in today's careers

- Use teaching methods based on how the faculty were once taught, rather than research-based practices that promote student learning and success
- Offer student support services based on what they think may help students succeed, rather than on systematic evidence of their students' barriers and research on practices that promote student success
- Offer cultural and arts programs to the region based on what they think will be good for the region, rather than on informed assessments of needs, interests, and gaps in regional cultural and arts programs

An example of higher education's isolation comes from surveys by the Association of American Colleges and Universities (AAC&U) and the Higher Education Research Institute (HERI) (Jaschik, 2013): 78 percent of employers want to know that graduates have used real-life examples in coursework, but just 55 percent of faculty report doing so, just 42 percent of college seniors believe their professors have given them chances to apply classroom learning to real-life situations, and only 29 percent of seniors say they are satisfied with the relevance of course work to real life.

A Culture of Reticence

U.S. higher education has come under fire in part because of its slow steps to communicate meaningfully with its stakeholders. The higher education community has kept its light under the proverbial bushel basket. It has been historically reticent about its achievements, the public good of higher education, and the benefits to college graduates beyond higher pay. One reason for this reticence, I think, is that those in higher education do not recognize their own successes. In some of the workshops I conduct, I give participants a scenario describing very positive—but not perfect—student learning assessment results and ask them how the results might be used. More often than not, their conclusion is either that something must be wrong with the assessment to yield such good results or that, because the results are not perfect, improvement is needed. Colleges cannot share successes that they themselves do not recognize!

U.S. higher education has also come under fire in part because of its slow steps to acknowledge its shortcomings. As discussed in Chapter 1, this has led to suspicion among some stakeholders about higher education's quality or what Peter Ewell (2005) has called a crisis of confidence: "the point is not so much that outcomes are visibly deficient as the fact that no one seems to know *what* they are" (p. 122). Chapter 6 explains that, whether your college is public or private, it is a steward of resources that others have provided, and it has an obligation to demonstrate that it uses those resources prudently, efficiently, and effectively.

Change Is Hard

After years of accreditors emphasizing the culture of evidence, many colleges are now sitting on considerable piles of data, but too often either the data sit unused or are used to make only what one faculty member described to me as "tweaks around the edges." Why? Change is never easy, but it can be particularly hard at colleges because academic traditions, cultures, and structures have not historically emphasized or valued change. Margaret Miller (2013) is blunt: "The culture, governance structures, and leadership of higher education typically prevent colleges . . . from making the radical changes that may be necessary" (para. 4).

Change is not part of the tradition of scholarly research. Charles Blaich and Kathleen Wise have explained that the goals of research "are communication with colleagues . . . and, ultimately, more research. The goal of assessment, on the other hand, is to create changes. . . . Research and assessment are not just different processes; at some point the goals of each process are in opposition. . . . The challenge then is to engage faculty's interest in inquiry without engaging the other familiar scholarly skills that will lead them to gather more data and write reports rather than taking concrete actions" (2011, pp. 12–13).

Acknowledging the need for change can be painful. As Richard Morrill has explained, "Issues of fundamental change are avoided because the conflicts are too deep and the conversations too painful" (2013, "The Culture of Academic Decision Making," para. 1).

Some are satisfied with the status quo and see little meaningful incentive to change. Years ago, I was getting decent teaching evaluations, despite my old-fashioned lectures. I tried collaborative learning—having my students discover their own learning through group work—and it was a disaster. I did not know what I was doing, some of the groups were frustrated and unproductive . . . and my students' evaluations of my teaching tanked. Of course, I learned from the experience, made adjustments, and the following semester my groups—and evaluations—were fine, but what if I had been coming up for promotion or tenure right after that disastrous semester? I probably would not have risked changing my teaching methods . . . and might still be holding lecture-based classes to this day.

At some colleges, there is no real incentive to change what one does—to be innovative, to try new research-based teaching methods—or indeed to acknowledge any areas for improvement. Colleges with cultures of preserving the status quo are the ones who report to their accreditors that all their assessment results are great and there is no need for change except, perhaps, those minor tweaks I mentioned earlier.

Patricia O'Brien challenges this culture beautifully when she says, "I have yet to meet a college president willing to stand up in front of the campus community and say, 'We are as good today as we are ever going to be. We are never going to get any better.' No president says that because no president believes that. As good as an institution is, there is always room for improvement" (personal communication, August 1, 2013).

Innovation requires some degree of risk taking, and risk taking is, well, risky. "It's far less risky and complicated to analyze data than it is to act" (Blaich & Wise, 2011, p. 13). There is the chance that an innovation will fail, that time and resources will be wasted. Sticking with the tried-and-true can seem a much safer course.

Some are threatened by the prospect of change. In today's economic and political climate, such fears can be legitimate. If a president invests considerable college resources in an innovative program that fails to achieve its intended purpose, he can be out of a job. Some faculty are rightly concerned that changes in program or general education offerings may lead to the elimination of the courses they teach or the downsizing or closure of their departments.

Change means work, and everyone already feels overloaded. Implementing cultures of evidence and betterment can force a college to address underlying issues that it may have been procrastinating on for far too long, creating more work. As you plan to assess student achievement of your curriculum's key learning outcomes, for example, you may come to realize that the curriculum is not designed to achieve those outcomes and has to be rethought. As you plan to use systematic evidence to inform resource allocation decisions, you may realize that you need to reconceive your annual budgeting process with new forms and procedures so that funding decisions are based on your college's vision and goals, rather than on the whim of a college leader.

A Culture of Silos

Some colleges have very little true communication and collaboration. Despite cultures of shared governance, "divisions and departments that operate as silos and independent actors . . .[remain] prevalent in academe" (Hinton, 2012, p. 27). Examples that I have seen include:

- Student survey results and other relevant information and evidence that are not shared with faculty, administrators, staff, and students

- Instructions for budget requests without specifics on the criteria that will be used to decide what is funded and what is cut

- Decisions to start or cancel programs without explaining why

- Strategic directions set by boards after only lip service attention to the input of faculty and staff

- Faculty and student life staff who do not collaborate on helping students achieve key learning outcomes in and out of the classroom

- Faculty teaching courses for a general education requirement who do not talk together about the requirement's learning outcomes and how best to achieve—and assess—them

- Department faculty who do not discuss their programs' curricula: how program courses fit together to create an integrated learning experience

- Faculty teaching the same course on campus and off who do not collaborate to ensure appropriate consistency in curricula, goals, and standards

- Faculty teaching sections of a course who do not talk about the course's key learning outcomes or share ideas on how to help students achieve them

This culture of silos is present in the greater U.S. higher education community as well. National blue-ribbon panels, commissions, and other high-level conversations rarely include faculty, assessment directors, deans, student development staff, or others working "on the ground." Conferences on teaching, assessment, and student success are rarely attended by college leaders.

Lack of communication and collaboration can lead to a culture of disrespect, which I discuss in the next section, and even "parallel realities," in which different college groups (say, faculty and board members) have perceptions of what is happening—and why—that do not even intersect.

Chapter 7 suggests ways to break down silos by fostering a culture of community.

Colleges Are Not Always One Big Happy Family

When I am on my way home after a visit to a college, I find myself thinking either "Gee, I wish I worked there" or "Boy, I'm glad I don't work there." It never takes me more than a couple of hours visiting a college to pick up its "vibes." Usually, everyone I meet is respectful and cordial, but sometimes the tension feels so thick that I could cut it with the proverbial knife. The five cultures of quality require working together collegially—to identify goals and plans, to collect evidence, to improve programs and services—and that cannot happen when people behave disrespectfully or feel disrespected. The root causes of a culture of disrespect can include the following.

Marginalization. Colleges have incredibly knowledgeable, well-educated faculty (including adjuncts), administrators, staff, and students. These people can feel disrespected if their knowledge, expertise, and perspectives are not tapped, if they feel that no one is listening to them, or if no one has taken the time to keep them informed on what is going on.

Distrust. People do not wake up one morning and decide to be distrustful; they become distrustful when they feel they have been betrayed. A past president may have changed their working conditions for the worse. They may have spent a lot of time participating in an assessment process that died when the last accreditation review ended. Unfortunately, broken trust is very hard to fix, because memories are long. Faculty and staff have vented to me about incidents that took place over a decade earlier.

Self-centeredness and narrow-mindedness. Every college has a few people who care only about what is best for them, not the college as a whole. Others stick stubbornly to their own narrow perspectives and refuse to consider alternatives, such as teaching differently from how they were once taught. The results of such self-centeredness can include general education and degree program requirements that are political machinations, based on what faculty want to teach rather than on what students need to learn.

Bullying. Every workplace seems to have a bully or two who throws weight around, threatens and intimidates others, and holds up progress with objections and roadblocks. Colleges are no exception. Bullies can be presidents, senior faculty members, department chairs, deans . . . almost anyone with real or perceived authority. I have never understood why colleges tolerate bullies, and I hope that increasing public attention to bullying will empower colleges to stop this behavior.

Academic Freedom Is Misunderstood

I meet many faculty who are misinformed about what academic freedom means in the classroom and in academic programs. The 1940 "Statement of Principles on Academic Freedom and Tenure" of the American Association of University Professors (AAUP) has only one line on academic freedom in the classroom: "Teachers are entitled to freedom in the classroom in discussing their subject" (p. 1). The statement does not provide for faculty autonomy in choosing their subject or deciding whether or how to assess student learning in their subject. While he was general secretary of AAUP, Gary Rhoades clarified that AAUP sees the assessment of student learning and reform of teaching and academic programs as the primary responsibility of faculty—individually *and collectively*—and that "there is no reason that faculty cannot collectively take on the task of identifying student learning outcomes, conducting those assessments, and revising curriculum accordingly" (Gold, Rhoades, Smith, & Kuh, 2011, p. 7).

Jargon Alert!

Academic Freedom

Academic freedom (AAUP, 1940) is the right to engage in research, scholarship, inquiry, and expression without fear of repercussion.

Fuzzy Focus and Aspirations

To paraphrase the Cheshire Cat in *Alice's Adventures in Wonderland* (Carroll, 1865/1997), if you do not know where you are going, it does not matter which way you go. Some colleges aim to be all things to all people, trying to go everywhere at once and stretching everyone too thin to do any one thing really well. Chapters 8 through 11 talk about focusing your college's priorities, including your goals for student learning.

We Do Not Put Our Money Where Our Mouth Is

Some mission statements and strategic plans talk a good talk, but they are little more than meaningless paper exercises to satisfy accreditors or other stakeholders; their colleges do not truly commit to and invest in their stated priorities. Too many colleges, for example, profess to focus on providing a learning-centered environment, while they base faculty hiring decisions largely on the applicant's research record and a sample lecture—when we know that lectures are the worst way for students to learn (Chapter 12). Chapter 17 talks more about putting your money where your mouth is.

A Culture Relying on Antecedents and Anecdotes

A college dean once told me, "We have a great math program. Our math team won the state championship!" My reaction? "That's wonderful for the five or so students on the team, but what about the other 19,995 students at your college, including the ones who struggle with math?" Your most exceptional students and alumni are "hardly representative of the vast majority of current or former students" (or, by definition, they would not be exceptional) (Halpern, 2004, p. 11). Today "many now want hard facts instead of anecdotes and intuitions" (Dickey, 2014, p. 58). A college needs *systematic* evidence of the quality and effectiveness of its

math program, not just information on the experience of a hand-
ful of students.

I have always been intrigued by college administrators and faculty with backgrounds in research who fail to apply those methods
of systematic inquiry to their daily work (other than their scholarly research). I am equally intrigued by college administrators
and faculty with backgrounds in business who fail to apply basic
quantitative analysis methods to their work. A lot of decisions are
still made simply because someone has a whim or notion based
only on anecdote, antecedent, a 30-second elevator pitch, scat-
tershot evidence, or a squeaky wheel, with no systematic evidence
to support its viability or potential. This is a culture that is simply
no longer viable in the 21st century. Chapter 17 talks about using
evidence to inform decisions and plans, including resource deployment decisions.

Emphasizing Assessment Over Learning

I have had the pleasure of working with some Canadian colleges
that were not required by their quality assurance agencies to assess
student learning. (The colleges invited me to work with them
on student learning assessment simply because—you will be shocked
by this—assessment is a good idea!) The conversations were completely different from those I have at U.S. colleges. The entire focus
was on assessment as a good classroom teaching practice. The workshops were fun, because faculty found the focus on the classroom
practical and useful, and because they therefore participated enthusiastically. Toward the end, they began to observe that it would be a
good idea for faculty teaching in each program to get together and
talk about teaching and assessing common learning outcomes across
courses. In other words, they were very quickly seeing the connection from classroom-level assessment to program-level assessment.

Compare this with how the U.S. assessment movement began
in the 1980s. Faculty were immediately asked to identify and assess

program-level learning outcomes and use the evidence to make improvements. For many faculty, these were a lot of new ideas to absorb and, as noted earlier in this chapter, for some a 180-degree change in their approach to teaching. Imagine if the U.S. assessment movement had begun by focusing on disseminating and applying research on classroom teaching practices and curriculum design and on revising faculty promotion and tenure (P&T) guidelines to emphasize efforts to understand and improve one's teaching. The focus could have then progressed to good assessment practices in the classroom, and then to program-level and general education curricular design, assessment, and improvement. This would have been a more natural progression, and we might be further along today.

We Have Pockets of Mediocrity

Higher education has pockets of mediocrity just as anyplace else does:

- Some colleges lack the capacity or integrity to offer courses and programs at appropriate and consistent levels of rigor.
- Some colleges hire adjunct faculty and give them virtually no guidance or support on expectations for student learning and how to help students meet those expectations.
- Some college presidents lack the courage or capacity to take on meaningful reforms.
- And I have an untested theory that a good chunk of the faculty who are "hard core resisters" to assessing student learning are mediocre teachers . . . and, down deep, they know it. They have learned to game the system, getting decent student evaluations, but they subconsciously fear that systematic assessment may expose them as the mediocre teachers they are.

Someone said to me decades ago that higher education is the one commodity for which customers want the least for their money, meaning that many students simply want a degree or credential, not necessarily the learning that goes with it. There is a germ of truth in this. Pockets of mediocrity in higher education can exist only if they are tolerated by students, their families, faculty, administrators, employers, and society.

For More Information

"The Challenge to Deep Change: A Brief Cultural History of Higher Education" (Shugart, 2013) is a thoughtful and thought-provoking article. Chapter 5 of *Assessing Student Learning: A Common Sense Guide* (Suskie, 2009) reviews some of the key sources of resistance to student learning assessment.

DIMENSION I:
A Culture of Relevance

CHAPTER 5

INTEGRITY
Doing the Right Thing

Your college's stakeholders expect you to look out consistently for the best interests of your students, your college, and your stakeholders. They expect your college to demonstrate that it meets its responsibilities and keeps its promises. They expect honesty, discussed in Chapter 16, and fairness, discussed in Chapter 7. In short, they expect your college to do the right thing.

Jargon Alert!

Stakeholders

A *stakeholder* is simply someone whom your college serves, who has an interest in your college, who is involved with your college, or who is affected by what it does.

Meet Your Responsibilities

Quality is defined in Chapter 3 as excellence: a quality college does an excellent job at whatever it does. Easy, right? Too easy. Under this simplistic definition, a quality college might be one that is doing things excellently, but not the right things: offering courses that no one wants to take, constructing beautiful, energy-efficient buildings that are not designed in ways that help students learn, graduating students who lack the skills and competencies that employers need.

Quality, then, is not just a matter of doing things excellently but doing the *right* things excellently. A quality college is not just excellent per se, but excellent in fulfilling its responsibilities. What are those responsibilities? The concerns about U.S. higher education discussed in Chapter 1 suggest that your college has five fundamental responsibilities:

1. Meet stakeholder needs, especially its students' needs.
2. Keep its promises.
3. Ensure its health and well-being, and deploy resources effectively, prudently, and efficiently. This is stewardship, discussed in Chapter 6.
4. Serve the public good.
5. Demonstrate its quality and effectiveness in fulfilling these responsibilities. This is accountability.

Jargon Alert!

Institutional Effectiveness

Institutional effectiveness refers to the effectiveness of an entire college, as opposed to specific programs, services, or initiatives. Many people—and some accreditors—think of institutional effectiveness as a college's effectiveness in achieving its purpose (mission) and goals. I think that is too narrow; it ignores the other fundamental responsibilities discussed here. I therefore define institutional effectiveness as a college's effectiveness in meeting all five fundamental responsibilities listed here.

Put Your Students First

At a quality college, everyone's focus is on ensuring the five dimensions of quality and that the college is effectively fulfilling the responsibilities listed above. But everyone's *top* priorities are making sure that students receive the best possible education, that the college helps students achieve their educational goals, and that it gives students an appropriate return on their investment of tuition dollars and time. Looking out for the best interests of your students might include, for example:

- Offering accelerated programs only to students whose responsibilities and schedules allow them to devote the out-of-class time needed to succeed to the same degree as students in traditionally scheduled programs
- Offering graduate credit only for courses whose content and rigor exceed those of undergraduate courses
- Offering an online program in leadership or management only if leadership and management skills can truly be developed online, without face-to-face practice

Put your students first consistently. A quality college ensures consistency in whatever it does, wherever and however it operates. Your students should see a culture of pervasive consistency in quality and rigor in your academic offerings and support services, no matter where, when, or how students learn:

- *Platforms:* Expected and actual learning outcomes should be consistent no matter how they are delivered: in online, face-to-face, or blended classes.
- *Venues:* Expected and actual learning outcomes should be consistent no matter where they are offered: at off-campus locations or on the main campus.

- *Formats:* Expected and actual learning outcomes should be consistent across accelerated, self-paced, and traditional semester-long courses.
- *Control:* Expected and actual learning outcomes should be consistent no matter who develops or delivers the course or program: your college or a contracted third party, such as another college or private vendor.
- *Course sections:* Students who pass a course should have mastered its key learning outcomes, no matter which section they enroll in or who their professor is.

This is harder than it may seem. A college needs structures, policies, and people in place to ensure these consistencies, and the actual process of verifying consistency (and documenting it for accreditors) takes time and work. The larger and more disparate the college, the greater degree of coordination that is required. But the alternative is unacceptable.

Know Your Key Stakeholders and Meet Their Needs

Key higher education stakeholders include current and prospective students and their families, employers, and government policymakers. Others may include your accreditors, donors and investors, community residents, and taxpayers (Suskie, 2009). If research is part of your college's purpose, your stakeholders include foundations, corporations, and public agencies that can fund that research. Your internal stakeholders—members of your college community—are also part of the mix.

In order to meet your key stakeholders' needs, you first need to learn about their perspectives, interests, and priorities. What do they care about? Why? While today's key higher education stakeholders are broadly concerned about economic development, return on investment, and the changing college student, as I discussed in Chapter 1, each stakeholder has somewhat different interests within this mix.

To meet the needs of your current and prospective students and their families, for example, first find out:

- What are their interests and concerns? The Cooperative Institutional Research Program (CIRP) Freshman Survey (www.heri.ucla.edu/cirpoverview.php), the National Survey of Student Engagement (NSSE) (http://nsse.iub.edu/), and the Community College Survey of Student Engagement (CCSSE) (http://ccsse.org) are examples of published surveys that can provide helpful information on this.

- What are your alumni doing, both immediately after graduating and perhaps five to ten years later? Are they satisfied with their lives (Busteed, 2013), or have they found that they do not have the knowledge, skills, and dispositions they need or want? Alumni surveys, interviews, and focus groups can be helpful here.

To meet the needs of employers of your alumni, first find out:

- Who employs your graduates? Who are the key employers in the region that your college aims to serve? Alumni surveys and regional labor statistics (trends and projections) from state and county agencies may be helpful here. The *Federal Occupational Outlook Handbook* (www.bls.gov/oco) may also provide insight, but it does not list many specific positions and provides only national, not regional, information.

- What traits do employers most need in their workforces? Chapter 11 gives general answers, but employer advisory councils (for example, business advisory councils or health professions advisory councils), your local chamber of commerce, and industry groups can provide more relevant insight.

To meet the needs of government policymakers, first find out the most pressing unmet economic, social, cultural, and environmental needs of the region your college aims to serve. Surveys of community needs by local charities, arts councils, and government agencies can be helpful here, as can regional economic development plans.

Your college's internal stakeholders include faculty, administrators, your college's leadership team, board members, and assessment and accreditation committees and coordinators. They all need to see evidence that your college is fulfilling its fundamental responsibilities, listed at the beginning of this chapter, and that it is ensuring all aspects of the five cultures of quality.

Keep Your Promises

Your college's statements of its purpose, values, and goals, along with the stated learning outcomes of its general education program, each academic program, and the college as a whole, are promises it is making to its students and other stakeholders. Your college is promising that it *is* the college described in its mission statement. It is promising that it *will* achieve the goals it has established for itself. It is promising that your students *will* learn the learning outcomes you have articulated by the time they graduate. In order to keep these promises, your college must design and appropriately support its curricula, programs, and services to ensure that all students *will* achieve those learning outcomes.

Serve the Public Good

The public good of higher education is an important return on the investment of students, taxpayers, and donors, but it is one that is largely absent from U.S. conversations. People with college educations lead lives that benefit themselves and their communities in myriad ways (Baum & McPherson, 2011; Bowen, 1997; Schramm, Aldeman, Rotherham, Brown, & Cross, 2013) that go beyond economic development. They are more likely to become engaged citizens, to vote, to volunteer, and to support programs that benefit their communities, such as arts programming and social service agencies. They are in better health (Buckles, Hagemann, Malamud, Morrill, & Wozniak, 2013), less likely to commit crimes and be imprisoned, less likely to need food stamps, and more likely to save for retirement. Because they earn more, they pay more taxes (Berger & Fisher, 2013). Their communities attract new businesses seeking skilled employees. In short, people with college educations change the world (Block, 2013).

But today government policymakers see a college education as a private good that primarily benefits the individual student through higher income, rather than a public good that benefits society at large and is therefore worthy of taxpayer investment (Mintz, 2013). State investment in higher education plummeted from $11 per $1,000 of state personal income in 1976 to $6 in 2011 (Mortenson, 2012), even though "providing expanded access to high quality education will . . . likely do more to strengthen the overall state economy than anything else a state government can do" (Berger & Fisher, 2013, p. 2).

Nonetheless, "American higher education remains collectively responsible to the broader public good" (Association of Governing Boards of Universities and Colleges [AGB] and the Council for Higher Education Accreditation [CHEA], 2009, p. 2). It is a responsibility that your college cannot ignore.

Demonstrate That You Are Ensuring Quality and Meeting Your Responsibilities

All those supporting your college have a right to expect good quality evidence that your college is doing the right thing: that it is ensuring quality and that it is meeting its responsibilities, including putting students first, meeting stakeholder needs, keeping its promises, and serving the public good. They have a right to expect good quality evidence that their resources are being used appropriately to achieve the goals that they are underwriting. In short, your college has a duty to be *accountable*.

Jargon Alert!

Accountability

Accountability is demonstrating to your stakeholders the effectiveness of your college, program, service, or initiative in meeting its responsibilities, as listed at the beginning of this chapter. A good synonym for accountability is *assurance*. Indeed, the Association to Advance Collegiate Schools of Business (AACSB) refers to assessment of learning as assurance of learning (www .aacsb.edu).

Your college's stakeholders also want to be able to quickly and easily find and understand answers to their questions about your college's quality and effectiveness. In short, your college has a duty to be *transparent*; this is discussed in Chapter 16.

Jargon Alert!

Transparency

Transparency means making evidence clear, concise, easy to find, and relevant to your stakeholders.

For More Information

Your go-to resource for further information on integrity is your accreditor and its requirements on integrity. The Association of Governing Boards (AGB) (www.agb.org) offers a variety of publications and other resources on board integrity. Two other sources on integrity are Chapter 3 of *Assessing Student Learning: A Common Sense Guide* (Suskie, 2009) and "Fair Assessment Practices: Giving Students Equitable Opportunities to Demonstrate Learning" (Suskie, 2000).

CHAPTER 6

STEWARDSHIP
Ensuring and Deploying Resources Responsibly

Colleges run on other people's money, and colleges have an obligation to those people and organizations. I like to say that my higher education mentor is Spiderman (or, more accurately, his uncle): with great power comes great responsibility. Your college has been entrusted with millions of dollars in resources from other people. Those people expect you and your colleagues to be wise stewards of their resources, managing and using their resources carefully, responsibly, and judiciously.

This chapter looks at three responsibilities of stewardship:

- Ensuring your college's health and well-being
- Deploying resources effectively to achieve your college's purpose and goals, meet your college's responsibilities, and ensure the five dimensions of quality
- Deploying resources efficiently

A fourth critical stewardship responsibility is deploying resources prudently: using good-quality evidence to inform resource deployment decisions. That responsibility is discussed in Chapter 17.

Recognize That People and Their Time
Are Your Greatest Resources

When I advise college faculty and administrators on what needs to be done regarding assessment, accreditation, accountability, or any of the dimensions of quality, the most common question I hear is: "Where do I find the time to do this?" Human resources consume the vast majority of most college budgets, and time is a resource to be safeguarded, deployed, and analyzed just like any other resource. I offer suggestions regarding this throughout this chapter.

Ensure Your College's Health and Well-Being

Part of the fiduciary responsibility of a college's leaders and board is to ensure the college's health and well-being. Is the college solvent? Safe? Does it have enough resources to achieve its purpose and goals and to ensure ongoing quality? To weather any unexpected expenses or revenue downturns?

A college may not have a formal strategic goal to keep the books balanced and maintain a healthy cash flow, but obviously these measures of financial health nonetheless need to be monitored on an ongoing basis. Similarly, a college may not have a formal strategic goal to provide its students with a safe campus environment but, no matter how safe its campus is, it should monitor crime statistics to make sure problems are not developing.

I do not pretend to have any great financial expertise, but I have found that the following truisms are as relevant as ever to ensuring a college's financial health and well-being.

Understand your financial picture. Someone once confessed to me: "I don't know why our accountant said we need this month-by-month breakdown of revenues and expenditures." (The answer? You have cash flow problems.) When it comes to finances, there is no such thing as a stupid question. Keep asking questions until you are comfortable that you understand every financial document you are seeing. Among the measures you should track regularly are your income sources (tuition revenue, gifts, and endowment size and yield), expenditures by object (such as personnel, equipment, and facilities), and expenditures by cost center (such as the biology department, admissions office, and tutoring center).

If your college is private, one of the most important financial health measures to monitor is its federal financial responsibility composite score, partly because it affects your ability to offer Title IV financial aid and partly because it is publicly available and can therefore affect your college's reputation and perception of credit-worthiness. The score is a composite of three ratios that the U.S. Department of Education (ED) calculates from audited financial statements:

Jargon Alert!

Financial Ratio Analysis

As explained in Chapter 15, numbers have meaning only when they are compared against other numbers. *Financial ratio analysis* is the practice of deriving meaning from various financial figures by comparing them against one another through ratios or percentages. Cost per credit hour (in other words, the cost of offering one credit of education to one student), facilities cost per square foot, and reserves as a proportion of annual expenditures are all examples of financial ratios.

- The *primary reserve ratio* is the ratio of expendable resources to total expenditures. It is a measure of your college's liquidity—its access to ready cash.
- The *equity ratio* is the proportion of assets that is not subject to claims by third parties. It is a measure of your college's capacity to borrow.

- The *net income ratio* is your college's net income gain or loss: revenue minus expenditures as a proportion of revenue. It is a measure of your college's ability to operate within its means.

Federal financial responsibility composite scores are interpreted as follows:

- 1.5 to 3.0: Financially responsible
- 1.0 to 1.4: Financially responsible, but requiring additional ED oversight
- −1.0 to 0.9: Not financially responsible

For more information, visit http://studentaid.ed.gov/about/data-center/school/composite-scores.

The federal financial responsibility composite score is only one indicator of financial health. Bond rating services such as Standard & Poor's, Moody's, and Fitch monitor their own indicators of financial health, including not only the financial ratios examined by ED but also qualitative factors, such as the college's leadership, its market, its strategic plan, and the viability of its educational offerings. Feasible enrollment management plans, based on well-founded realistic assumptions, are thus vital to financial health.

Live below your means. Develop not one financial plan but three: a reasonable budget based on prudent assumptions informed by past experiences, an optimistic budget assuming that your plans for improvements in enrollments, gifts, and other revenues and expenses do indeed materialize, and a pessimistic budget based on unanticipated shortfalls in enrollment or investment value or on expenses running significantly higher than anticipated.

Diversify your assets. The more flexible your facilities, the better positioned you are to respond to students' changing needs. The greater the range of experience and expertise in your faculty, staff, and board members, the greater your flexibility and capacity to respond to unforeseen developments. The more diversified your endowment and other investments, the better your capacity to weather market fluctuations.

Diversify your revenue sources. The Great Recession of 2008–2009 hit every sector of higher education, but in different ways. Public colleges saw their state funds cut, sometimes dramatically. Some small regional private colleges saw drops in enrollment . . . and in tuition revenue. Some older, well-established private colleges saw the values of their endowments dip . . . along with the endowment revenue they counted on for their operating budgets. The colleges that weathered this fiscal storm best generally seemed to be those who were not overly reliant on any one source of revenue for their annual operating budgets. Monitor the diversification of your revenue sources by tracking the proportions of annual revenue derived from tuition, annual fund gifts, endowment income, auxiliary enterprises, and athletics, as appropriate.

Have enough people, including a sufficient core of full-time faculty and student support staff. Full-time faculty are the linchpins of your college. They are the ones who, more than anyone else, bring everything contributing to the student learning experience into a cohesive whole: their disciplinary expertise, articulation of program- and college-wide learning outcomes, curricular design and review, teaching, guidance and support to students, and assessment of learning outcomes. They also contribute significantly to your college's system of collegial governance (Chapter 7). Separate these responsibilities among people serving narrower roles, and you run the risk that the student learning experience may be provided in uncoordinated fragments and therefore decline in quality and effectiveness.

Put Your Money Where Your Mouth Is

Just because your college has resources in place does not necessarily mean that it is achieving its purpose and goals, that students are learning what they are supposed to, or that a culture of quality is being advanced. *Your college's key responsibilities* (Chapter 5) *should be central to how you deploy resources.* Put more simply, a quality college puts its money where its mouth is. It deploys its resources in ways that meet stakeholder needs, serve the public good, achieve its purpose and goals, and ensure and demonstrate its quality and effectiveness.

As your college leaders develop various college budgets (annual operating budget, capital budget, and so on), they should do so with your college's purpose and goals in hand, asking questions like these:

- What human, capital, and technology investments will *most* help our college achieve its purpose and goals, help students achieve key learning outcomes, and advance a culture of quality?
- What is consuming significant resources but not contributing substantively toward achievement of our college's purpose and goals?
- How might our college be different if a particular course, program, or service did not exist? Would our college still be able to achieve its purpose?

Your college leaders should then give funding priority to requests and needs that flow from your college's purpose, goals, responsibilities, and quality agenda and that are supported by systematic evidence. Provosts have told me that they have advised department chairs: "If your budget request isn't supported by systematic evidence, don't bother giving it to me." Resource deployment decisions made by buttonholing or lobbying a college leader are poor stewardship . . . and unfair. Across-the-board budget cuts are politically expedient but poor stewardship. Think what you would do with your own family budget if you faced a pay cut. You probably would not cut every expense across the board by an equal proportion. You would cut back the most on vacations, eating out, and entertainment, while minimizing cuts to more vital expenses such as groceries. Your college should do the same.

Deploying resources to support your college's key aims is hard today. Money is so tight that funds and time for college priorities must often come not from new resources but by redeploying existing resources (Lederman, 2013). It may be time for your college to limit and focus its priorities, rather than aiming to be all things to all people, as I discuss in Chapters 9 and 10.

Scale back time spent on tangential activities. The vast majority of people I meet at colleges are hard-working and spend their time trying to accomplish important things, but there are only so many hours in a week. The only way to help everyone find time to address key goals and advance the five cultures of quality is to hone back time spent on less important things, at least temporarily, while you get quality initiatives going. If you do not do this, you are essentially telling your college community that your college's stated priorities and the cultures of quality are less important than whatever else they have been doing.

Review low-enrollment courses. Here is an example I used at a small college with an average class size of 13 students. A faculty member teaching eight courses a year, with an average of 13 students per class, teaches 104 students per year. If the faculty member taught an average of 15 students per class instead of 13—just two more—in seven courses a year, she would teach roughly the same number of students per year (105 versus 104) with one less course preparation, giving her more time for advising students, working on the curriculum, assessing student learning, and so on.

Consider streamlining course and co-curricular offerings. It takes a lot more work to offer 20 courses from which students may fulfill a general education requirement than to offer 10. Faculty need to develop twice as many syllabi and spend more time collaborating to ensure that the courses all address—and assess—the requirement's key learning outcomes.

I offer this advice with a heavy heart, because one of the delights of my own college experience was sating my intellectual curiosity by sampling from an incredible array of courses. But today's college students are different from many of us. There are probably no more than 20 courses that the vast majority of your students take to fulfill their general education requirements. Research the costs and benefits of offering all the others. Why do your students choose the general education classes they take? Do they choose each class because of intellectual curiosity about the topic, or the time of day it is offered, or the reputation of its professor?

You can ask similar questions about elective courses in your academic programs, co-curricular activities, and student development programs. How many students enroll in or participate in each? What is the cost of each course, activity, or program, and what is its impact? What is the value of these offerings to your college and your students as a whole?

Monitor Where Your Money Is Being Spent

Deploying resources effectively requires looking regularly at where your money is being spent.

What proportion of revenues goes toward your priorities? A good portion of any college's resources is, of course, deployed simply to ensure its ongoing health and well-being. The electric bill must be paid, snow must be plowed off roads and sidewalks, debts must be paid off, and contributions to employee health plans must be submitted. But I have seen colleges whose "fixed" costs consume up to 90 percent of the annual budget and whose strategic plan is a set of special little add-on projects. These are not colleges that are advancing their quality and effectiveness. Your college's purpose and goals should be supported by the deployment of significant portions of its budget and everyone's time.

What proportion of revenues goes toward meeting student needs, including the proportions spent on academics, student development, and student support programs? Are those proportions in line with the emphasis that your mission and key goals place on academics and student development and support? (Proportions that are too low do not necessarily mean that students are not receiving a good education, but they may be paying too much for what they are receiving.)

How does everyone spend his or her time? Imagine asking faculty and staff to keep logs on how they spend their time each week. How would their time usage match up with your college's stated purpose and goals? Or the next time you are in a meeting, imagine adding up the time the participants spend in the meeting, as well as preparation time and follow-up time. Now imagine calculating the pay and benefits that your college is spending on that time. Was enough accomplished toward achieving your college's purpose and goals and ensuring quality and effectiveness to make that expenditure worthwhile?

Are you bringing in the right people? In other words, are you hiring people who can help your college move forward substantively with its quality agenda? All accreditors require—and your stakeholders expect—that faculty, administrators, and staff bring appropriate experience and expertise to their positions. (College board members and presidents are discussed in Chapter 8.) This means hiring people with the capacities your college needs to achieve its purpose and goals. If your college is focusing on student learning, for example, give hiring priority to faculty applicants whose research focuses on the scholarship of teaching as well as the traditional scholarship of discovery (Boyer, 1997). If your college is focusing on serving its community, give hiring priority to faculty applicants whose research focuses on the scholarship of application to real-world problems. If your college is serious about providing a learning-centered environment, instead of asking interviewees for teaching positions to deliver a sample lecture, ask them to provide a record of creating environments for learning and to demonstrate how they do this during their interviews.

Jargon Alert!

Scholarship of Teaching

Faculty at most colleges are evaluated on three broad criteria: excellence in teaching, scholarship, and service. (Scholarship includes research and other scholarly endeavors, such as creating an original work of art.) Ernest Boyer's groundbreaking book *Scholarship Reconsidered* (1997) observed that faculty are traditionally expected to engage in what he called the *scholarship of discovery*: making an original research discovery, such as the habitat of a microorganism or the influence of one author on another. He proposed encouraging faculty to engage in other forms of scholarship, including the *scholarship of teaching*—research on effective teaching practices—and the *scholarship of application*—applying research to solve real-life problems—among others.

Watch for both high turnover and stagnation. Part of the experience and expertise that a college needs is with its own history, culture, processes, and realities. When turnover is high, a college loses these, and its progress slows as new incumbents go through the inevitable learning curve.

I worry just as much, however, about colleges that have hired very few people in the last 20 years. New hires bring fresh perspectives and expertise. If your college has low turnover, make a special effort to encourage faculty, administrators, and staff to participate in professional development opportunities to make sure your college remains relevant and responsive and uses current, research-informed practices.

Monitor the Impact of Your Investments

Your college's stakeholders probably have questions about how your college's resources are impacting things they care about. It is not enough to tell today's stakeholders that your college has invested, say, $50,000 in an initiative to improve students' writing skills.

People investing in this initiative want and deserve to see evidence that the $50,000 is spent effectively—that students who complete the program do indeed have stronger writing skills. You should be asking the same questions. Are your investments— your deployments of resources—having the impact you intend? Chapter 13 provides examples of measures for gauging the success of your endeavors.

Monitor student success. I do not care for the widely bandied term "productivity" that is used to describe the proportions of students who complete a program and land an appropriate job; it sounds like colleges are rolling students off an assembly line rather than providing personalized, individualized learning experiences. But concerns about student success are understandable, given stakeholder expectations that U.S. colleges contribute to economic development. One can legitimately raise questions about a college that does not help a sizable proportion of its students achieve their eventual goals to earn a degree or other credential and earn higher pay. So part of a college's stewardship responsibilities is monitoring the percentage of students who persist through completion of their degrees . . . or achieve whatever other goals they might have. Student success is discussed further in Chapter 12.

Deploy Resources Efficiently

Accreditors tend to focus on *effective* deployment of resources: using your goals and substantive evidence as the basis for resource deployment decisions, as discussed above and in Chapter 17. But another obligation of stewardship is *efficient* deployment of resources, yielding an appropriate cost/benefit ratio or return on stakeholder investment. It is perfectly reasonable for students and their families, taxpayers, and donors to expect you to deploy their investments in your college efficiently, keeping a college education affordable. One of stakeholders' greatest concerns today is how the tuition and fees paid by students compare to their likelihood of graduating and landing a job and their post-graduation pay. Monitor your answers to these questions regularly.

Similarly, track how successfully you are achieving your goals, but also compare those successes against their costs in both time and money. Does your college leadership know and use basic information such as the following?

- Percentage of students who graduate with significantly more than the number of credits required for a degree
- Cost of providing one credit's worth of education
- Distribution of class sizes (for example, the proportions that are either very large or very small)
- Student/faculty ratio
- Percentage of instructional space that is occupied by scheduled classes, labs, and so on each hour of each day of the week
- Energy use per square foot of space
- Residence hall occupancy rate
- Cost per attendee of cultural events
- Cost of enrolling one new student (admissions and student marketing budgets divided by the number of new students enrolled)
- Cost of each dollar raised (funds raised divided by development, fundraising, and alumni office budgets)

Fold evidence of efficiency into reviews and decisions. Incorporate cost-effectiveness into program reviews and proposals for new initiatives, for example, as discussed in Chapter 20.

But do not let efficiency adversely affect effectiveness. You may save money by moving courses online or increasing class size, but that savings is moot if students do not learn as much or as well. Prudent stewardship requires examining the effectiveness as well as the efficiency of what you are doing. Are you considering increasing class sizes? Try offering a course with two or three different class sizes and comparing student learning outcomes.

Keep the governance structure lean and focused. No matter what its fiscal circumstances, almost every college I know has one thing in overabundance: committees. The problem is that work expands to fill the time allotted. Appoint a committee and it will meet, no matter how important or unimportant its work in advancing the college's purpose, goals, or quality. Too many layers of committee review can bog a college down and make it unresponsive to stakeholder needs. Try putting some committees on hiatus for a year and see what happens. Or try merging committees to help "move away from the passive and disconnected work that often now occurs, for example, in separate educational policy, curriculum, and assessment committees" (Morrill, 2013, "Faculty Educational Leadership," para. 1). McKendree University, for example, has one Student Learning, Assessment, and Teaching Effectiveness Committee, whose first responsibility is to improve the quality of teaching and learning (Tami Eggleston, personal communication, June 24, 2013). Ohio State University, meanwhile, integrates assessment oversight into the charges of its curriculum committees (Alexis Collier, personal communication, April 25, 2014). These kinds of practices integrate assessment into teaching and curriculum development, rather than presenting it as a standalone activity.

Proceed carefully with alternative education models. The high cost of the traditional face-to-face teaching model has prompted the exploration of alternative models aimed at improving affordability and effectiveness in meeting today's needs. These models include:

- Online courses and programs
- Problem-based learning, in which students construct their own learning through hands-on collaborative work solving real-life problems, with a faculty member available as a resource
- Competency-based programs in which progress toward a degree or certificate is judged by what students have learned and can do, rather than by the number of hours they spend in a course

Jargon Alert!

Massive Open Online Courses (MOOCs)

MOOCs are online courses that are open, at no charge, to anyone who wants to enroll in them. They can attract thousands of students throughout the world, and they are generally characterized by interactive online communities of students.

Jargon Alert!

Competency-Based

In *competency-based* courses, grades are based solely on how well students have achieved the course's learning objectives. All assignments and coursework are designed to help students achieve those objectives, and students must earn a passing grade on every learning objective in order to pass the course. In a writing course, for example, an A for persuasive arguments cannot be averaged with an F for grammar to yield a C. Factors such as attendance, class participation, or submitting assignments on time do not count toward grades unless the course's learning objectives include things like time management.

Competency-based courses could be combined into competency-based degrees; students would earn a degree by completing and passing every assignment in every course. But competency-based degrees instead consist of all those assignments without chunking them into courses; students do not earn credits or grades for courses. Students often have the option of working through assignments at their own pace.

While competency-based degrees are not for everyone, the principles of competency-based education—evaluating or grading students based on whether or not they have achieved important learning outcomes, and not letting an A on one key outcome balance an F on another—is simply good educational practice and something that anyone can apply.

A common characteristic of these models is that students are expected to take greater responsibility for constructing their own learning. These models all have potential to deliver courses and programs more efficiently and to reach students for whom face-to-face on-campus courses are not feasible, such as those living in remote locations or working odd hours. They are not a panacea, however. Some skills, such as using laboratory equipment and client counseling, require face-to-face or hands-on experiences (although simulations can be helpful), and some students learn more effectively when they interact meaningfully with faculty, as discussed in Chapter 12.

These initiatives all require careful planning and significant investment if they are to succeed. Online courses, for example, require an appropriate technology infrastructure, structures for student support, and considerable support for faculty as they transition from teaching face-to-face to the very different model of online education. Develop a "business plan" before moving ahead with any of these ventures, addressing the questions in Table 20.1 in Chapter 20.

For More Information

Your go-to resource for all things financial is the National Association of College and University Business Officers (NACUBO) (www.nacubo.org). Its book *Strategic Financial Analysis for Higher Education* (Salluzzo & Tahey, 2010) is particularly helpful in understanding measures of financial health.

Sally Johnstone and Louis Soares' "Principles for Developing Competency-Based Education Programs" (2014) offers thoughtful ideas. Carol Moore and Bob Whittaker's "A Four-Step Plan to 'Right-Size' the Curriculum" (2013) offers practical strategies for examining the breadth of course and program offerings.

DIMENSION II:
A Culture of Community

CHAPTER 7

A COMMUNITY OF PEOPLE

A quality college cannot function without many people: students, faculty, administrators and staff, governing board members, alumni, donors, and community and business leaders. As Robert Delprino says, "Change is a people process" (2013, p. 7). None of the five cultures of quality can be achieved by one individual or a small group. Identifying purpose and goals, assembling evidence, using that evidence to advance quality, acting with integrity, deploying resources, and providing students with the best possible education—these all need people working together as a community to take the college on its journey. A quality college thus has pervasive cultures of respect, communication, collaboration, growth and development, shared collegial governance and, mundane though it may sound, documentation.

There is no one right or best way to organize a college and its people. A quality college is simply organized in a way that best helps it achieve its purpose, goals, and the five cultures of quality. If your college focuses on student research experiences, for example, design your organizational and governance structures to foster those opportunities by bringing the right people at your college together to work on them.

A traditional organizational model may not be the most effective. For example, if one of your key aims is to help students appreciate diverse perspectives by making connections across disciplines and approaches, you might want to consider an organization that fosters interdisciplinary connections, which may not be one with traditional academic departments.

A Culture of Respect

At a college with a true atmosphere of mutual respect, everyone is open with everyone else. Disagreements are expressed and received civilly. Everyone feels treated fairly, equitably, and consistently. Their diverse skills, expertise, viewpoints, and values are respected.

A culture of disrespect can be hard to turn around. Tackle it with root cause analysis (Chapter 10), asking: "Why does this culture exist here?" (I list some potential root causes in Chapter 4.) Then use the answers to identify strategies to foster a culture of respect. Here are some ideas to consider.

Be fair. Fairness is about treating your college's current and prospective students, your college's community, and your college's other stakeholders equitably and consistently. It includes, for example, putting college policies and practices in writing, sharing them, and sticking to them, as discussed later in this chapter.

Trust. Here is an example. Some colleges insist on assessing the learning outcomes of programs or general education curricula through independent "blind" scoring of student work: student names are removed, the work evaluated by people other than the students' professors, and inter-rater reliabilities (Chapter 14) are calculated, comparing the evaluators' scores for consistency. This is a good research practice, but what does it say about your trust in your faculty to evaluate their students' work fairly and consistently? If you have evidence that faculty are not evaluating student work credibly, first try to find out why before investing in independent blind scoring. Perhaps it is a matter of clarifying a fuzzy rubric, or training faculty on how to use it properly, or providing support to address any shortcomings in student learning identified by the rubric. I talk more about the costs and benefits of independent blind scoring in Chapter 18.

Tap faculty expertise. I worry when I see a business college with an ineffectual strategic plan or financial plan or a college offering a communication or graphic design major whose evidence is impossible to find or incomprehensible. What are you teaching your students, I wonder? If you are teaching this well, how can you be doing this so badly? It often turns out that administrators are not tapping faculty expertise.

Involve students. A great deal of the work to implement a culture of quality can be done by students through class projects, independent study, or co-curricular activities:

- Students, especially those in teacher education, can help identify a program's learning outcomes and design rubrics and test blueprints to assess student achievement of them.

- Student government organizations can collaborate with faculty and administrators to design programs to improve student success.

- Business students can help identify dashboard indicators.

- Marketing, statistics, and social science students can help design and analyze surveys, do market research on your college's stakeholders and their needs, and analyze competitors.

- Economics students can measure the economic impact of your college and the cost-effectiveness of your programs and services.

- Accounting students can review various ratios of your college's financial health and performance.

- Information technology students can design ways to record and process evidence.

- Graphics, communications, and information technology students can help develop infographics, slide presentations, and websites to share evidence.

Let people learn from their mistakes. Some colleges require faculty and administrators to submit assessment plans to a committee for approval before they are allowed to implement them. While I understand the intent—we all want to do things right the first time—critiques can make people defensive and uncooperative. Trying and initially failing, on the other hand, can be a valuable learning experience. Let administrators try to assess poorly worded goals, and they will quickly see the need to state them more clearly. Let faculty with a history of working in silos design and implement their own assessments, and they will soon see that they are drowning in apples-and-oranges data. Let the student development staff send out a survey without strategies to maximize the response rate, and they will soon see that they do not have enough responses. After these experiences, people will be willing to move to more thoughtful and collaborative models (Frye, 2012).

I offer words of caution here. As I discussed in Chapter 4, people in higher education would much rather improve methodologies than use results. Treat these initial trials like a research pilot study. Pilot studies are conducted once, and then the actual research project gets underway. Do the same with any quality effort, including assessment: move from one trial run to implementation.

A Culture of Communication

Open, honest communication is vital to a quality college because it affects so many aspects of the cultures of quality, including integrity, transparency, respect, and collaboration. As Richard Morrill has noted, "Providing information creates a sense of common circumstance and ownership that builds trust and motivates action" (2013, "Communication," para. 2).

Here are some of the suggestions I have offered to colleges:

- Just sending out e-mail announcements may not work; we all know how many e-mails are never read. Plan your communications with an understanding of your stakeholders and how they prefer to receive information.

- Do not overwhelm students and employees with so much communication that they cannot discern the signal (important information) from the noise (irrelevant information). Monroe Community College found that honing and targeting its communications to students increased student attention to announcements about early fall registration, leading to a 30 percent increase in registrations (Nelson, 2013). Try putting routine college announcements into one daily e-mail coordinated by one office.

- Communication is a two-way street, of course, not just telling but also listening. Create forums for input . . . and make sure they are taken seriously. This is where collaboration, which I discuss next, comes into play.

Chapter 16 offers suggestions on sharing evidence effectively.

A Culture of Collaboration

A culture of collaboration is another indispensable component of quality (Morrill, 2013). Learning experiences, for example, ". . . need to be integrated into a coherent whole for each and every student. And this integration needs to occur as a result of enhanced collaboration among faculty across departments, as well as closer collaboration between faculty and student affairs professionals—including academic advisors, career counselors, and other campus educators who work every day to help students make sense of their educational experiences" (Humphreys, 2013, para. 13).

Yes, there are people who will never appreciate the bigger picture, but these kinds of people seem to be in the minority at most of the colleges I have worked with—except, perhaps, those whose courses, programs, or services are facing declining interest and demand and who are fighting to keep their jobs above all else.

Most people I have encountered are ready to work with their colleagues on key issues of quality.

The best way to build a culture of collaboration is to deploy resources—people and facilities as well as dollars—in ways that address broad rather than narrow needs. Give budget priority to projects (identified through systematic evidence, of course, as discussed in Chapter 17) that cross department and disciplinary lines. Target professional development funds for collaborative projects, such as for a group of faculty who want to work together to learn how to improve their students' critical thinking skills. A sizable portion of the President's Innovation Fund at Lebanon Valley College, for example, which was created to encourage pilot projects with wide-reaching potential for fostering transformative learning, is reserved for collaborative teaching/learning experiences between disciplines and programs (Lewis Thayne, personal communication, August 19, 2013).

Other strategies to foster a culture of collaboration include the following:

- Use videoconferencing and online forums to facilitate meetings across locations.

- Carve a time slot out of weekly class schedules—say Wednesdays at noon—that is dedicated to faculty meetings, with no classes scheduled.

- Block off dates in the academic calendar for faculty and staff retreats to perhaps discuss collected evidence and identify strategies for addressing any shortcomings.

A Culture of Growth and Development

A quality college cannot be static, so neither can its community. Everyone's expertise needs to grow and develop. Most people at colleges are eager to learn (Suskie, 2013). Help them! Help your college community learn about and discuss stakeholder needs, external forces affecting your college, and current research and good practices on student learning and student success (Alexander & Gardner, 2009).

Then provide ongoing venues for faculty, administrators, and board members to discuss and use this information to help your college achieve its purpose and goals and advance the five cultures of quality. Possible venues include:

- A teaching-learning center
- On-campus workshops, brown-bag lunch discussions, online forums, and webinars
- A network of mentors or champions to provide one-on-one assistance and support with particularly challenging work, such as student learning assessment
- If you use rubrics, training so that faculty interpret and apply them consistently and fairly

Jargon Alert!

Teaching-Learning Center

A *teaching-learning center (TLC)* is an office that provides professional development and support to faculty on curriculum design and effective teaching methods. Many focus on technological support, helping faculty use new technologies in the classroom or move classes online. The best centers provide support for student learning assessment, helping faculty see that assessment is simply part of teaching.

Focus on your college's priorities. As with any other resource, focus professional development programs and opportunities (and this can include travel and sabbatical leaves) on helping your college achieve its purpose and goals and advance its quality agenda (Kuh, Jankowski, Ikenberry, & Kinzie, 2014). If one of your college's priorities is developing in students a commitment to civic engagement, for example, give priority to funding professional development activities on civic engagement.

Provide coordination and guidance. Just as students learn best when they are given clear guidelines for their assignments, so faculty and staff do their best work in implementing a culture of quality when they are provided with clear expectations, guidance, and coordination. Hancock College, for example, helped faculty learn about student learning assessment through a flexible combination of drop-in sessions, group training, one-on-one training, going to faculty offices, and even having the institutional research and planning office enter results for them if need be. After less than a year of this guidance and support, the proportion of courses with reported student learning assessment data jumped from 8 percent to 92 percent (Jennie Robertson, personal communication, June 26, 2013).

The best people to provide coordination and guidance (Suskie, 2009) are those with:

- Sensitivity and open-mindedness
- Flexibility: readiness to encourage and facilitate multiple approaches
- A passion for your college's purpose and goals, especially teaching and learning
- Recognized expertise

Because so many aspects of the five cultures of quality are about student learning, look to your teaching-learning center director or someone else with respected experience in curriculum design and teaching methods to help provide leadership, coordination, and guidance. Long Island University (LIU), for example, created the position of General Education Faculty Fellow, filled by an experienced, respected faculty member, to coordinate the assessment of LIU's core curriculum (Frye, 2012).

Support adjunct faculty with training and supervision. Today, nearly half of all college faculty are part-time/adjuncts (AFT Higher Education, 2010) and, at U.S. community colleges, 58 percent of all courses are taught by adjuncts (Center for Community College Student Engagement, 2014). Adjuncts can enrich student learning through their real-world experiences, but they can provide a quality learning experience only if they understand and convey their courses' key learning outcomes and standards and how their courses fit into the program or general education curriculum. Training, supervision, support, and clear, appropriate expectations are thus essential. If possible, consider including in adjuncts' contracts requirements that they fulfill key responsibilities before receiving their final payment. Examples of such responsibilities include:

- Incorporating certain core elements into their syllabi,
- Including a common set of questions on their final exams,
- Engaging in certain professional development activities, and/or
- Participating in assessments of learning outcomes by submitting student work or completed rubrics.

Offer constructive, collegial feedback. Just as students learn best when they receive feedback on their work, so faculty and administrators do their best work in implementing a culture of quality when they receive constructive feedback on their efforts. Consider, for example, charging a committee of peers with reviewing annual reports on assessment efforts and offering commendations for good assessment efforts, constructive feedback, and support such as mentoring.

A Culture of Shared Collegial Governance

An effective governance system balances power, authority, and responsibility appropriately among:

- The board
- The president
- The college's leadership team and other administrators

Jargon Alert!

Institutional Governance

Institutional governance is simply a balance of power, a lot like the system of checks and balances enshrined in the United States Constitution, that leads to collaborative, integrated decisions (Morrill, 2013).

- Faculty
- Students

To people who have spent their careers at traditional colleges, the concept of shared collegial governance is self-evident. But to those from outside higher education or at what I call outlier colleges, the concept may be foreign. In the business world, for example, "governance" traditionally refers only to the responsibilities of the corporate board and officers.

Does your college really need a system of collegial shared governance? After all, there are plenty of companies and non-profit organizations that operate successfully without the governance system prevalent in U.S. higher education. Do dysfunctional governance systems really hurt the quality of student learning? And do not elaborative governance systems, with multiple layers of committees and review, slow down progress?

These are legitimate questions, but I have seen plenty of examples of what happens when a governance system is dysfunctional and the balance of power gets out of whack. Faculty go up in arms because their president has announced major new initiatives without consultation. Presidents depart in frustration over micromanaging boards. Assessment committees set college-wide learning outcomes without input from or approval of the faculty . . . and then wonder why the faculty are not helping to assess those outcomes. Faculty step in to fill the power void left by weak college leaders, doing end runs directly to the board.

Do these problems kill a college? Of course not. But they sap morale, time, and energy and can lead to high turnover and a chaotic campus environment. People focused on these kinds of issues cannot spend time on far more critical issues, such as improving the quality of the educational experience.

A Culture of Documentation

Part of fairness and effective shared governance is documenting in writing what I call "the rules of the game" and then applying them consistently and equitably.

Provide clear statements of everyone's responsibilities and how their work is integrated into organizational and governance structures. Make clear the role of every individual and group in making college decisions, including whether each has an advisory role or final authority regarding particular decisions. When faculty or students have a proposal, for example, where do they take it? What is the process to ensure that appropriate groups offer feedback on the idea? What is the process by which the idea is considered formally by appropriate groups and individuals, such as the chief academic officer, the president, and/or the board? Similarly, to whom does the college assessment committee report? What decisions can it make on its own, and which must it forward elsewhere for review and ultimate approval? Keep in mind that many accreditors expect that faculty have leadership and responsibility for student learning, including learning outcomes, curriculum design, teaching methods, and assessment.

I am not talking about simply pulling together existing bylaws and position descriptions. Bylaws provide the legal framework for the establishment of a board or other governance body, but they typically do not list the board's specific responsibilities or how it conducts its work.

Document policies, evidence, and decisions. Have a clear, written research-based definition of effective teaching, for example, that your college uses in decisions on promotion, tenure, professional development, and resource deployment.

Pull together and share documentation. For example, organize all governance and organizational documents into one college
website, so that all members of the college community can see their
roles in your college's governance and organizational structures.

For More Information

I often suggest that colleges looking for institutional governance
models contact peer colleges to request access to their governance documents. Sometimes these documents are publicly
available on college websites. But do not look to adopt another
college's governance structure wholesale; your college's culture
and needs are unique.

The American Association of University Professors (AAUP)
(www.aaup.org) offers resources on the faculty role in shared governance, and the Association of Governing Boards (AGB) (www
.agb.org) offers resources on the board's role, which is discussed
in Chapter 8. For insight into the administration's role, I like
"The Art, Science, and Craft of Administrative Support" in *Using
Quality Benchmarks for Assessing and Developing Undergraduate
Programs* (Dunn, McCarthy, Baker, & Halonen, 2011). An important new resource is *Governance Reconsidered: How Boards,
Presidents, Administrators, and Faculty Can Help Their Colleges
Thrive* by Susan Resnick Pierce (2014).

CHAPTER 8

LEADERSHIP CAPACITY AND COMMITMENT

Your college has two kinds of leadership—presidential leadership and board leadership—to further the balance of power in college governance discussed in Chapter 7.

Board responsibilities. Your board has no greater responsibility than ensuring that your college has effective leadership through its president and board members. Its other fundamental responsibility is one of oversight, especially in assuring your college's:

- Quality (Chapters 3 and 17)
- Integrity (Chapter 5)
- Stewardship (Chapter 6)
- Focus and aspirations (Chapters 9 and 10)

Presidential responsibilities. Your president is responsible for leading the college toward its goals and the fulfillment of its purpose, with the board supporting the president through any challenges the president faces in implementing the strategic plan and making other changes necessary to achieve the five cultures of quality.

Jargon Alert!

Chief Executive Officer

In the corporate world, the *chief executive officer* (CEO)—first-in-command and responsible for vision, strategy, and integrating policy into day-to-day operations—is often called *chairman of the board.* The *chief operating officer* (COO)—second-in-command and responsible for day-to-day operations—is often called *president*. In contrast, at most colleges the CEO is called *president*. At many colleges, the president serves as both CEO and COO, but some colleges have a separate COO with a title such as *executive vice president* or *senior vice president*.

Capacity and Commitment

A quality college has leaders with the *capacity* and *commitment* to facilitate the college's journey toward its goals. *Boards and presidents especially need the capacity to do what needs to be done.* Whether or not a troubled college survives—or a mediocre college improves—boils down to two kinds of capacity. Obviously, colleges need resources to fix whatever problems they are facing. But the other equally critical capacity issue is one of leadership itself. Do the college's leaders recognize what needs to be done to put the college on the right course? Are they able to get things going? Are they capable of deploying the college's resources effectively to address problems?

At a quality college, the board and president are also *committed* to the best interests of the college and its students. Their time, energy, and active support concentrate on ensuring the five dimensions of quality and that the college is effectively fulfilling its responsibilities to its students and other stakeholders. And support is not just a matter of throwing money at something, say by sending a few people to a conference (Suskie, 2009). It is keeping priorities at the forefront and providing active, vocal, visible, personal support.

Capacity and commitment are embodied in the following traits, all discussed in this chapter:

- Empowered leadership
- Independent leadership
- Putting your college's interests ahead of a third party
- Collaborative leadership
- Board engagement
- The right people
- Ongoing education and development

Empowered Leadership

Quality colleges have boards and leaders who are sufficiently empowered to act in the college's best interests. Colleges must have a president empowered to act as chief executive officer, providing vision, strategy, and leadership, not just overseeing day-to-day operations. One president once defined empowerment to me this way: "I can say no."

Independent Leadership

Quality colleges have boards and leaders who are sufficiently independent that they can view the college with an objective eye. When I ask a college's board members how they came to be on the board and most of them say, "I'm an alum," I worry. Will they be able to recognize that the college today cannot be the college they attended? Will they embrace the need for appropriate transformations?

When most board members tell me, "I'm a friend of the president," again I worry. Will they be able to give the president the objective support he or she needs? Will they be able to recognize when the president is no longer effective and it is time for a change?

Do they have a clear, impartial picture of the traits the college most needs in a president and what the president most needs to accomplish?

The Securities and Exchange Commission, New York Stock Exchange, and NASDAQ all expect a majority of corporate board members to be independent. This is a good rule of thumb, although my definition of independent board members is different from theirs, comprising only those with *no* affiliation with your college—even alumni status—or any affiliated entity. A silent majority of independent board members is inadequate, however. Independent members need to have backgrounds and credentials sufficient for their views to be treated with respect and given full consideration in decisions.

Putting Your College's Interests
Ahead of a Third Party

Leadership empowerment and independence may be a particular challenge when a college is overseen or controlled in some way by another entity or third party. These colleges may have boards or leaders who are responsible to the oversight entity. Such colleges include those that are

- Part of a public or private system of colleges or other operations, such as a high school, museum, or hospital
- Operated by a government agency
- Owned by an individual or corporation
- Sponsored by a church, order, or other religious organization

Many colleges in these circumstances operate successfully, of course, when the oversight entity recognizes that the path to a successful future, both for itself and the college, is fulfilling the college's responsibilities listed in Chapter 5 and ensuring the five dimensions of quality. But sometimes the oversight entity may have goals that differ from—or are even at cross-purposes with—the college's goals:

- If a college is operated by a church (or other organization) that is struggling financially, the church board may want to use college resources or excess revenue to support the church, rather than the college's mission.

- If a college is public, its board's priority may be furthering a political agenda such as minimizing taxpayer support, rather than ensuring the college's ongoing quality.

- If a college is owned by a corporation (or private owner), the corporate board may want to maximize immediate shareholder return by expanding too quickly to maintain quality.

- If a college's board is responsible for an affiliated high school or museum as well as the college, it may struggle to reconcile its dual responsibilities. If the high school or museum is struggling more than the college, will the college continue to receive its fair share of board attention and resources?

Solving these kinds of dilemmas is not always straightforward; the board of the oversight entity may have legal responsibility for the college and ultimate authority for approval of decisions affecting it. Possible solutions include establishing a separate board or a board committee that reports to the third-entity board but is charged with college oversight. Then the proof is in the pudding: whether the oversight board respects and endorses the actions and advice of the college board or committee or whether it often overrides them.

Collaborative Leadership

The work of college leaders is part of the work of the college community. As I discussed in Chapter 7, a quality college is characterized by a culture of communication, collaboration, and shared collegial governance. An effective board does not fulfill its responsibilities in isolation but consults with the college community, especially when determining the college's purpose and goals and establishing broad policies.

Board Engagement

I have read through two years of some board minutes without seeing a single motion, just unending reports from administrators on how great everything is. I have seen other minutes that show attention to the college's finances . . . but none to the college's academic quality. I have seen others in which the strategic plan is never mentioned; the annual budget is approved without any apparent discussion of how the budget should help move the college toward its key goals. Board members need to ensure that the right items are on their agendas and that critical questions are raised and discussed during board and committee meetings. In particular, they need to make sure that they regularly receive information on student success, including student achievement of key learning outcomes (Bok, 2006; Kuh, Jankowski, Ikenberry, & Kinzie, 2014).

The Right People

Your board needs members who bring experience and expertise in all the board's areas of responsibility, as well as in the significant directions that your college is pursuing. Consultants and advisory groups can be helpful, but they are not a substitute for board members who actively participate in board discussions and vote on board actions. If your college has made improving student retention and completion rates a priority, for example, consider adding board members with expertise in this. Planning, financial management, higher education administration, and higher education academics are other areas in which board expertise is needed. Here I counsel diversity, especially in financial expertise and in layers of financial review. Some college leaders and boards place too much faith in one financial officer, one board member with a financial background, or one financial advisor.

As I noted at the beginning of this chapter, perhaps the board's most important responsibility is ensuring effective leadership. When a longstanding president leaves and some significant changes are needed, I encourage boards to consider hiring an interim president for one or two years. An interim president can make tough, unpopular, but necessary changes and pave the way for a smooth, successful transition to a new long-term president.

Ongoing Education and Development

Most presidents cannot possibly bring the vast array of knowledge and skills they need to succeed in their leadership positions at their colleges. Boards can support them by encouraging them to attend programs for new presidents, join relevant organizations, and develop networks with other presidents. This is especially important at what I call "outlier" colleges: those outside the higher education mainstream, such as proprietary colleges, and those serving a very narrow segment of the college-going population, such as those sponsored by a very small religious denomination or offering only a very specialized program. Outliers often want college leaders with backgrounds reflecting their college's mission. Depending on how narrow the mission is, these colleges can have a hard time finding leaders with appropriate experience and expertise. Board encouragement of these presidents' ongoing professional development is particularly important.

While board members generally bring some experience and expertise to their roles, their backgrounds are in contexts different from those of your college. Board members must understand your college's history, culture, environment, students, and needs, but they generally do not have time to pore through lengthy reports or sit through long presentations. Chapter 16 offers ideas on sharing information concisely and effectively.

For More Information

Your go-to resource on board roles and responsibilities is the Association of Governing Boards (AGB) (http://agb.org), which offers publications, events, and consultants. Another excellent, comprehensive resource on leadership is *Academic Leadership and Governance of Higher Education: A Guide for Trustees, Leaders, and Aspiring Leaders of Two- and Four-Year Institutions* (Hendrickson, Lane, Harris, & Dorman, 2013). Derek Bok's "Seizing the Initiative for Quality Education" (2006) and Peter Ewell's *Making the Grade: How Boards Can Ensure Academic Quality* (2012) offer terrific suggestions on the board's role in supporting and ensuring academic quality.

The Harvard Institute for Higher Education (www.gse.harvard .edu/ppe/programs/higher-education/index.html) offers a variety of face-to-face programs for presidents, including the Harvard Seminars for Presidents. I also encourage presidents to partici-pate actively in whatever associations serve their colleges' higher education sectors or cohorts, such as the American Association of Community Colleges or the Association of Catholic Colleges and Universities.

DIMENSION III:
A Culture of Focus and Aspiration

PURPOSE
Who Are You?
Why Do You Exist?

A quality college knows what it is, where it is going, and how it wants to get there. Put another way, it can answer the questions that journalists traditionally ask:

- *What? Why? Who?* The answers to these questions state the college's purpose: its essential activities and distinctive traits, its values, and its target clientele, respectively.
- *Where?* The answer to this question states the college's key goals: its destinations, using the analogy of a road trip from Chapter 3.
- *How? When?* The answers to these questions are the college's plans to achieve its goals: to reach its destinations.

A clearly delineated purpose is the foundation of your college's journey. It focuses the college community and its resources in ways that give your college its best shot at enduring quality. Without a clear sense of purpose, critical resources can end up going to nonessential, sidebar projects. As Richard Morrill has said, "Institutions and their major units need above all to define a compelling sense of purpose that authentically reflects their narratives of identity and core capabilities, and that translates into an ambitious agenda for action. The work of strategy is always about integrating the powerful intrinsic values and motivation that come from a strong sense of educational purpose with the need to gain advantage in a competitive and precarious world of limited resources" (2013, "Collaborative Strategic Leadership," para. 1).

Or, to cite a quotation widely attributed to W.H. Auden, "You owe it to all of us to get on with what you're good at." A quality college knows what it is good at. Some examples:

- The home page of Hamilton College, a private liberal arts college, says simply, "A national leader in teaching students to write effectively, learn from each other, and think for themselves" (www.hamilton.edu).

- The mission of California State University East Bay, a public university, includes offering "culturally relevant learning experiences" (2012, p. 1).

- The mission of Central Penn College, a proprietary college, is to prepare students to obtain "employment or advancement in their chosen field, continue their education, and be contributing members of society" (2011–2013, "Mission & Vision," para. 1)

- Oakton Community College's stated purpose in part challenges its students "to experience the hard work and satisfaction of learning" (1998, para. 3).

- The mission of Wilmington University, a private non-profit university, notes its commitment to "relevancy of the curriculum" (n.d., "Mission," para. 1).

A college's purpose is articulated by defining its essential activities, its distinctive traits, its underlying values, and its target clientele. These are not necessarily discrete; a college's underlying values or target clientele may define what makes it distinctive, for example.

Jargon Alert!

Mission

Mission simply means purpose. A mission statement is a statement of purpose.

Essential Activities:
What Would You Keep Doing No Matter What?

The stated purposes of the vast majority of U.S. colleges and universities fall into three broad categories: education, research and scholarship, and service. Within these three broad categories, most colleges try to do many things: provide a variety of academic offerings, engage in research and scholarship on a broad array of issues and ideas, and offer wide-ranging services to the community.

To gauge which of these are your college's essential activities, imagine the unimaginable: that your college's budget is cut in half. What would happen? Some programs, services, and initiatives would have to end, but there would be some for which you would say, "No, if we stop doing this, this would change what we are; we would no longer be the college we purport to be." What kinds of degree programs would you continue to offer? What would be your balance between teaching and scholarship? What kinds of community service would you continue to provide? Why?

Limit your essential activities. Many colleges are stretched too thin, offering too many programs and services, too many courses, and engaging in too many research and service activities. There is simply no way so many things can be done well.

Jargon Alert!

Mission Creep

Mission creep is expanding the array of a college's essential activities to the point that it is doing a broad array of things passably, rather than focusing on those things that it does excellently and that its stakeholders most need.

Focus on what your stakeholders need most. If your college's fundamental purpose is student learning and success, consider focusing research support on investigating effective teaching strategies (the scholarship of teaching, discussed in Chapter 6). One model in this regard is the University of Wisconsin–Oshkosh (Kuh & O'Donnell, 2013). If your college aims to serve your community, consider focusing your college's service activities on addressing key unmet community needs and using research to solve real-world problems (the scholarship of application, also discussed in Chapter 6). Chapter 5 talks more about meeting stakeholder needs and the public good.

Distinctive Traits:
Why Should Anyone Enroll or Invest Here?

Distinctive traits are what set your college apart from its peers and competitors. Today's higher education environment has become incredibly competitive, especially for small regional private colleges. Why should a student enroll at your college when there are other perfectly good colleges offering similar programs? Why should a foundation award your college a grant for a new initiative when there are other equally good colleges trying to do something similar?

Diversity is one of the historic strengths of U.S. higher education, and some U.S. colleges are truly unique. Gallaudet University, for example, is the only liberal arts college in the

United States with a mission to serve the deaf and hard of hearing (2013, "Mission Statement," para. 1). But many colleges have no clearly distinct identity, and in today's competitive environment these colleges may be struggling for students, funds . . . and their eventual survival. As Bev Taylor has said, some colleges "are going to need to do some serious work to get themselves noticed" (Pearce, 2013, para. 6).

Each of the colleges I mentioned earlier not only has a clear sense of purpose, but a *distinctive* sense of purpose. The focus of each—service to society at Central Penn, writing and thinking at Hamilton, curricular relevance at Wilmington, and so on—are the kinds of distinctive traits that attract both students and support.

Underlying Values: What Are the Rationales for Your Decisions?

Values are the fundamental principles that underlie how your college makes decisions and goes about its business. Think of how your family and other families you know spend their money. If you have any discretionary income, you all have different priorities for how it is spent. Some families think it is especially important to have as nice a home as they can afford. Others think it is especially important to drive a relatively new car. Others place a high priority on their children's education, wearing the latest styles, traveling, or simply saving for a rainy day. Few families have enough money to do all these things, so each family sets priorities that reflect its values.

Values come into clearer focus when families face financial changes. Either a pay cut or a pay raise leads to changes in what families do with their resources. What you decide to cut from the family budget or what you do with a windfall says a lot about your values.

The same is true for colleges. Look at how you spend your college's budget: how you decide what to fund and what to cut. What do those decisions say about your college's values? Some colleges' stated values are so generic—integrity, respect for diverse view-points, and the like—that, although they are important, they cannot help inform decisions. Quality colleges articulate distinctive values that sharpen their sense of purpose and help them make decisions. Central Penn's belief that "the end purpose of education is to make this world a better place for others" (2011–2013) informs its decision to sponsor a college-wide community service day each term.

Target Clientele: Whom Do You Aim to Serve?

If your college's primary mission is education, your primary clien-tele is your students, and your target clientele is the specific kinds of students you aim to serve. Does your college focus on serving full-time students or part-time commuters? Traditionally aged stu-dents straight out of high school or older working adults? Students from your immediate region, or contiguous states, or across the nation? Students who are largely self-directed learners or who need extra support? Students who are well prepared to succeed in college or who need to come up to speed?

I find too many colleges silent on their target clientele. Students want and deserve to find a college that will be a good "fit" for them, but too many colleges seem ready to take all comers. Except for highly selective colleges, how many are willing to tell students, "Yes, we can admit you, but we're not sure we're a good match with what you're looking for"? The University of Phoenix, which offers much of its curricula online, offers a self-screening for prospective applicants (https://www.phoenix.edu/experience.html) to help them gauge their readiness for success in an online environment.

Use Systematic Evidence and Collaboration

Nowhere are the cultures of community, evidence, and betterment more important than in deciding what your college is all about. Collaboration is discussed in Chapter 7, and using systematic evi-dence is discussed in Chapter 17.

How to Articulate Your Purpose

Unless your accreditor requires otherwise, no law says that your college's purpose must be articulated in a particular format. I have often suggested articulating the four elements of purpose—essential activities, distinctive traits, underlying values, and target clientele—into one statement. But Karen Hinton (2012) suggests keeping the mission statement to just a few lines that delineate essential activities and putting values, target clientele, and distinctive traits into separate statements. This may make sense, because many accreditors require assessment of each aspect of the mission, and it may not be appropriate or feasible to assess a college's underlying values or distinctive traits. On the other hand, however, some values and distinctive traits, such as, "to help students learn through hands-on experiences" or "to prepare students to arrive at ethical decisions," represent assessable aims.

For More Information

Your go-to source for information on strategic planning in higher education, including delineating purpose, is the Society for College and University Planning (www.scup.org). It offers a variety of resources, including books and events. Diane Cordero de Noriega's "Institutional Vision, Values, and Mission: Foundational Filters for Inquiry" (2006) is a wonderful, succinct introduction to articulating your college's purpose.

CHAPTER 10

GOALS AND PLANS
Where Are You Going?
How Will You Get There?

While your college's purpose defines what it is and why, its goals define its destinations: where it will be at some future point. Those destinations can be expressed in two ways.

- A *vision* is a compelling narrative description of your college's destinations that inspires and engages stakeholders, such as potential students, alumni, and community residents, and helps them understand and support your college.

- *Key or strategic goals* are more concrete statements of your college's destinations that provide pragmatic guidance to your college community as it plans and makes decisions. Clear statements of goals also help major donors and investors understand where your college is going and how they can support its journey.

Jargon Alert!

Strategic Goals, Strategic Directions, and Strategic Aims

Strategic goals, *strategic directions*, and *strategic aims* all describe your destinations. Use whatever term fits best with your college's culture. Because these terms all come with some baggage, in this book I generally use *key goals* or simply *goals*.

Some colleges have both vision statements and strategic goals, but I am not convinced that you need both. Well-stated goals alone can be compelling and inspiring, as well as clear and concrete. SUNY College of Environmental Science & Forestry's *Vision 2020* (n.d.), for example, states seven compelling goals without a separate narrative statement of vision.

Identify Your Destinations

Simply put, your goals should focus on what is truly important.

Quality is more important than quantity. I have seen strategic plans with 100 objectives. There is no way that so many things can be done well. "A few well-conceived goals that address identified priorities will engage, unite, and inspire the institutional community, while a long 'laundry list' of goals may cause the institutional community to lose focus and diffuse its energies. . . . The process of honing many possible goals . . . down to a few essential ones is valuable, as it generates critical discussions throughout the institutional community about institutional values and priorities" (Middle States Commission on Higher Education [MSCHE], 2006, p. 5).

I rarely give very prescriptive advice, but I often suggest a "3-to-6" rule. Focus on just three to six key goals, three to six program-level learning outcomes, three to six strategies for each key goal . . . you get the idea. With more than six, you may be spreading yourselves too thin and losing focus. Hone your goals by focusing only on those that are most important to achieve your college's purpose and that build on your college's distinctive traits and values.

Focus on student learning, stakeholder needs, and the public good. A quality college ensures that there is appropriate congruence among its purpose, its goals, the interests and needs of its stakeholders, and the public good. Aim for a suitable balance among your goals. I worry, for example, when a college's goals focus almost exclusively on its finances and factors affecting them.

If the fundamental purpose of your college is education, your goals should focus on student learning and success. Yes, you may need goals to shore up your college's financial position, but you do not want to achieve them at the price of neglecting student learning and success and the five cultures of quality.

Focus on what is significant and aspirational. Your goals should tackle things that really need to be addressed in order to advance your college, meet your students' and other stakeholder needs, and serve the public good. *Meaningful goals are significant, aspirational destinations that will take several years to reach, not one-year projects that are quick operational fixes.* An important lesson here comes from those colleges that grew rapidly in recent years in order to generate immediate income and (for corporate proprietaries) return to stockholders. By focusing on short-term returns rather than long-term position, some of these colleges have not maintained quality . . . and have seen an aftermath of accreditation issues, diminished reputation, and enrollment declines.

Use external as well as internal evidence to inform your discussions. A faculty member once commented to me that evidence of achieving goals and student learning outcomes can inform incremental changes, but it cannot alone lead to innovative changes. His point is well taken. To make innovative changes, you also need to consider evidence of what is going on in the world outside your college. Some examples:

- Know your key competitors for students and funds and what they think, say, and do, including evidence of how successful they are in doing the kinds of things that you want to do.
- Use evidence of emerging research on strategies that promote student learning and student success to inform capital facilities expenditures. The movement toward flipped classrooms (Chapter 12), for example, suggests that lecture halls with fixed seating may go the way of the dinosaur in the next decade.
- Surveys of public perceptions of your college can be enlightening.

Chapter 5 offers suggestions on information you might collect about your key stakeholders' needs, interests, and priorities, and Chapter 17 talks more about using evidence to refine goals.

Jargon Alert!

SWOT Analysis

A *SWOT analysis* is a review of your college's strengths and weaknesses and potential opportunities and threats in the environment. A SWOT analysis calls for systematic evidence, not anecdotal or unsupported assertions, such as, "We have a beautiful campus."

Jargon Alert!

Environmental Scan

An *environmental scan* is the part of the SWOT analysis that gathers and reviews systematic evidence on what is happening in the various environments in which your college operates: demographic, geographic, economic, political, and so on.

Collaborate. Collaborative deliberations are at the heart of good strategic planning (Morrill, 2013). Colleges are fortunate to be permeated with talented, well-educated, well-informed people as well as a history and values, whether articulated or unspoken. If you ignore your college community and its history and values, articulating your college's future becomes an uphill, divisive battle. But if you involve people representing a broad cross-section of stakeholders, such as faculty, staff, students, alumni, business leaders, and donors, their input will doubtless lead to stronger, better goals. And you will need the help of all these people to realize your college's goals, so their buy-in, through active collaboration from the very beginning, is important. Collaboration is discussed further in Chapter 7.

Articulate Your Destinations

What is a well-stated goal? Consider these examples, similar to real college goals that I have seen:

- Student distinction
- Promote student growth and development
- Exceptional academic programs
- Create and enhance partnerships

Now consider these:

- Encourage a recognition and understanding of personal and cultural differences (Dutchess Community College, 2013, "Institutional Goals," para. 15)
- Provide an outstanding student experience (SUNY College of Environmental Science & Forestry, n.d., p. 7)
- Integrate academics with experiential learning and career preparation (Stevenson University, 2013, "Strategies," para. 1)
- Create vibrant, distinctive, and collegial campus identities (Pace University, 2010, p. 5)

What makes the first examples poor and the latter examples more effective? The latter incorporate many of the following suggestions.

Describe outcomes, not the processes to achieve them. A goal is not adding a service learning component to your curriculum but what students gain from the experience. A goal is not building smart classrooms but the richer, deeper learning that results. A goal is not increasing partnerships but the benefits of those partnerships to your college, students, and community.

Describing a destination rather than the route to reach it can be surprisingly hard. Some people think and reason abstractly, others concretely. Colleges need both; the abstract thinkers can envision the destination, while the concrete thinkers can plan the practical steps to get there. But you can help concrete thinkers see the destination—the outcome—through root cause analysis (Rooney & Vanden Heuvel, 2004). Repeatedly ask, "Why?" Why, for example, does your college want to increase revenues? Perhaps it wants to offer more scholarships. Why? To make college more affordable—the true goal. Or perhaps it wants to increase revenues to buy equipment that gives students more hands-on practice using cutting-edge technologies. Why? To prepare students better for successful careers—a different true goal.

Avoid "fuzzy" terms. If you ask people to paraphrase a clearly stated goal, everyone will pretty much say the same thing. Paraphrases of the vague "Student distinction" example above would probably vary considerably, while paraphrases of the clearer "Integrate academics with experiential learning" example would probably be far more consistent.

If clarifying a fuzzy goal is a struggle, imagine visiting two colleges, both with goals similar to yours. As you observe and interact with people at each, it becomes clear to you that one has achieved your goal and one has not. What might you see or hear that would help you tell them apart? Those concrete differences will give you clues on how to express your goal more clearly.

Sometimes, relatively fuzzy statements of goals are more inspirational or motivational than clearer statements might be. If this is the case, perhaps a second parallel statement that translates the goal into more concrete terms (what social scientists call an operational definition) might provide clearer, more explicit guidance to those implementing or assessing the goals.

Sometimes goals need a degree of fuzziness to be meaningful. A goal that your college will provide a learning-centered environment is fuzzy, for example (What *is* a learning-centered environment?), but explicating this goal would mean coming up with a laundry list of the traits of an effective learning-centered environment—too much to express in one goal statement. Explicating such fuzzy goals through action steps can help . . . but still try to keep the goals themselves as clear as you can.

Use observable action verbs. Observable goals make the destination clearer and therefore make it much easier to figure out how to track progress toward the goal.

Plans: How Will You Get There?

Your college's stated purpose and goals are promises that your college is making to your students and other stakeholders, so a key responsibility of your college is making sure it achieves them. Plans come in two forms: strategic and operational.

A *strategic plan* is a broad overview of a college's route to its destinations (goals). Like a GPS map, it shows in broad terms how your college will achieve its goals. It uses terms that are clear, compelling, and neither fuzzy nor too specific. One example that I have already mentioned is *Vision 2020* of the SUNY College of Environmental Science and Forestry (n.d.).

Operational plans are the nitty-gritty details, akin to a GPS's step-by-step directions and a road trip's pre-departure plan of what to pack, what to check on the car (Are tires properly inflated? Is the gas tank full?), and so on.

Jargon Alert!

Objectives, Tactical Plans, Operational Plans, and Action Steps

These terms all refer to the details of a strategic plan, with some perhaps referring to greater levels of detail than others. These terms are not used consistently. While I refer to the nuts and bolts of a strategic plan as an *operational plan*, choose whatever terms work best with your college's culture.

Operational plans are where things can become really complicated really quickly. If your college has a goal to improve student graduation rates, for example, its strategic plan might include several strategies, perhaps strengthening the first-year experience, implementing an "early warning system" identifying students at risk of failure, and increasing hands-on learning experiences. Each of these strategies requires a plan with specific action steps, timelines, and budgets. Some divisions, units, and offices will need their own goals and plans to contribute to this goal and these strategies. So there can be multiple layers of goals and plans between lofty aspirations and nitty-gritty how-to. Aim to minimize the layers and amount of detail; you do not want to spend more time planning than doing.

Put your money where your mouth is. This means not only investing dollars in support of your college's purpose and goals but also focusing everyone's time and energy on your priorities. Consider, for example, a goal of many colleges: "Provide a learning-centered environment." If this is one of your college's goals, is your college really putting its money where its mouth is, doing what it takes to accomplish this truly well?

- Is your college undertaking the challenging discussion of what it means to provide a learning-centered environment?
- Do faculty and staff hiring practices give priority to applicants with successful experience in providing a learning-centered environment?
- Do employee evaluation procedures, including promotion and tenure criteria, place strong emphasis on faculty and staff contributions toward a learning-centered environment? Are college leadership team members evaluated on the steps they take to nurture a learning-centered environment within their areas of responsibility?
- Does your college place a priority on supporting faculty scholarship that is related to learning-centered environments?
- Do professional development programs focus on how to provide a learning-centered environment?

Bottom line: Do not put anything in your purpose or goals that you are not prepared to follow through on . . . or monitor for success.

Limit your plans and activities. Carnegie Mellon University (CMU) is an example of a university that successfully focuses its activities on priorities articulated in its strategic plan. For instance, CMU has expanded its global footprint over the past decade, but it has not done so indiscriminately. Instead, it applies three criteria to inform decisions regarding future partnerships: the degree to which a location is becoming a center of growth and influence, how CMU's strengths would be used to address pressing global challenges, and a review of financial considerations (Kamlet, 2010). These priorities flow directly from Carnegie Mellon's mission to "enhance society in meaningful and sustainable ways" (n.d., "Mission Statement," para. 1), its values of entrepreneurship and compassion, and its strategic goal to build new models for "global knowledge creation, education, and citizenship" (2008, p. 14). What makes these statements and criteria compelling is that they enable Carnegie Mellon to carve a distinctive niche for itself in a competitive environment.

Integrate Goals and Plans Throughout Your College . . . Reasonably and Appropriately

Because no part of a quality college can afford to be static, every part of your college—divisions, departments, programs, services, and so on—should have goals and plans to reach them. The budget office, for example, might have a goal to improve the clarity and readability of budget reports, and a service learning program might have a goal that most undergraduates participate in meaningful service learning opportunities. I am not convinced, however, that every unit needs a lot of goals. Earlier in this chapter I suggested a "3-to-6 rule," aiming for no more than three to six goals per program or department. But for some units, especially very small ones (a one-person institutional research office, for example), just one or two meaningful goals may be plenty.

When possible, everyone's goals should support one another and your college's overall purpose and goals (Hinton, 2012). If your college has a goal to provide students with an improved educational experience, for example, most college units should have their own goals that help achieve it. But should *every* unit have goals that contribute to this college goal? Use common sense here. The budget office should probably be more concerned with making sure that the college's financial affairs are in order, and the grounds crew should probably be more concerned that roads and walkways remain safe and passable.

Colleges often have a variety of plans, not only a strategic plan to achieve the college's key or strategic goals but also an academic plan, financial plan, enrollment management plan, capital facilities master plan, technology plan, and so on. Obviously, all these plans should support the strategic plan and each other. The enrollment management plan, for example, must aim to enroll enough students to generate sufficient tuition revenue to help achieve the financial plan. The financial plan, meanwhile, must ensure that each goal in the strategic plan is supported with adequate resources. But again use common sense as you interrelate these plans; the capital facilities plan may need to focus more on resolving critical safety issues than on achieving key goals.

Unless your accreditor requires otherwise, there is no law that says all these goals and plans must be articulated in a particular format. Express and organize them in whatever documents will best help your college achieve its purpose and advance its quality and effectiveness.

Be Prepared to Attune and Adjust Your Goals and Plans

I worry when I see a long, multilayered, complex process to develop strategic goals and plans. Invariably, such a process leaves everyone so exhausted that they consider the goals and plans immutable for the next five years. Only rarely do goals and plans remain fully relevant after two or three years. In fact, sometimes it becomes apparent that goals or plans are not working out after only one year. You may find that a stated goal is being misinterpreted. A goal may turn out to be a minor project rather than a major destination. You may realize that a key goal has been omitted. A wholesale annual rewrite should not be needed, but a quality college revisits its strategic goals and plans annually, or at most biennially, and recognizes when adjustments are warranted. What often seems to work best are rolling plans that lay out several years of strategies but are updated annually and extended one year further after each update.

For More Information

Your go-to source for information on strategic planning in higher education is the Society for College and University Planning (SCUP) (www.scup.org). It offers a variety of resources including books and events. Its "Trends in Higher Education" newsletter offers great environmental scanning of the U.S. higher education landscape.

CHAPTER 11

WHO IS A SUCCESSFUL STUDENT?

O f all your college's goals, none are more important than those for student learning and success. I define successful students relatively broadly, in ways that flow from your college's responsibilities (discussed in Chapter 5).

- Successful students have achieved their goals, which for many students is a higher standard of living. To achieve this end, their goals at your college might be earning a degree or certificate, preparing to transfer successfully to another college to continue their studies, or simply developing new skills.

- Successful students' needs have been fulfilled: they have learned whatever they need to succeed at subsequent pursuits. They have the knowledge and skills for a career, or for study at a more advanced level, or to contribute to their communities, or simply to live a richer, fuller life.

- Successful students have learned what your college thinks is important: its key learning outcomes, which may go beyond their own goals and needs and serve the public good.

- Successful students have learned all these things at appropriate levels of rigor.

- Successful students have achieved their goals in an appropriately cost-effective fashion, not spending inappropriate amounts of time and money.

What Do Students Need to Learn?

There has been a great deal of thinking and writing on this in recent years. Within the world of higher education, two statements have garnered the most attention.

- The Essential Outcomes (www.aacu.org/leap) are part of an initiative of the Association of American Colleges and Universities (AAC&U) called Liberal Education and America's Promise (LEAP); the outcomes are often referred to as the "LEAP goals."
- The Degree Qualifications Profile (DQP) (www.degreeprofile .org), sponsored by the Lumina Foundation, is intended to define "what students should be expected to know and be able to do once they earn their degrees" at the associate, bachelor's, and master's levels (Adelman, Ewell, Gaston, & Schneider, 2011, p. 1).

Outside higher education, there have been numerous surveys of the knowledge, skills, and competencies that employers seek in new hires (for example, see Carnevale, Smith, & Strohl, 2013; Gallup, Inc., 2014; Hart Research Associates, 2013; and Wiseman, 2013).

Putting together these and other sources from inside and outside higher education (Fink, 2003; Sharp, Komives, & Fincher, 2011) shows that the knowledge, skills, and competencies that students need today fall into three broad categories.

- *"Hard" skills* are the particular skills required for a specific occupation. An ultrasound technician, for example, needs to operate ultrasound equipment. A lawyer needs to interpret legal documents. A chemist needs to conduct chemical tests.

- *"Soft" skills* are the generalizable skills that are applicable to a wide range of careers and are often required to advance beyond a specific position. All managers and supervisors, for example, need to be able to communicate effectively with their staffs and colleagues.

- *Attitudes, values, and dispositions* that contribute to the public good and quality of life (Busteed, 2013) might include such things as an appreciation of the arts, a commitment to a healthy lifestyle, and a dedication to community service.

A few things are noteworthy about this short list. First, these three categories are not discrete. Some soft skills are required for specific occupations; social workers must be able to use interpersonal skills effectively, for example. Many soft skills, such as listening and teamwork, contribute to quality of life and the public good, while some dispositions, such as a tolerance for ambiguity, contribute to career success.

Second, while a certain level of head knowledge is necessary and important, today it is no longer sufficient for college students only to acquire knowledge; graduates need to be able to *use* that knowledge in some way.

Third, while most jobs require a combination of hard and soft skills, soft skills are rising in importance. Over 90 percent of employers agree that a "capacity to think critically, communicate clearly, and solve complex problems is more important than . . . undergraduate major" (Hart Research Associates, 2013, p. 1). Today, 80 percent of all U.S. jobs are in the service sector, and the more one works with people, the most important soft skills become. A majority of employers now believe that both field-specific and broad knowledge skills are important to advancement and long-term career success (Hart Research Associates, 2013), rather than just one or the other.

What soft skills and dispositions are most valued by employers today? The following crop up most often, in roughly the following order:

- Teamwork and collaboration, including listening
- Written and oral communication, especially articulating ideas clearly and effectively
- Real-world problem solving, especially complex problems, under pressure or "on the fly" (Wiseman, 2013)
- Critical thinking and analysis, especially in evaluating information and conclusions
- Flexibility and adaptability to change, including the capacity to continue learning
- Creativity and innovation

Jargon Alert!

Bloom's Taxonomy

Bloom's taxonomy (Anderson, Krathwohl, Airasian, & Cruikshank, 2000) is a framework for viewing various kinds and levels of student learning. It divides learning into three domains: cognitive, affective (attitudes and values), and psychomotor (athletic skills, laboratory skills, and so on). Cognitive skills are organized into six categories: remember, understand, apply, analyze, evaluate, and create. Many people still refer to the original names of these six categories (Bloom, 1956): knowledge, comprehension, application, analysis, evaluation, and synthesis.

Bloom's taxonomy does not highlight many of the skills and dispositions needed today, such as teamwork and flexibility, and many interpret its hierarchy erroneously to mean that students must master one level before proceeding to the next (for example, that students must thoroughly understand a concept before they can begin to apply or analyze it). Consider other taxonomies such as that of L. Dee Fink (2003): knowledge, application, integration, human dimension, caring, and learning how to learn.

- Intercultural knowledge and skills, especially working with people from diverse cultural backgrounds
- Ethical judgment
- Quantitative and computer skills, especially understanding numbers and statistics

Jargon Alert!

Information Literacy

Information literacy is (Suskie, 2009):

- Recognizing the need for information to answer a question or solve a problem
- Determining what information is needed
- Finding that information
- Evaluating the information for credibility and relevance
- Using the information to answer the question or solve the problem
- Using the information legally and ethically, respecting intellectual property

Identify Your Learning Outcomes

Here are some things to consider as you identify key learning outcomes.

Jargon Alert!

Learning Outcomes, Learning Goals, Learning Objectives, and Learning Competencies

These are all terms used to describe what students are supposed to learn in order to pass a course or exam or to graduate (Suskie, 2009). Unless an agency or accreditor requires otherwise, use whatever terms work best with your college's culture.

Be relevant and responsive to student needs. How many of the skills and dispositions that are valued by employers are reflected in your college's learning outcomes? Teamwork, flexibility, and creativity receive particularly light attention in many college curricula. I often suggest that colleges struggling to distinguish themselves in a competitive market carve a niche for themselves by focusing on these throughout their curricula.

Reflect your college's values and distinctive traits. If a commitment to serving one's community is an important value of your college, for example, make it a key learning outcome. While the LEAP goals and DQP are valuable resources, they should not be construed as dictating your college's learning outcomes. In fact, the VALUE rubrics, which explicate the LEAP goals, are "meant to be adapted in order to reflect the individual mission, program mix, and student demographics of the institutions where they are used" (Rhodes & Finley, 2013, p. 7). A college or program that largely prepares students for research careers through further graduate study may have somewhat different learning outcomes, for example, than one that largely prepares students to be high school teachers.

Limit your learning outcomes. I have seen associate degree programs with 45 learning outcomes and general education curricula with more than 100 learning objectives. There is no way that students can learn so many things well. As I suggested in Chapter 10, consider the "3-to-6" rule: focus on just three to six key learning outcomes for each program and each general education requirement. McKendree University (2013) is an example of a university with just a few university-wide learning outcomes that are tied to its mission.

Use systematic evidence and collaboration. I discussed this in Chapter 10, but this is worth reiterating here. Effective learning outcomes come from collaborative discussions and systematic evidence not only on what is happening at your college but on what is happening in the world around your college. Chapter 7 talks more about fostering a culture of collaboration, and Chapter 17 talks about using systematic evidence to inform goals.

Articulate Your Learning Outcomes

The principles for articulating goals in Chapter 10 apply to learning outcomes. Here are some examples of well-stated learning outcomes that follow those principles:

- Accurately interpret representations of quantitative data and create truthful representations to deepen understanding and inform debate and decision making (Lebanon Valley College, 1995–2013, "Intellectual and Practical Skills," para. 2).

- Set individual goals and devise strategies for educational, personal, and professional development in a changing world (Community College of Baltimore County, 2013, "4. Independent Learning and Personal Management," para. 1)

- Critically engage with multiple cultural traditions and perspectives, and with interpersonal situations that enhance understanding of different identities and foster the ability to work and live productively and harmoniously with others (Hamilton College, 2013, para. 8).

- Integrate effective written and oral communication into daily business practices (Central Penn College, n.d., p. 46).

- The essential characteristic of the educated person is the ability to weigh alternatives and make thoughtful choices. The rapidly changing world in which we live demands that we all make enormously difficult decisions, choosing wisely and responsibly in an area of competing persuasions (Slippery Rock University, 2013, "Goal VII: Challenges of the Modern Age," para. 1). (The learning outcomes embedded in these lovely statements are "weigh alternatives and make thoughtful choices" and "choose wisely and responsibly in an area of competing persuasions.")

A few points from Chapter 10 are worth repeating here. **_Describe outcomes, not learning products or activities._** Learning outcomes, like other goals, are destinations, not the route students take there. Consider this general education goal: "Critically assess and express ideas about cultural diversity and individual roles in society." This goal states what students will do *in* the courses they take to complete this general education requirement, not what they will be able to do *after* they complete the requirement. How will they use these skills in their lives? Root cause analysis (Chapter 10) can be helpful here.

Avoid fuzzy terms. The clearer and more explicit your students' destinations, the clearer the path you and your students will take to get there, and the easier to confirm that they have indeed arrived. One fuzzy term I see frequently is *critical thinking*. Unless your college has defined it clearly, if you ask any two people at your college what it means, you will likely hear two different answers. Another frequently fuzzy term is *demonstrate*. A goal that nursing students will demonstrate the proper technique for drawing a blood sample is fine, but a goal that students will demonstrate critical thinking skills is fuzzy.

Jargon Alert!

Critical Thinking

Critical thinking is a term whose meaning lacks popular consensus (Suskie, 2009). I use it as an umbrella term for thinking skills that go beyond basic conceptual understanding, including analysis, synthesis, evaluation, and problem solving, among others.

If you are struggling to clarify a fuzzy learning outcome, use a version of the scenario I suggested in Chapter 10. Imagine that you run into two alumni of your college. As you talk with them and learn about what they have been doing and what they are thinking, it becomes clear to you that one has achieved your (fuzzy) goal and one has not. What might they say that would help you tell them apart? For example, graduates who "demonstrate cultural sensitivity" might continue to learn about other cultures, listen to and consider viewpoints different from their own, and incorporate cultural nuances into their work and interactions with others.

Use observable action verbs. If you see students doing something, you can assess their achievement of it. A goal that students will *explain* or *describe* a concept is clearer and more straightforward to assess than a goal that students will *understand* a concept.

Integrate Learning Outcomes Throughout Your College . . . Reasonably and Appropriately

Students learn more effectively when their learning is purposefully integrated and, for this to happen, learning outcomes must be integrated across levels and experiences. One course, for example, might have a goal that students develop skill in a particular type or style of writing. This course, along with others, helps students achieve a broader program goal that students write effectively in the discipline. The program goal, in turn, contributes to a college-wide goal that students communicate effectively in writing.

For More Information

Chapter 2 of *Effective Grading: A Tool for Learning and Assessment in College* (Walvoord & Anderson, 2010) and Chapter 8 of *Assessing Student Learning: A Common Sense Guide* (Suskie, 2009) discuss learning outcomes more thoroughly.

Transparent Pathways, Clear Outcomes: Using Disciplinary Tuning to Improve Teaching, Learning, and Student Success (Midwestern Higher Education Compact, 2014) offers many excellent suggestions for developing collaborative processes to articulate meaningful learning outcomes.

● **CHAPTER 12**

HELPING STUDENTS LEARN AND SUCCEED

O nce you have identified your students' destinations—what they should know and be able to do by the time they graduate or accomplish whatever other goal they might have—you can identify how they will get there: curricular, teaching, development, support, and other strategies that help students learn and succeed.

What Helps Students Learn?

While in many ways these are extraordinarily challenging times for American higher education, in some respects we are living in a golden age, because we have a quarter-century of really good research on strategies that help students learn (Ambrose, Bridges, DiPietro, Lovett, & Norman, 2010; Association of American Colleges & Universities, 2011; Bain, 2004; Connor, 2011; Kuh, Kinzie, Schuh, Whitt, & Associates, 2010; Kuh & O'Donnell, 2013; McClenney, Marti, & Adkins, n.d.; McCormick, Gonyea, & Kinzie, 2013; Pascarella & Blaich, 2013; Pascarella & Terenzini, 2005). Table 12.1 summarizes these strategies, throughout which two themes pervade.

TABLE 12.1. Strategies That Help Students Learn

A growing body of research evidence indicates that students learn most effectively when:

1. They see *clear relevance and value* in their learning activities.

2. They are instilled with a *"can do" attitude*.

3. They are academically challenged and given *high but attainable expectations*, such as through assignments with scaffolding.

4. *Learning activities and grades focus on important learning outcomes.* Faculty organize curricula, teaching practices, and assessments to help students achieve important learning outcomes. Students spend their time and energy learning what they will be graded on.

5. They understand course and program learning outcomes and the *characteristics of excellent work*, often through a rubric.

6. They spend *significant time and effort studying* and practicing.

7. They *interact meaningfully with faculty*—face-to-face and/or online.

8. They *collaborate with other students*—face-to-face and/or online—including those unlike themselves.

9. New learning is *related to their prior experiences and what they already know*, through both concrete, relevant examples and challenges to their existing paradigms.

10. They *learn by doing, through hands-on practice engaging in multidimensional "real world" tasks*, rather than by listening to lectures.

11. They use their learning to *explore, apply, analyze, justify, and evaluate*, because facts memorized in isolation are quickly forgotten.

12. They participate in *out-of-class activities* that build on what they are learning in the classroom.

13. They can *obtain support* when they need it: academic, social, personal, and financial.

14. They receive *frequent, prompt, concrete feedback* on their work, followed by opportunities to *revise* their work.

15. They *integrate and see coherence* in their learning by reflecting on what and how they have learned, by constructing their own learning into meaningful frameworks, and through synthesizing capstone experiences, such as first-year experiences, field experiences, community-based or service learning experiences, independent study, and research projects.

16. Their college and its faculty and staff truly *focus on helping students learn and succeed and on improving student learning and success*.

Jargon Alert!

Scaffolding

Scaffolding is the clear written instructions and guidance for an assignment that help students produce their best work (Suskie, 2009). An assignment with scaffolding explains what students should learn by completing the assignment, what the completed assignment should look like, how students should spend their time and energy in completing the assignment, and how the completed assignment will be evaluated or graded. Students submit large, complex assignments in stages, so their professors can help them get back on track before they go too far off course.

Jargon Alert!

Capstones

A *capstone* is an opportunity for students to see the big picture as they approach the end of their course, program, or general education curriculum: to integrate, synthesize, apply, and reflect on what they have learned throughout their studies. The best capstones use many of the strategies in Table 12.1, including working collaboratively and addressing complex, real-life problems. Examples of capstone experiences include senior projects, performances, and exhibits; research projects and papers; independent studies; field experiences such as internships, clinicals, practicums, and service learning experiences; and theses and dissertations.

Engagement. Students who are actively engaged in their learning learn more effectively than those who sit passively listening to a lecture. "Learning is not something done *to* students, but rather something students themselves do" (Ambrose, Bridges, DiPiertro, Lovett, & Norman, 2010, p. 3).

Faculty and students share responsibility for learning. Yes, students are still ultimately responsible for their learning; you can bring the proverbial horse to water, but you cannot make it drink. But faculty share that responsibility by using strategies that help students learn (Barr & Tagg, 1995). Merely delivering a lecture and being available to answer questions is not enough.

Jargon Alert!

Learning-Centered

Learning-centered classrooms are those in which the strategies in Table 12.1 are implemented; students are actively engaged in their learning, and faculty and students share responsibility for learning. A learning-centered college actively fosters these practices.

What Helps Students Persist and Complete a Degree?

The strategies in Table 12.1 that help students learn also help them persist through their studies (Greenfield, Keup, & Gardner, 2013; John N. Gardner Institute, 2005a, 2005b; Pascarella & Terenzini, 2005; Tinto, 2012). Especially important are those strategies that not only help students succeed in their studies but "make students want to come back," as Ken O'Donnell has explained (Kuh & O'Donnell, 2013, p. 25):

- Engagement with faculty and other students
- Clear and high expectations
- Academic, social, personal, and financial support
- Frequent, prompt, and concrete feedback
- Exposure to diverse viewpoints
- Opportunities to analyze, justify, evaluate, integrate, and reflect

Jargon Alert!

Completion, Persistence, Retention, and Attrition

Completion refers to students earning a college degree or certificate. *Persistence* refers to students staying enrolled in college until they earn a degree or certificate. *Retention* refers to students staying enrolled in the same college from one semester, term, or year to the next. *Attrition* refers to the opposite: students leaving a college before earning a degree or certificate.

Underlying all of these strategies is *a college that truly focuses on helping its students learn, persist, and succeed* (John N. Gardner Institute, 2005a, 2005b) by addressing the five cultures of quality:

- *Relevance*, in which the college understands its students and what they most need in order to succeed
- *Community*, in which responsibility for student success is broadly shared and strategies for student success are appropriately integrated
- *Focus and aspiration*, with student success made a high priority and strategies purposefully designed to help students succeed
- *Evidence*, in which good quality, useful evidence is collected regarding student success
- *Betterment*, in which evidence is used to understand and improve student success

Jargon Alert!

Student-Centered

Student-centered colleges actively focus on helping students learn, persist, and succeed. A student-centered college is thus also a learning-centered college (see previous sidebar).

These are generalities, of course. While it is important to be familiar with research on strategies that help students persist and succeed, it is even more important to understand why *your* students leave before graduating. Gallaudet University, for example, found that class attendance patterns correlated especially highly with persistence. It acted on this evidence by implementing a system of tracking class attendance and communicating with students missing classes during the first two weeks of the semester . . . and saw persistence improve as a result (Catherine Andersen, personal communication, July 23, 2013).

Designing Curricula to Help Students Learn and Succeed

If you have ever renovated a kitchen, you know how many components go into it: floor plan, plumbing, electrical, and heating systems, walls and ceiling, cabinets, countertops, flooring, appliances, and lighting. Each component is important, but what is even more important is how they all integrate with one another to fulfill their purpose: a kitchen that is beautiful, functional, and durable. The overall kitchen design and plan are judged, not by the individual elements, but by the overall result—the completed kitchen—which is greater than the sum of its parts.

This applies to a course or program curriculum as well. A collection of courses is not a program, and topics in a textbook are not a course. At a quality college, the courses in a program and the activities in a course all integrate with one another to fulfill their purpose: student achievement of key learning outcomes and preparation for post-college success. The curriculum is judged, not by the program's individual courses or the course's activities, but by the overall result—student learning—which should be greater than the sum of its parts.

Design each program so students will achieve its key learning outcomes by the time they graduate (Strategy 4 in Table 12.1). Use a simple chart called a curriculum map to do this. In the left column,

EXHIBIT 12.1. Curriculum Map for a Hypothetical Four-Course Certificate Program

	Introductory Course	Problem-Solving Methods Course	Advanced Course	Capstone Course
Choose and apply appropriate problem-solving methods and tools	✓	✓		✓
Collect, analyze, and evaluate evidence and information		✓		✓
Lead a team charged with solving problems			✓	✓
Convey findings and solutions clearly in writing		✓	✓	✓

list the key learning outcomes of the program and, along the top row, list the courses in the program. Then check off those courses for which achievement of a key learning outcome is a significant part of the final grade. Exhibit 12.1 is a simple example. Some faculty (and some assessment information management systems) use codes instead of checkmarks to indicate whether students are introduced to, develop, or demonstrate mastery of the outcome.

Jargon Alert!

Curriculum Alignment and Curriculum Maps

Curriculum alignment is ensuring that your course, program, or general education curriculum is designed to give students enough opportunity to achieve your key learning outcomes. It is an important way to make sure that you keep your promises to your students that they will achieve those outcomes. A *curriculum map* is a tool to ensure curriculum alignment.

EXHIBIT 12.2. Template for a Curriculum Map for a Course Syllabus

This is what you'll learn (course objective)	This is how you'll learn it (homework, class work, assignment, and so on)	This is how you'll show me that you've learned it (test, paper, project, presentation, and so on)

Notice that, even in this simple example, each learning outcome is addressed in at least two courses. It is unfair to any one faculty member—and his or her students—to be expected to bear sole responsibility for achievement of a key program learning outcome. Students generally need repeated practice of a skill or competency, in a variety of contexts, in order to master it. So important program learning outcomes should be the responsibility of multiple faculty and addressed in more than one course.

Design each course so students who pass it will have achieved its key learning outcomes. I have a fantasy of every accreditor requiring every course syllabus to replace the usual list of the topics or objectives to be covered with the three-column chart in Exhibit 12.2 (Bain, 2004; Fink, 2003).

Jargon Alert!

Backwards Curriculum Design

Backwards curriculum design develops a course or program by first articulating its key learning outcomes, then designing the course or program so students achieve and demonstrate those learning outcomes. Some faculty describe this as first writing the final assignment or exam for a course, then designing the course so that students will be able to earn an A on it.

Include integrative, synthesizing capstone experiences (Strategy 15 in Table 12.1). This is especially important for students who have "swirled" through several colleges or programs because, as I explained earlier, a collection of courses does not constitute a program or degree; capstones provide the integrative experience that makes the program greater than its courses. Capstones are also a great opportunity to collect evidence of student achievement of key program or general education learning outcomes.

Ensure appropriate consistency across sections of a course. As a matter of your college's integrity, every student who passes a course, no matter the section in which he or she enrolls, should have achieved the course's key learning outcomes and be prepared for whatever comes next, whether further study, a career, or life. I therefore often recommend that faculty teaching sections of a course collaborate to develop a shared core "package" that includes the course's key learning outcomes, key concepts that all students must learn, and perhaps one or two common assignments or a half-dozen questions to be included on all final exams. Beyond that core, faculty can flesh out their own syllabi and class materials as they see fit.

Periodically review syllabi to confirm that key learning outcomes continue to be taught and assessed. For courses in degree or certificate programs, this can be part of program reviews (Chapter 20). General education course syllabi can be reviewed by a general education committee on a rolling multi-year schedule.

The Role of the Liberal Arts and Sciences and General Education

Most U.S. colleges incorporate study of the liberal arts into undergraduate curricula through general education requirements and through programs or majors in liberal arts subjects such as art, Spanish, history, sociology, and biology. While a purely professional or technical education prepares students for one job (and that may be all that some students want or need), a liberal arts education, with its greater emphasis on transferrable soft skills,

Jargon Alert!

Liberal Arts

The *liberal arts* are those studies addressing knowledge, skills, and competencies that cross disciplines, yielding a broadly educated, well-rounded individual. The term liberal comes from *liber*, the Latin word for free; in the Middle Ages a liberal arts education was for the free individual, as opposed to an individual obliged to enter a particular trade or profession. Today, many people use the term *liberal arts and sciences* or simply *arts and sciences* to make clear that the liberal arts comprise study of the sciences as well as the arts and humanities. The Association of American Colleges & Universities (AAC&U), a leading advocate of liberal arts education, refers to liberal arts as a *liberal education* (Humphreys, 2013).

attitudes, and dispositions, can do far more. As Steve Jobs said, "Technology alone is not enough. It's technology married with liberal arts, married with humanities, that yields the results that make our hearts sing" ("Steve Jobs," 2011). A liberal arts education has the potential to prepare students to transition into a host of careers. As a result, liberal arts graduates actually earn more in the prime of their careers than professional and pre-professional graduates (Humphreys & Kelly, 2014). Those with a liberal arts education lead richer, more fulfilling lives as well as serve the public good (AAC&U, 2002; Busteed, 2013).

Jargon Alert!

General Education

General education is the part of a liberal arts education that is shared by all undergraduates at your college (Humphreys, 2013). It may go by another name, such as *liberal arts core* or *core curriculum*. In recent generations, general education curricula have traditionally comprised study of arts, humanities, social sciences, natural sciences, and mathematics.

Unfortunately, many general education curricula and liberal arts programs are not yet fulfilling their potential. I often advise the following:

Articulate in concrete terms the purpose and benefits of your general education requirements. State their learning outcomes, then go a step further, explaining why they are important. It is not enough to tell students they must take certain courses or fulfill certain requirements "because it's good for you" or "Someday you'll thank me for making you do this." Explain clearly (with supporting evidence) *why* the learning outcomes of your general education curriculum are important to students and how achieving them will contribute to student success . . . and to the public good. As Ken O'Donnell has explained. "When they see . . . how college learning can be applied in life and the real world, then they don't have those nagging questions, 'Why am I taking this course?' 'Is this really the best use of my time?' 'Shouldn't I be earning money?'" (Kuh & O'Donnell, 2013, p. 25).

Make your general education and liberal arts curricula relevant and responsive to your stakeholders, including students, employers, and the people of your region (Maxwell, 2013). Evergreen College, for example, has offered a course called "Why Shakespeare?" (http://academic.evergreen.edu/curricular/whyshakespeare/home.htm) that not only studies Shakespeare's works but explores why they remain valued today. Throughout your liberal arts curricula, emphasize the skills that employers are seeking, such as analysis, creativity, flexibility, and teamwork. Look to the institutions participating in AAC&U's "Give Students a Compass" initiative (www.aacu.org/compass) for models and ideas.

Design your general education and liberal arts curricula purposefully, following the steps outlined earlier in this chapter.

Helping Students Learn and Succeed in Non-Traditional Venues and Modalities

Fewer and fewer students are attending college solely by taking semester-long courses in traditional classrooms on college campuses. In Fall 2012, for example, one-third of all U.S. college students took at least one online course (Allen & Seaman, 2013). Students today take courses at off-campus locations, on accelerated schedules, and in "blended" modalities that combine online and face-to-face learning. Some colleges offer courses or programs developed and/or delivered by third parties, such as other accredited colleges and non-accredited ventures.

These non-traditional venues and modalities pose challenges. A quality college provides consistent learning experiences, with consistently high expectations for student learning, wherever and however those learning experiences are offered. This cannot happen without careful, consistent oversight and coordination, which takes time and money. But emerging venues and modalities also represent opportunities to implement the strategies in Table 12.1 more effectively by "flipping" the classroom experience.

Jargon Alert!

Flipped Classrooms

For generations, many college courses have been designed so that students are first taught in the classroom, then they reinforce and deepen their learning through homework. In a *flipped classroom*, students first learn basic content outside the classroom. They then reinforce and deepen their learning in the classroom (be it face-to-face or online) through interactive engagement with fellow students, under the guidance of their professors, applying their learning to new situations, analyzing, evaluating, creating and, above all, thinking. While the initial flipped classroom model called for students to learn content by watching a recorded lecture (Sams & Bergmann, 2012), in a learning-centered flipped classroom students teach themselves by engaging in interactive online learning experiences, potentially including a "rich media screen culture of video, games, hyperlinks, and simulation" (Gonick, 2013, "It takes a village," para. 1).

Facilitating Transfer

Students who attend multiple colleges on their path to earn-ing a degree face a variety of barriers, all flowing from one fact: while one of the great strengths of U.S. higher education is its diversity, this means that U.S. colleges and programs do not all offer the same curricula and do not have the same degree require-ments. Courses completed at one college or in one program may not count toward another's requirements.

The more distinctive or extensive a college's curricular requirements, the harder it is for transfer students to complete a degree in a timely fashion. Some college curricula require 48 to 50 general education credits, plus 60 credits in a major, leaving practically no room for those transfer credits that do not fit any-where . . . or for those courses that students explore on their way to finding a major. If your general education curriculum requires, say, a course addressing social issues unique to your college's region, for example, a student who has completed all the general education requirements of another college may still need to take this additional general education course.

There are several ways to help students move past these barriers:

- Develop articulation agreements with the colleges that stu-dents most frequently transfer to or from. Delineate course or requirement equivalences, so that a course or requirement completed at one college counts as the equivalent at another.

- Let prospective students know, before they commit to enroll-ing at your college, how many of their transfer credits count toward general education and program requirements.

- To make sure that incoming transfer students are up to speed before they graduate, consider adding a capstone requirement to general education, the major, or both that reviews and reinforces key skills and competencies such as writing and critical thinking.

- If your general education or program curricula are extensive or distinctive, make sure that the benefits of those requirements outweigh the barriers to graduation that they may create, especially if your college's stated purpose or goals include meeting the needs of transfer students. Or consider scaling back your requirements. Only one of the regional accreditors (New England Association of Schools and Colleges Commission on Institutions of Higher Education [NEASC], 2011) requires that the general education requirements of a bachelor's degree consist of more than thirty credits.

- Track progress toward a degree by competencies rather than credits, an idea rapidly gaining traction (Fain, 2013).

For More Information

The books and articles cited in this chapter are all worthwhile reading. An excellent resource on curriculum design is *Designing and Assessing Courses and Curricula: A Practical Guide* (Diamond, 2008). From the title, *Effective Grading* (Walvoord & Anderson, 2010) might appear to be a book about assessment, but it is really a terrific book about teaching. The Lilly Conferences on College & University Teaching (http://lillyconferences.com) are another great resource on good teaching practices, as are the newsletter and events of the Teaching Professor imprint of Magna Publications (www.teachingprofessor.com).

The Quality Matters Program (www.qmprogram.org) has a rubric of eight standards for online courses (Quality Matters Program, 2011), many of which are applicable to face-to-face courses as well. And the Council of Regional Accrediting Commissions (C-RAC) has published guidelines for reviewing distance education programs (2011).

Your go-to resource on general education and the liberal arts is the Association of American Colleges & Universities (www.aacu.org). And your go-to resources on student persistence and success are the National Resource Center for the First-Year Experience and Students in Transition (www.sc.edu/fye) and the John N. Gardner Institute for Excellence in Undergraduate Education (www.jngi.org).

DIMENSION IV:
A Culture of Evidence

CHAPTER 13

GAUGING SUCCESS

A quality college continually gauges its progress toward its goals so it can ensure that it will achieve those goals—arrive at its destinations—safely and on time or so it can make adjustments if warranted. It also continually gauges its success in fulfilling its other responsibilities that are discussed in Chapter 5. This chapter reviews some of many potential gauges of a college's success. (See Chapter 6 for information on gauging success in ensuring your college's health and well-being and for deploying resources effectively and efficiently.) *This chapter provides examples, not recommendations;* your measures must fit your college's purpose, values, goals, and stakeholder needs, and the examples here may not.

Jargon Alert!

Performance Indicators, Metrics, Performance Measures, Key Performance Indicators, and Dashboard Indicators

Performance indicators, metrics, and *performance measures* are all terms for measures of quality and effectiveness. Those measures that are particularly critical to tracking quality and effectiveness are called *key performance indicators* or *dashboard indicators.* Use whatever term fits best with your college culture. In this book, I generally use the term *measure.*

Jargon Alert!

Institutional Assessment

Institutional assessment refers to gauging a college's *effectiveness* or *institutional effectiveness*. In Chapter 5 I define *effectiveness* more broadly than some. I include not only achieving purpose and goals but also meeting stakeholder needs, serving the public good, ensuring ongoing health and well-being, and deploying resources effectively, prudently, and efficiently.

Gauging Student Success

Many stakeholders are particularly interested in evidence that your college uses student tuition and fees effectively, prudently, and efficiently to help students achieve their goals. The most important gauges of student success concern student learning, which is discussed later in this chapter. But many stakeholders also want to see information such as the following:

- Proportion of students who achieve their educational goals such as earning a degree, earning a certificate, progress toward more advanced study elsewhere, or simply boosting skills (Examples of measures include student retention and graduation rates, such as the proportion of degree-seeking students still enrolled one year after entering and the proportion of students who, three years after entering a community college, have earned an associate's degree or are still enrolled in college, either at your college or elsewhere.)

- Proportion of students who achieve their educational goals in a timely fashion (Students who take an extra year to achieve their educational goals may pay more in tuition and fees, plus lose a year of the higher earnings they anticipate.)

- Proportion of students who, after achieving their educational goal, are in the jobs for which they prepared

- Ratio of tuition and fees paid by students against what they earn after achieving their educational goals

- Debt-to-income ratio, comparing graduates' student loan debt against their earnings

Student experiences and outcomes vary considerably within any college, so students may want answers to these questions broken down for their program of study or college experience (say, for working adults or online students).

Gauging Responsiveness to the Changing College Student

Government policymakers want to know how effectively your college meets the needs of today's students, while prospective students and their families want to know about specific "fit": how effectively your college meets the needs of students like them, specifically information such as the following:

- Profile of the students your college aims to serve: your "target clientele," as discussed in Chapter 9
- Profile of the students your college actually enrolls
- How your college helps students succeed, including what your college does to provide students with optimal learning experiences and the extent to which your college engages in research-based teaching-learning practices
- Average debt load of students who graduate from your college or leave before graduating

Gauging Economic Development Contributions

Government policymakers and employers want to know how effectively your college contributes to the regional or national economy, specifically information such as the following:

- Proportions of your college's students who graduate with the types and levels of knowledge, skills, competencies, and dispositions that employers want and need (Employers may want evidence broken down by occupation.)

- Number of graduates prepared for high-demand fields
- Proportion of your graduates who stay and work in your region after graduating
- Economic impact of your college—including the economic contributions of its students, employees, and their families—on your region
- Impact of research conducted at your college on the economies of your region and the country

Gauging Contributions to the Public Good

Potential gauges of contributions to the public good depend on your college's goals, but two examples include:

- Number of internships at regional non-profit community agencies
- Attendance by community residents at cultural events

Gauging Achievement of College Purpose and Goals

College goals vary widely; only very rarely do I see any two colleges share even similar goals. Because of this, there is no neat list of measures for college goals or other aspects of institutional effectiveness. (Measures of student learning outcomes, discussed in the next section, do generally fall into a few common categories.) The preceding sections of this chapter offer some examples of potential dashboard indicators for college goals; Table 13.1 offers some additional examples.

Gauging Student Learning

A quality college continually gauges not only its progress toward its goals but also its students' progress toward its learning outcomes.

TABLE 13.1 Examples of Dashboard Indicators for Some Hypothetical College Goals

Goal	Potential Dashboard Indicators
Provide a student-centered environment.	Responses to relevant questions on the National Survey of Student Engagement (NSSE) or Community College Survey of Student Engagement (CCSSE)
Students engage in active learning.	Proportion of faculty participating in professional development opportunities to incorporate active learning in their classes
	Proportion of students participating in field experiences such as internships, practicums, and service learning
Increase the diversity of the college community.	Student, faculty, and staff profiles
Strengthen the faculty profile.	Proportion of faculty holding degrees in fields appropriate to what they are teaching
	Proportion of faculty using learning-centered teaching strategies
	Proportion of classes taught by full-time faculty
Promote research and scholarship.	Support for research and scholarship (funds, space, sabbaticals, etc.)
	Number of peer-reviewed research publications and presentations

Student learning assessment is really about answering just the following questions:

- Do you have evidence that your students are achieving your key learning outcomes?
- Does that evidence meet the characteristics of good evidence (Chapter 14)?
- Are you using evidence not only to evaluate individual students but also to improve what you are doing (Chapter 17)?

Jargon Alert!

Assessment

Assessment, a term originally coined because it had less baggage than *evaluation*, now has plenty of baggage of its own, so this book talks instead about *gauging success* and *evidence*. One exception: I do talk about *student learning assessment* because that language is so pervasive.

Thanks in part both to the learning centered movement discussed in Chapter 12 and pressures from accreditors and other quality assurance agencies, higher education has seen considerable progress in efforts to assess student learning, including the following:

- A growing number of books, conferences, webinars, and other resources on student learning assessment
- The work of AAC&U described in Chapter 12 that has advanced us light years in our capacity to understand and assess our general education and liberal education curricula
- Significant research papers on assessment practices and issues sponsored by NILOA (learningoutcomesassessment.org)
- A number of published instruments, although evidence of the quality and value of some remain a work in progress
- Commercial assessment information management systems that can make it easier to collect and make sense of evidence, as discussed in Chapter 18

Because of this wealth of resources, this chapter provides just a 30,000-foot overview of options for student learning assessment, not detailed information.

Rubrics (Walvoord & Anderson, 2010) are simply rating scales or scoring guides used to evaluate student work. They can be used to evaluate virtually any evidence of student learning short of an objective multiple-choice test. Exhibit 15.1 in Chapter 15 is one example of a rubric. Exhibit 18.2 in Chapter 18 is another example, with a different format, used to appraise a college rather than student learning. For more examples, simply do an online search; plenty will pop up, no matter what the subject or competency. Increasingly popular are the Valid Assessment of Learning in Undergraduate Education (VALUE) rubrics developed by AAC&U (www.aacu.org/value/index.cfm), which assess the association's LEAP learning outcomes that I discuss in Chapter 11.

Rubrics—and the term "rubric"—now pervade higher education (Kuh, Jankowski, Ikenberry, & Kinzie, 2014). Fifteen years ago, few faculty were using rubrics to evaluate student learning. Today, many if not most faculty do, and they almost always talk enthusiastically about them. It is one of the great success stories of the assessment movement.

Rubrics are the most useful tool we have to assess most learning. If a rubric is given to students with an assignment, students understand faculty expectations and standards . . . and therefore often do a better job learning—and demonstrating—what faculty want. Rubrics help faculty evaluate student work more consistently and fairly. Rubrics can make the grading/evaluation process go faster, because faculty do not need to write as many individual comments on student papers. Completed rubrics give students a clear sense of their strengths and areas for improvement.

Rubrics are not a panacea, however. They are not appropriate with small numbers of students; average scores will bounce up and down too much from one cohort to the next to be meaningful. While scoring student work is far more consistent with a rubric than without one, it is still subjective, and you will not get it right the first time you use one.

Assessment information management systems and published rubrics have sometimes led faculty to feel pressured to use a particular rubric or to format their rubric in a particular way. My response is *rubrics have no rules*. You can choose from a variety of formats, and there are several ways to arrive at an overall score (Suskie, 2009).

While rubrics are among the easiest and fastest student learning assessment strategies we have, they can nonetheless be a challenge to develop and use across courses or programs. Faculty need to agree on the rubric (not an easy task!) and often need to go through some practice sessions in order to interpret and apply the rubric consistently and fairly. Then there are the logistical details to be worked out. What examples of student work will be collected? How and when will they be scored? How will the results be shared? The larger and more complex your college—the more courses, adjunct faculty, and locations—the greater the logistical challenges. There is no one best answer to these challenges, because what works will depend on campus culture and organization. Assessment information management systems, discussed in Chapter 18, can help, *if* you choose the best system for your needs.

Published instruments have gained increasing attention over the last fifteen years or so. Most fall into one of four broad categories:

- Subject-specific tests and examinations, such as the Major Field Tests (MFTs) (www.ets.org/mft) and the National Council Licensure Examination (NCLEX) for nurses (www.ncbsn.org/nclex.htm)

- Tests that aim to assess the intellectual skills and competencies typically developed in general education curricula or throughout undergraduate studies, such as the Proficiency Profile (PP) (www.ets.org/proficiencyprofile) and the Collegiate Learning Assessment (CLA) (www.collegiatelearningassessment.org)

- Surveys of student experiences, perceptions, and attitudes, such as the National Survey of Student Engagement (NSSE) (http://nsse.iub.edu) and the Your First College Year (YFCY) survey (www.heri.ucla.edu/yfcyoverview.php)

- Rubrics such as the VALUE rubrics mentioned earlier and the American Council of Teachers of Foreign Languages (ACTFL) proficiency guidelines (http://actflproficiencyguidelines2012.org), which define various proficiency levels of reading, writing, speaking, and listening

The main advantage of published instruments is that they get you out of the ivory tower; they let you see how your students compare against their peers (Chapter 15). A key concern about published instruments is their usefulness in identifying and making improvements in teaching and learning. In a survey by the National Institute for Learning Outcomes Assessment (NILOA), for example, roughly 80 percent of colleges reported that "[published] test results were not usable for campus improvement efforts" (Jankowski, Ikenberry, Kinzie, Kuh, Shenoy, & Baker, 2012, p. 13). Locally designed student learning assessments are often a better fit with a college's goals.

Portfolios (Light, Chen, & Ittelson, 2011) are collections rather than single examples of student learning, often evaluated using a rubric. Effective portfolios are learning experiences as well as assessment opportunities; students develop skills in synthesis and integration by choosing items for the portfolio and reflecting on them (Suskie, 2009). A decade ago, portfolios were typically stored in cumbersome paper files, but today a variety of assessment information management systems can store them as electronic portfolios or "e-portfolios."

Portfolios are rich sources of evidence of student learning. They are great for programs with small numbers of students and for individualized curricula in which students design their own programs of study and set their own learning outcomes. If they include early examples of student work, they can provide evidence of student growth and development. Their key drawback is the time needed to review even a relatively small portfolio. I suggest a score-as-you-go approach: as faculty grade each item that will go in the portfolio, they can concurrently complete a simple rubric or other analysis to be included in portfolio records.

Reflective writing, in which students reflect on what and how they have learned, is a great choice for assessing many attitudes, values, and dispositions that could be faked by students on tests, surveys, and graded papers. They promote students' skills in synthesizing what they have learned and can thus help them prepare for lifelong learning. I am a big fan of reflective writing, because it can reveal not only what students have learned but *why*. My favorite reflective writing tool is the "minute paper" (Angelo & Cross, 1993), so named because students should complete it in no more than one minute. I ask students to share the one most important or meaningful thing they have learned and the one question uppermost in their minds. Their replies have transformed my teaching in ways that rubrics or rating scales cannot. Reflective writing is qualitative evidence of student learning and can be analyzed using qualitative research methods (Creswell, 2012).

Local tests and examinations—multiple-choice or essay—have the advantage of being designed by your college's faculty, so the results are more likely to be relevant and useful than the results from published tests. Their key shortcoming is that, because faculty are typically not assessment experts, local tests can be poorly designed and written, with confusing items or too many questions addressing basic content knowledge rather than thinking skills.

Surveys and self-ratings can add insight, especially regarding attitudes, values, and the impact of out-of-class experiences, all situations for which tests and rubrics may be inappropriate. Their main shortcoming is that, because survey evidence is self-reported rather than observed, it is generally insufficient evidence of student learning. Another concern is survey fatigue (Jankowski, Ikenberry, Kinzie, Kuh, Shenoy, & Baker, 2012; McCormick, Gonyea, & Kinzie, 2013): people today can feel deluged with surveys and therefore disinclined to respond to yet one more.

Grades provide some basic information on student learning; you know you have a problem if most of your students are failing. But grades alone are insufficient evidence of student learning. There are several reasons why (Walvoord & Anderson, 2010), but here is the big one: a course, assignment, or test grade alone is too global to tell you *what* students have and have not learned.

If a student earns a B on a midterm exam, for example, you know that he learned some things well, or he would have earned a C or D, and that he did not learn some things, or he would have earned an A. But the grade alone tells you nothing about what the student has and has not learned well. The evidence that went into the grade, however—scores for each test item and rubric criterion— are more meaningful and useful evidence of student learning.

Jargon Alert!

Direct and Indirect Evidence of Student Learning

Direct evidence of student learning is simply evidence that a critic cannot argue with, such as test results or samples of student work evaluated using a clear rubric. *Indirect evidence* is less convincing to a critic, even though it can be very useful in understanding and improving student learning. A critic might dismiss grades as evidence of student learning, for example, saying they are inflated, and student self-ratings, saying they are full of misperceptions. Job placement rates are indirect evidence of student learning because they are affected by the economy and market; when unemployment rates are high, even highly competent graduates can struggle to find jobs.

What About the "Ineffables"?

There are some who argue that focusing on concrete measures of student learning takes the soul out of higher education, focusing on what is easily quantified at the expense of more important aims that are harder to assess. I share their concern. I worry, for example, that the push for online education and career readiness will lead to a focus on specific competencies, such as analyzing data or citing evidence correctly, at the expense of other aims of a traditional college education, such as thoughtful reflection on works of art or compassion for others. A world where these traits are a rarity would be a dismal place.

There are ways to deal with the ineffables, however:

- Try to articulate that ineffable goal clearly, following the suggestions in Chapters 10 and 11. "Ethics" may seem impossible to measure, for example, but it can be articulated as understanding the ethical principles of the discipline and reasoning ethically—both assessable goals.
- Use qualitative research approaches (Creswell, 2012) for tools such as reflective writing and interviews, analyzing them by looking for common themes in responses.
- Ask how an ineffable student learning outcome is taught. What class work, homework, and assignments do students complete to help them achieve the outcome? Some outcomes, such as instilling a love of the discipline or a passion for inquiry, are really hard or almost impossible to teach, although everyone hopes students will be inspired. Do not assess what you cannot teach.

For More Information

Today there are many books on assessing student learning, including *Effective Grading: A Tool for Learning and Assessment in College* (Walvoord & Anderson, 2010), the second edition of *Assessment Essentials: Planning, Implementing, and Improving Assessing in Higher Education* (Banta & Palomba, 2014), and *Assessing Student Learning: A Common Sense Guide* (Suskie, 2009). *Designing Effective Assessment: Principles and Profiles of Good Practice* (Banta, Jones, & Black, 2009) offers dozens of real-life examples of good practices. Also check out *Assessment Update* (www.assessmentupdate.com/), a peer-reviewed periodical of good student learning assessment practices, and *Assessing and Improving Student Writing in College: A Guide for Institutions, General Education, Departments, and Classrooms* (Walvoord, 2014).

Good resources on electronic portfolios (e-portfolios) include:

- The Association for Authentic, Experiential, and Evidence-Based Learning (AAEEBL) (www.aaeebl.org)
- The Inter/National Coalition for Electronic Portfolio Research (http://incepr.org)
- The International Journal of ePortfolio (http://theijep.com/)
- "Catalyst for Learning: ePortfolio Resources and Research" (http://cl2.mcnrc.org), a website of e-portfolio resources sponsored by Connect to Learning, a project coordinated by LaGuardia Community College's Making Connections National Resource Center

There are many assessment conferences every year, such as the Indianapolis Assessment Institute (http://planning.iupui.edu/conferences/national/nationalconf.html), which attracts over 1,000 participants each year, and the annual conference of the Association for Assessment of Learning in Higher Education (AALHE) (http://aalhe.org).

The Association for Institutional Research (AIR) (www.airweb.org) and the Society for College and University Planning (SCUP) (www.scup.org) offer resources on assessing other aspects of institutional effectiveness, including AIR's *Institutional Dashboards: Navigational Tool for Colleges and Universities* (Terkla, Sharkness, Cohen, Roscoe, & Wiseman, 2012), which includes examples of potential dashboard indicators. The strategic plan of Finger Lakes Community College (http://flcc.edu/pdf/StrategicPlan.pdf) is a good example of a plan with clear measures for each of its goals.

CHAPTER 14

GOOD EVIDENCE IS USEFUL

You do not need a formal background in social science research to recognize whether or not your evidence is good quality. Almost everyone I have worked with in higher education, regardless of academic background, has a good gut instinct for this. Simply ask yourself whether you are comfortable using your evidence to inform your plans, decisions, and actions and, if not, why not. This chapter, along with the chapters that follow on setting targets and transparency, will help you figure this out.

Know Your Stakeholders and What Is Useful to Them

Many years ago, I gave my college president what I thought was a very nice presentation of the results of a survey I had conducted. His reaction? "Linda, this is what I call 'gee whiz' data. I think, 'Gee whiz, this is interesting,' but I don't know what to do with it." Today, none of us can afford to spend a dime or a moment collecting "gee whiz" evidence—the kind that ends up on a (perhaps virtual) shelf.

I am often asked to suggest measures appropriate for a particular college unit, such as the institutional research office or a service learning program. I always ask, "Who needs to see evidence for this unit, and why?" Your measures should be determined by the decisions that the measures will inform. Do not feel obliged to adopt measures used by others; choose only measures that will be useful to your stakeholders.

Focus on what people care about. Good evidence is "driven by genuine inquiry" (Hawthorne & Kelsch, 2012, p. 1) into questions of real interest to your college community and your stakeholders. If your evidence is clearly tied to your college's key goals, but nonetheless no one is interested in it, you have a signal that your goals are no longer relevant, and it is time to reconsider them.

Is it good for your students? One of President Barack Obama's initial principles for determining federal education priorities was: "Is it good for the kids?" (Alter, 2009). The parallel questions at your college are

- Is your work collecting this evidence good for your students?
- Will it help them obtain a better, more effective education?
- Will it help them achieve their goals more efficiently?

Tie Evidence to Key Goals

Evidence should tell you about your college's effectiveness in meeting its responsibilities, including meeting stakeholder needs, serving the public good, ensuring your college's health and well-being, deploying resources appropriately, and achieving your college's purpose and goals.

Any measure is only as good as the goal it is intended to assess. To return to the road trip analogy in Chapter 3, if your goal is clear—to reach a specific street address in Seattle—it is easy to track your progress and tell whether you have arrived. But if your goal is fuzzy—simply to head west—it is impossible to tell whether you have reached your destination or whether you are reaching key milestones in good time. Likewise, a concrete goal to spend less than $130 on the trip is easy to monitor, but a vague goal to make the trip "economically" is harder to assess. Chapter 10 offers suggestions on articulating goals clearly and effectively.

Aim for Reasonably Accurate and Truthful Evidence

Most people have a good feel for the accuracy and truthfulness of their evidence. No one would make decisions based on a rubric, survey, or test whose scores bounce up and down erratically from one semester to the next. No one would draw conclusions about a college-wide writing program based on a review of half a dozen student papers. Keep the following ideas in mind here.

Evidence needs to be reasonably accurate and truthful, not perfect. It should be simply good enough quality that you can use it with confidence to inform meaningful plans and decisions.

Maintain an appropriate balance among the quality, dependability, and usefulness of your measures. Barbara Wright expresses this beautifully when she asks, "Are we sacrificing validity on the altar of reliability?" (personal communication, August 9, 2013). You can spend a lot of time and resources making sure that evidence is dependably consistent, but that evidence will be meaningless—and your time and resources wasted—if your evidence is not clearly tied to important goals.

Jargon Alert!

Validity

Validity means that your test, survey, or other measure gives you good-quality information on whatever you are trying to assess. There are several kinds of validity. The most important when examining quality in higher education are *content validity*, which is whether your evidence gives you meaningful information on your goals, and *consequential validity* (Pike, 2012), which is whether the evidence can be used to make meaningful, substantive decisions and solve problems—the embodiment of the culture of betterment.

Jargon Alert!

Reliability

Reliability is simply the consistency or dependability of a measure. If you assess the learning of a group of students repeatedly, the results should be consistent. There are several kinds of reliability, including *inter-rater reliability*, the consistency between two evaluators who review the same student work, and *internal consistency* among those items in a test or survey that are all supposed to assess the same thing. Note that *reliability* refers only to the consistency or dependability of a measurement tool, such as a test, rubric, or survey. This is very different from the consistency of quality and effectiveness across a college's learning venues, programs, and modalities that is discussed in Chapter 5.

This is particularly important to keep in mind when considering published tests and surveys. It is a lot easier to measure reliability (dependability) than validity (quality and usefulness), and some publishers tout reliability evidence as evidence of their instrument's "quality," glossing over a lack of substantive evidence of content validity or consequential validity. Ask some tough questions. What is this test or survey supposed to be measuring, in concrete terms? What is the evidence that this test or survey really provides meaningful, useful information on those things? For example, how do the publishers of a "critical thinking" test define the kinds of critical thinking skills that the test purports to assess? And what evidence shows that it truly assesses critical thinking as defined and not, say, aptitude or skills developed over a lifetime, rather than just at your college?

Focus on outcomes, not just efforts. Effective measures track progress toward your goal, not the processes to get there. Progress toward a fundraising goal is gauged not by the number of fundraising events you sponsor but by how much they generate in gifts. The success of a graduate program in clinical research is assessed not just by what students learn but by whether its graduates are indeed contributing to and impacting clinical research. A goal to increase student retention is gauged not by the fact that you have launched three new student support programs but by the retention rate of students who have completed them. *Checklists are not measures. If your measures consist of checking completed tasks off a list, you are measuring the wrong things.*

Look at current evidence. You would not use your bank statements from five years ago to decide whether you can afford a new car today. The same holds true for evidence at your college. Suppose you assess students' writing skills and they are poor. Do you really want to wait another three or five years to assess them again? Disappointing evidence calls for frequent reassessment to see whether planned improvements are having their desired effects.

Assessments that have yielded satisfactory results are fine to move to a back burner, however. Put those reassessments on a staggered schedule, freeing up time to focus on more pressing matters. But do not let that schedule run more than every two or three years. If you wait until the fourth or fifth year, chances are good that you will not find or remember what was done four or five years earlier, and you will need to start from scratch.

For More Information

Chapter 3 of *Assessing Student Learning: A Common Sense Guide* (Suskie, 2009) concludes with a list of published statements of principles of good practice in testing and measurement.

CHAPTER 15

SETTING AND JUSTIFYING TARGETS FOR SUCCESS

Today, many colleges have collected considerable evidence, only to see things then come to a screeching halt. Why is it so hard to use evidence to identify and implement improvements? Why is it so hard to use evidence to demonstrate quality and effectiveness to stakeholders and accreditors? Chapter 4 lists plenty of reasons, but I have seen one more frequently than any other: *You cannot share your successes or identify areas for improvement until you have a clear definition of what constitutes success.* You need a good sense of the kinds and levels of results that are good enough to conclude that your college is successful in achieving its goals, as well as the kinds and levels that indicate that you are not where you want to be.

Here is an example: A group of faculty has evaluated student writing using a rubric. The results are shown in Exhibit 15.1.

Now what? Faculty often do not know what to do with this kind of evidence, because they have never had a conversation about what rubric results they would consider good enough. What kinds of results would indicate that students have successfully achieved the outcome: that they can communicate effectively in writing? What kinds of results would indicate the need for improvement in students' writing skills?

EXHIBIT 15.1. Rubric Results for a Hypothetical Assessment of Written Communication Skills

	3	2	1
Purpose and Audience	**65% of students:** Paper has a clear purpose and shows awareness of audience.	**30% of students:** Paper shows limited awareness of purpose and audience.	**5% of students:** Paper does not show awareness of purpose and audience.
Organization	**30% of students:** Paper clearly presents a central idea supported throughout the paper. Well-planned organization. Organizational devices (title, opening/closing paragraphs, transitions) are always effective and smooth.	**65% of students:** Paper vaguely presents a central idea supported throughout the paper. Overall organization is good enough to be understandable, but devices may lack smoothness, be missing, or be ineffective.	**5% of students:** Central idea is unclear. Paper is difficult to follow.
Paragraph Structure	**55% of students:** All paragraphs have clear points with effective organizational devices (e.g., topic sentences and transitions).	**40% of students:** Most, but not all paragraphs have clear points, organizational devices, and transitions.	**5% of students:** Multiple paragraphs fail to make clear points or use effective organizational devices and transitions.
Content/ Reasoning	**45% of students:** Exceptionally sound reasoning; ideas and positions are well developed and supported with convincing evidence and relevant facts, examples, details, etc.	**45% of students:** Reasoning is sound; ideas and positions are supported with some evidence, but are not always well developed.	**10% of students:** Ideas and positions are often not supported with evidence.
Sentence Structure	**30% of students:** All sentences are clear, well-structured, and varied in pattern.	**70% of students:** Sentences are generally clear and well-structured, but some are awkward or unclear.	**0% of students:** Multiple sentences are awkward or unclear.
Tone and Word Choice	**35% of students:** Style options (tone, word choice) are appropriate for audience and purpose, are varied, and make the paper interesting.	**65% of students:** Style options are largely reasonable for audience and purpose, but some are inappropriate, or the paper is somewhat flat and dull.	**0% of students:** Style options are largely inappropriate, or the paper is unengaging.
Conciseness	**55% of students:** Paper is appropriately concise.	**40% of students:** Paper has several wordy sentences/phrases.	**5% of students:** Paper has numerous wordy sentences/phrases.
Grammar/ Mechanics	**30% of students:** Impeccable grammar, spelling, punctuation, and mechanics	**55% of students:** Substantially free of errors in grammar, mechanics, etc.; errors do not impede meaning nor overly distract the reader.	**15% of students:** Multiple errors impede meaning or distract the reader.

This rubric uses ideas in the "Standards for a 'C' Grade in English Composition" approved by Maryland chief academic officers (http://mdcao.usmd.edu/engl.html).

Now let us repeat the scenario, but with a twist: The faculty have evaluated student writing using this rubric, but this time they have agreed that a score of 2 is the minimum they consider acceptable for each criterion. They have also agreed that they want no more than 5 percent of students to score a 1. They see from Exhibit 15.1 that these targets have been met for every rubric criterion except two: those for content/reasoning and grammar/mechanics. Now the faculty have a clear path to using the rubric results. They can celebrate that their students met their targets on most criteria, and they can identify and implement strategies to help students with reasoning and grammar.

There are two lessons from these two scenarios.

Defining success means having a clear sense of what is good enough. In the parlance of the road trip analogy in Chapter 3, how do you know that your college and your students have arrived at their destinations? In the second scenario, the faculty set a target that students should score at least a 2 on a 3-point scale in order to be deemed acceptable writers.

Numbers have meaning only when they are compared against other numbers. In the second scenario, the faculty compared the 15 percent of students earning a 1 for grammar/mechanics against their target that no more than 5 percent earn a 1.

Choose an Appropriate Perspective
for Comparison

Now let us look a bit further into that second point: numbers have meaning only when compared against other numbers. Consider one question from the National Survey of Student Engagement (NSSE) (http://nsse.iub.edu): "To what extent has your experience at this institution contributed to your knowledge, skills, and personal development in thinking critically and analytically?" Suppose that today 82 percent of your seniors say "quite a bit" or "very much." There are several numbers against which you could compare this number (Suskie, 2009).

The historical perspective compares this number against those from previous years. Suppose that, three years ago, 87 percent of your seniors said your college contributes "quite a bit" or "very much" to thinking critically and analytically. Today's 82 percent would be a drop.

The historical perspective is an important perspective for gauging the success of a strategic plan, because you will want to compare where your college started, where it is now, and where it wants to be. (Exhibit 16.1 in Chapter 16 does exactly this.) This perspective is not viable, of course, if you are just beginning to collect evidence or launching a new initiative.

The strengths and weaknesses perspective breaks down results into "sub-results" or sub-scores that can be compared against each other. Imagine that, on the same NSSE survey, 75 percent of your seniors said your college contributed at least "quite a bit" to writing clearly and effectively. This is less than the 82 percent who said your college contributed at least "quite a bit" to thinking critically and analytically.

Drake University used this perspective in its assessment of first-year students' critical thinking skills (Saunders, n.d.). It found that, while student papers were mostly satisfactory in terms of organization and grammar, many students struggled with presenting assumptions, alternatives, and evidence; they cited evidence but tended to select evidence that supported their arguments. This led Drake to offer focused professional development for faculty on strategies to help students develop these particular skills.

Sub-scores or sub-results of well-designed tests, rubrics, and surveys can all be "mapped back" in this fashion to specific goals or objectives. For example, Items 3, 7, and 12 on an exam might assess students' ability to choose the correct treatment for a particular medical diagnosis, while Items 2, 5, and 8 on a survey might ask students about their experiences learning how to work with others as a team. These breakdowns are often far more useful than an overall test score. If you are considering a published test, choose one that gives sub-scores for specific skills and competencies related to your key learning goals; a test that provides only one or two global scores will not help you identify specific areas for improvement.

The value-added perspective compares seniors' NSSE responses to those from when they were first-year students. Suppose that, when they were first-year students at your college, 78 percent of your seniors said your college contributed quite a bit or very much to thinking critically and analytically. Today's 82 percent is an increase.

The value-added perspective is often confused with the pre-post experimental research design used in the social sciences (Suskie, 2009). Unlike a pre-post design, value-added does not compare changes you see against those in a control group of students who have not attended your college. So you cannot tell whether any changes are due to your college or to something else going on at the same time, say normal maturation or work experience.

This perspective is difficult to implement at colleges serving large numbers of transfer students (transferring either in or out).

The peer perspective compares your students' responses against those of students at peer colleges. Suppose that 86 percent of seniors at peer colleges across the country said their college contributed at least "quite a bit" to thinking critically and analytically. Your seniors' 82 percent is lower than this.

Jargon Alert!

Carnegie Classification

The *Carnegie Classification* of Institutions of Higher Education (http://classifications.carnegiefoundation.org/) is a framework for categorizing U.S. colleges. At its most basic level, the framework organizes colleges into 33 categories based on degrees offered, size, setting (urban, suburban, rural), and control (public, private not-for-profit, and proprietary). The Carnegie classification can help identify potential peer colleges.

This perspective can get you out of the ivory tower, but only if your college and its peers adopt common measures. In recent years, there have been increasing pressures to do so and to publish common evidence. For example, the Voluntary System of Accountability (VSA) (www.voluntarysystem.org/) developed by the Association of Public Land Grant Universities (APLU) and the American Association of State Colleges & Universities (AASCU) has called for member colleges to use and share common evidence such as results of the Collegiate Learning Assessment (CLA) (www.collegiatelearningassessment. org), the Proficiency Profile (www.ets.org/proficiencyprofile), and the VALUE rubrics discussed in Chapter 13. The Degree Qualifications Profile (DQP) sponsored by the Lumina Foundation articulates competencies at the associate's, bachelor's, and master's degree levels with an aim to "align [institutional] expectations with those of other institutions" and to prompt regional accreditors "to reach the consensus on learning outcomes that is being sought by many leaders and opinion makers" (Adelman, Ewell, Gaston, & Schneider, 2011, p. 2).

As I note several times throughout this book, diversity is one of the great strengths of U.S. higher education. Your college may have distinctive traits and goals that make the peer perspective inappropriate or unhelpful. A study by the National Institute for Learning Outcomes Assessment (NILOA) concluded, "The assumption that information must be comparable across similar institutions to facilitate student choice . . . clearly appears to have limited the richness of information that might have been of potential use to students and the public" (Jankowski, Ikenberry, Kinzie, Kuh, Shenoy, & Baker, 2012, p. 12).

The peer benchmark perspective can be used to look at breakdowns within your college by student cohort, program, financial cost center, or financial line item. You may find that this internal peer perspective is more meaningful and useful than comparisons to external peers, because there is often more within-college variability than between-college variability. Knowing that the graduation rate of students in one of your college's programs is well below your college's average, for example, is probably more meaningful and useful than knowing that your college's overall graduation rate is one percentage point above the average of its peers. Similarly, knowing that Miller Hall costs $1.75 per square foot to heat and air condition, while Prince Hall costs $1.30, is more helpful than knowing only that the campus-wide average is $1.50. Keep in mind, however, that just as your college is distinctive from its peers, some things within your college are distinctive, perhaps making comparisons pointless. It might be inappropriate to compare energy costs of your beloved but irreparably drafty Victorian Old Main and a state-of-the-art eco-friendly facility built two years ago.

No one perspective is perfect. Notice that the survey results in the NSSE scenario look different under different perspectives. Compared to seniors' responses on writing or how they responded as first-year students, the results for seniors' responses on critical thinking look good. Compared to seniors' responses three years ago or to responses from students at peer colleges, the results look disappointing. Each perspective has both strengths and weaknesses and paints an incomplete picture of success (Suskie, 2009). Choose the perspective that is most meaningful and useful for you and, if you can, try to look at your evidence from more than one perspective.

Set Justifiably Rigorous Targets

Once you have identified appropriate perspectives for your targets, you can get down to the business of setting the actual targets and doing so at appropriate levels of rigor. If you set targets too low, your college risks falling short in terms of its quality and effectiveness. Students who graduate with a bachelor's degree in accounting should be prepared to do the kinds of work that employers generally expect of bachelor's degree graduates and to pursue graduate study, and your targets should reflect this. Your student learning targets for graduate courses should be more advanced than those for senior-level courses.

While I offer many suggestions on setting targets in this chapter, there is only one real hard-and-fast rule: targets must be *justifiable*. You must be able to convince your stakeholders that your targets are appropriately rigorous. You must be able to explain not only *what* minimally acceptable student achievement is, but *why* you consider that level minimally acceptable.

The analogy to scholarly research in Chapter 19 is apt. A scholarly research paper does not merely state a hypothesis, but justifies it; the researcher's professional judgment about an appropriate hypothesis is informed by evidence. Your stakeholders expect the same. It is insufficient to say, "Our college will double its annual gifts next year" or "65 percent of students should pass each exam" without sound, informed justification.

The following strategies help justify targets.

Set externally informed targets. Even if comparisons with peers are unavailable or inappropriate, your targets can be informed by external information. For example:

- Convene an advisory panel of employers to review drafts of rubrics to make sure that they address the skills employers seek in new hires at appropriate levels of rigor.
- Talk to your disciplinary association or to faculty teaching in peer programs and see whether your targets are in line with their standards or expectations.

Set historically informed targets. No matter which perspective you use for your targets, they will be more realistic and justifiable if you factor in where you and your students have been and where you all are now. Use a few samples of student papers, for example, to inform your conversations on targets for their writing skills.

Set consistent targets across venues, modalities, and course and program levels. Chapter 5 discusses the importance of providing consistent quality, including consistent levels of rigor, to all your students, no matter where or how they learn.

Essential goals need more rigorous targets. I would not want my tax returns prepared by an accountant who completes them correctly only 70 percent of the time. But no one expects 100 percent of college graduates to be brilliant leaders or superb public speakers.

Set a Range of Minimal and Aspirational Targets

A single target, perhaps that 85 percent of your first-year students will persist to their second year, can come across as arbitrary (Jose Jaime Rivera, personal communication, August 14, 2013). After all, your college will probably not close if only 84 percent persist, and there will probably not be fireworks if 86 percent persist.

So I sometimes suggest setting a range of targets. The lowest point in the range is what Universidad del Sagrado Corazon administrators call your critical level (Jose Jaime Rivera, personal communication, August 14, 2013): the point that raises a red flag signaling problems that must be addressed. The top end is the aspirational target that you hope to reach to see the meaningful improvement called for by your goal. Suppose, for example, that one of your goals is for your students to engage with people of diverse backgrounds and cultures. You might set an aspirational target that 30 percent of your students study abroad before graduating, but set 15 percent as your critical level.

Setting a range of targets is especially important in financial planning, and it is also important when assessing student learning. You will probably want all or the vast majority of your students to reach your minimally acceptable level of a student skill or competence. But I have yet to meet anyone who would be satisfied if all students performed at that minimally acceptable level, but none did any better. So you will likely want to set a second target for the proportion of students who demonstrate exemplary performance.

Have Clear Goals

Chapter 14 explains that any measure is only as good as the goal it is intended to assess. This is true for targets, too. If you are struggling to identify an appropriate target, take a look at your goal; it may be too fuzzy to be meaningful. To forestall this, include a conversation on measures and targets when you articulate your goals. If you cannot come up with ideas for clear measures or targets, your goals are probably too fuzzy.

Set Both Milestone and Destination Targets

As your college and students progress toward their destinations, you will want to check that they are on track to reach those destinations on time. If your college's three-year goal is that 80 percent of students engage in service learning experiences and only 65 percent do now, you might set an interim goal that 70 percent engage in service learning experiences in the coming year. Exhibit 16.1 in Chapter 16 is an example of a dashboard that lists targets for this year, next year, and long term.

For More Information

The DQP and the VALUE rubrics, both mentioned earlier in this chapter, can be a useful tool to kick off conversations on appropriate levels of rigor of your college's offerings. Chapter 15 in *Assessing Student Learning: A Common Sense Guide* (Suskie, 2009) discusses more thoroughly the perspectives presented in this chapter, along with several others.

CHAPTER 16

TRANSPARENCY
Sharing Evidence Clearly and Readily

If evidence is to be used, whether to better a college or to demonstrate effectiveness to stakeholders, it must be shared in ways that make it easy to locate and easy to understand. Chapter 5 explains that transparency means making evidence clear, concise, easy to find, and relevant—and thereby useful—to your stakeholders. This chapter offers suggestions on how to do this.

Form Follows Function

Have a clear purpose for everything that you summarize, analyze, and share, then design reporting structures and formats to fulfill that purpose. *Every piece of evidence that is shared should help inform decisions . . .* and not just decisions by your accreditor. Ask yourself:

- Who needs to see this report?
- Why? What decisions will they make that this evidence should inform?
- (If you ask that reports of evidence use a template) Why must each requested item be provided in the report? How will each item be used?

Organize evidence around key points your stakeholders want and need to know. Consider a question-and-answer format, for example. NILOA recommends presenting evidence "around questions of particular interest to students and other relevant stakeholders to tell a contextualized, institution-specific, evidence-based story" (Jankowski, Ikenberry, Kinzie, Kuh, Shenoy, & Baker, 2012, p. 3).

One size does not fit all. Different stakeholders want and need different information, at different levels of detail, and in different formats. Government policymakers typically want to see the "30,000-foot picture," for example, while prospective students are often more interested in information on specific programs. Employers want to see evidence that your students graduate with competencies they need, while non-traditional-aged prospective students most want to know that they will have teachers who "care about students and know how to teach" (Hagelskamp, Schleifer, & DiStasi, 2013).

Meanwhile, within your college, faculty and administrators often need to see detailed evidence about the quality and effectiveness of their own program, service, or unit. Administrators who are responsible for a number of programs, services, or units need more aggregated and less granular evidence for those units. College leaders and boards often need very concise, broad summaries of evidence for the entire college, rather than for specific programs (Allen, Bacow, & Trombley, 2011). Consider admissions statistics, for example:

- Your admissions director and staff need breakdowns of admissions statistics for various student cohorts to ensure that various admissions targets will be achieved.

- The vice president to whom the admissions director reports needs overall admissions statistics to ensure that enrollment targets will be met, perhaps needing breakdowns only if the overall statistics indicate a concern.

- Your college's leadership team needs a quick snapshot of the college's overall enrollment picture, including admissions, retention, and graduation, to verify, among other things, that tuition revenue targets are being met and your college's financial health and well-being thereby continue to be assured.

- Your college's leadership team also needs information beyond enrollment statistics. It has ultimate responsibility for ensuring that all programs and services affecting enrollment embody the five dimensions of quality: that enrollment management practices meet expectations for integrity, for example, and that decisions are made collaboratively, as appropriate. It needs to see indicators of these quality expectations.

Two lessons apply here. First, *no one report, database, or website will meet all your stakeholders' needs*. Different decision-makers want and need different evidence in different formats and in different levels of detail. Yes, preparing multiple reports takes time, but I would rather prepare several short, useful reports than one lengthy report that no one looks at and that is therefore a waste of my time.

Second, *no one reporting structure or form can tell the full story of quality and effectiveness throughout your college*. A single template adopted for college-wide use can simplify college-wide analysis of evidence, but it can force some programs and units to put the square peg of their stories into the round hole of the template. Unless your accreditor explicitly requires that evidence be presented in a consistent format, do not require everyone to contort their work to fit a common template. Instead, be flexible. Offer a template or an assessment information management system reporting feature (Chapter 18) as an optional tool, and also offer the option of telling the story of one's evidence in alternative ways, such as a narrative or a chart formatted differently from the template.

Make Clear, Meaningful Points

The points of your evidence should pop out at readers, so they can readily see the connection between your evidence and the decisions they are facing.

Keep things short and simple. The briefer and simpler your summary of your evidence, the more likely people will absorb it. Few people today have time or patience to wade through lengthy reports or complicated charts to find the evidence they seek. Consider the following (Suskie, 2009):

- Most evidence is useless; feel free to discard it (Harris & Muchin, 2002, "Information Architecture," para. 7). Do not feel obliged to share responses to every survey item, for example.
- Use consumer-friendly language, avoiding jargon (Jankowski, Ikenberry, Kinzie, Kuh, Shenoy, & Baker, 2012).
- Limit the amount of information in any one table or graph.
- Aim to make every table and graph self-explanatory.
- Round numbers, including percentages, to the nearest whole number.
- Percentages are generally more meaningful and easier to understand than averages.

Jargon Alert!

Data and Information

Data are a set of numbers (the singular is *datum*). *Information* makes clear the story that the numbers are telling.

Use visuals. Infographics, graphs, bulleted lists, dashboards, tables, sidebars, and callout boxes convey key points, differences, and trends more readily than text narratives. But note that a table or graph generated by the default settings of software or an assessment information management system may not convey your key points clearly; you may need to tweak the table or graph yourself before sharing. If you are considering investing in an assessment information management system, make sure that its reports can be customized to meet your audiences' diverse needs, or be prepared to create your own reports from information saved in the system.

Jargon Alert!

Infographics

Infographics combine graphics and text to convey the key points of complex information. Hundreds of examples (good and not so good) are available at http://dailyinfographics.com and http://visual.ly; click on the Education link of either site.

Use dashboards . . . but keep them balanced. Board members, understandably interested in their college's financial picture, tend to focus on financial and enrollment indicators, and their attention to "academic quality" is often limited to student persistence and graduation rates (Terkla, Sharkness, Cohen, Roscoe, & Wiseman, 2012). Unfortunately, "it is possible to produce so-called improvements in these [kinds of] measures while actually hurting teaching and learning" (Business-Higher Education Forum, 2004, p. 13). A focus on graduation rates, for example, can create a climate in which faculty feel pressured to set lower standards and pass students through, even if their learning is inadequate. Keep your eye on the prize: make sure your college-wide dashboards or infographics include measures on *all* your college's key goals, not just the easy-to-track ones.

Jargon Alert!

Dashboards and Balanced Scorecards

A *dashboard* is a set of dashboard indicators (Chapter 13) that give a snapshot of progress toward a goal or fulfillment of another responsibility. A *balanced scorecard* is a dashboard that aims to provide balanced information on a college's key or strategic goals. If your key goals focus on improving student success, for example, a balanced scorecard includes key measures of student success and not just, say, financial indicators.

EXHIBIT 16.1. A Dashboard for a Hypothetical College Strategic Goal

Strategic Goal: To sustain student enrollment at a level that ensures financial viability and fulfillment of the college's mission of providing personalized, responsive, interactive educational opportunities to qualified students.

	Baseline: Last Year's Results	This Year's Target	This Year's Results	Progress	Next Year's Target	Long-Term Target (five years from now)	Resulting Adjustments
Total full-time undergraduates	1,790	1,850	1,815	Yellow light	1,850	2,000	See below
Number of new full-time first-year students	550	600	559	Yellow light	580	600	Allocate $150,000 to recruitment plan
Percentage of new full-time first-year students whose high school rank is in the top 20 percent	45%	45%	47%	Green light	45%	45%	None warranted
Full-time first-year-to-sophomore retention rate	84%	86%	86%	Green light	88%	88%	Continue current retention initiatives

Overall Analysis of Achievement to Date

We are attracting and retaining qualified students; our priority is increasing the size of the first-year class. We are increasing our investment in recruitment strategies, as described in our enrollment management plan.

Exhibit 16.1 is an example of a dashboard that might be intended for the board of a private liberal arts college. Notice that it uses traffic signal coding: green for meeting or exceeding targets, yellow for potential areas of concern, red for areas falling short. This coding is a great way to help stakeholders use the dashboard to see progress and identify where adjustments may be needed.

Use plenty of headings, subheadings, and hyperlinks to cascade from major points to details and help stakeholders find quickly what they are looking for. Use engaging, meaningful titles and headings. "Students Successfully Integrate Ideas" says a lot more than "Critical Thinking Assessment Results."

Draw attention to the points you want to make using tools like brightlines, larger fonts, boldface, and italics and by sorting evidence in graphs and tables from highest to lowest.

Jargon Alert!

Brightline

A *brightline* is a line in a table that is highlighted with shading, boldface, or lines. The brightline highlights the average, norm, or some other target, such as a minimum pass score on an exam, against which other numbers in the table can be compared. Brightlines are most effective when the numbers in a table are sorted from highest to lowest and the brightline is inserted at an appropriate point.

Tell Your Story in Your Voice

The 2006 Spellings Commission conclusion that there was "a lack of clear, reliable information about the cost and quality of postsecondary institutions, along with a remarkable absence of accountability mechanisms to ensure that colleges succeed in educating students" (U.S. Department of Education, 2006, p. vii) led to an explosion in public information resources on higher education (see the listing below) and a call to colleges from the New Leadership Alliance for Student Learning and Accountability (2012b) to use common templates for communication with the public.

Information Resources on U.S. Colleges

- America's Top Colleges, sponsored by *Forbes* (www.forbes .com/top-colleges/)
- College Compass, sponsored by *U.S. News & World Report* (www.usnews.com/usnews/store/college_compass.htm)
- College Guide by *Washington Monthly* (www.washington monthly.com/college_guide/index.php)
- College Navigator, sponsored by the U.S. Department of Education (http://nces.ed.gov/collegenavigator/)
- College Portrait of Undergraduate Education, also known as the Voluntary System of Accountability (VSA), sponsored by the Association of Public and Land Grant Universities (APLU) and the American Association of State Colleges and Universities (AASCU) (www.collegeportraits.org/)
- College Rankings ("best college values") sponsored by *Kiplinger's* (http://kiplingers.com/fronts/special-report/college-rankings/index.html)
- College Results Online, sponsored by the Education Trust (www.collegeresults.org/)
- College Search, sponsored by the College Board (https://big future.collegeboard.org/college-search)
- University and College Accountability Network (U-CAN), sponsored by the National Association of Independent Colleges and Universities (NAICU) (www.ucan-network.org/)
- Voluntary Framework for Accountability (VFA), sponsored by the American Association of Community Colleges (AACC) (www.aacc.nche.edu/Resources/aaccprograms/ VFAWeb/Pages/VFAHomePage.aspx)

But your college has its own story to tell of its quality and effectiveness. As Lee Shulman has said, "The current quest for accountability creates a precious opportunity for educators to tell the full range of stories about teaching and learning" (2007, p. 25). Research by the National Institute on Learning Outcomes Assessment (NILOA) has come to the same conclusion, recommending "a platform through which institutions can speak to and engage their publics through evidence-based story telling" (Jankowski, Ikenberry, Kinzie, Kuh, Shenoy, & Baker, 2012, p. 4).

As I noted earlier in this chapter, *no one report, database, or website will tell the full story of your college's quality.* Research by NILOA has confirmed this, recommending that the College Portrait "be recast as a state-of-the-art electronic communication tool targeted for specific stakeholders, including prospective and current students, parents, and guidance counselors; faculty and staff; trustees; employers; accreditors; public policy-makers; and media" (Jankowski, Ikenberry, Kinzie, Kuh, Shenoy, & Baker, 2012, p. 3).

Your college's story needs to be told in your college's voice, using measures that reflect its purpose, goals, and values. Your college likely has goals that may not be on stakeholders' radar screens, but are nonetheless important; goals concerning civic engagement, social justice, and appreciation of the arts are just a few examples. The story you want to convey with evidence should therefore include (Douglas Eder, personal communication, February 8, 2013):

- How your college defines its success and successful students, including the knowledge, skills, and competencies students should have upon graduation
- Why you think these are important
- Evidence that your college and your students meet your definitions of success
- Whether you are satisfied with your evidence—and why or why not
- What you are doing about any unsatisfactory evidence

With the vital responsibility of U.S. colleges to serve the public good off many people's radar screens, consider also demonstrating to your stakeholders how your college serves the public good and making the case to them on why this is important.

Make Evidence Easy to Find

A few years ago, my advice in this regard was simply to make your evidence intuitively accessible from the home page of your college's website. To a degree, that advice still holds, and three great examples are the home pages of Hamilton College (www.hamilton.edu), Slippery Rock University (www.sru.edu), and St. Olaf College (http://wp.stolaf.edu/). Hamilton's and St. Olaf's home pages have "Outcomes" links, and Slippery Rock's has an "Accountability" link, all leading to web pages that are easy to navigate.

But making evidence easy to find today involves more than website navigation. Communication modalities have grown, and increasingly people expect information to come to them through their preferred modality, which may be tweets, e-mails, texts, postings on social media sites, snail-mailed reports, or face-to-face presentations. The NILOA study mentioned earlier (Jankowski, Ikenberry, Kinzie, Kuh, Shenoy, & Baker, 2012) recommended designing purposeful strategies to draw traffic to the website it studied.

Be Honest and Balanced

Honesty is being truthful with yourself and your stakeholders in how you share information and evidence (Suskie, 2009):

- Aim for evidence that is reasonably accurate and truthful.
- Share information and evidence completely, fairly, and openly with your college community, your stakeholders, and your accreditors.
- Provide full and balanced information, not just selected facts or the bare minimum required by a government or accreditation requirement.

- Help your stakeholders distinguish meaningful from trivial differences.

- Give appropriate attribution to the work and ideas of others.

- Respect students' privacy and dignity, while concurrently giving faculty, administrators, and other decision-makers sufficient evidence to make meaningful decisions.

In Chapter 19, I suggest viewing an accreditation report as a cousin of a scholarly research paper. That analogy holds here. The standard of honesty that you would use in a scholarly research paper is the standard that you should apply to sharing evidence and, indeed, to all five cultures of quality.

Delivering disappointing evidence honestly and fairly is always hard. Imagine a supervisor asking employees both for documentation that they have been doing their jobs well and for information on steps they are taking to improve their performance. The two requests can easily be seen as contradictory. Employees want to respond to the first request by documenting that they are doing a superlative job—after all, this way may lie pay raises and opportunities for advancement. The second request, however, implicitly requires them to admit that they are *not* doing the best possible job. Employees might therefore be tempted to respond to the second request incompletely, reporting only on minor areas for improvement. After all, acknowledging serious shortcomings might have serious consequences, perhaps even losing one's job.

Colleges face the same dilemma. The culture of relevance asks them to provide evidence of their quality, while the culture of betterment asks them to use evidence to improve themselves, which implicitly requires them to acknowledge shortcomings. Resolve this by using two classic public relations devices:

- Sandwich negatives between positives. Your college is doing some things well (if it is not, you really do have a problem!), so your evidence is bound to have some good news. Point out your successes as well as your disappointments.

- The story of the disappointing evidence is not the evidence itself but the steps you are taking to improve those results. The more concrete the plans you provide, the greater the assurance you are providing that shortcomings will be addressed as soon as possible. This is discussed further in Chapter 19.

For More Information

"Seven Maxims for Institutional Researchers" (Hackman, 1989) is a classic statement of principles for sharing evidence. Another good resource is *Making Student Learning Evidence Transparent: The State of the Art* (Jankowski & Provezis, 2011). The classic work on infographics is *Visual Explanations: Images and Quantities, Evidence and Narrative* (Tufte, 1997). *Effective Reporting* (Sanders & Filkins, 2009) offers great advice on sharing numerical data clearly and meaningfully. More suggestions are in Chapter 17 of *Assessing Student Learning: A Common Sense Guide* (Suskie, 2009).

Examples of effective presentations of evidence that incorporate much of the advice in this chapter include the following:

- Graduation rates at the University of Alaska Anchorage at www.uaa.alaska.edu/ir/publications/dashboard/upload/GraduationRate.html
- Employer perceptions of online and face-to-face degrees published by Drexel University at www.drexel.com/uploadedFiles/OnlineEdInfographic81213PDF.pdf
- Evidence of student learning at Capella University at www.capellaresults.com/bs_psych.asp

The NILOA Transparency Framework (www.learningoutcomeassessment.org/TransparencyFramework.htm) cites more examples of sharing evidence with public stakeholders.

DIMENSION V:
A Culture of Betterment

USING EVIDENCE TO ENSURE AND ADVANCE QUALITY AND EFFECTIVENESS

sraeli Prime Minister Benjamin Netanyahu has a habit of asking, "How do you know that?" (Stengel, 2012). At a college committed to a pervasive, enduring culture of betterment—one of evidence-informed decision making—everyone asks this on a regular basis. Decisions everywhere are consistently informed by systematic, compelling evidence: at board and department meetings, in administrative units and academic programs, in liberal arts and professional programs. A quality college is always learning about its students, its practices, its stakeholders, and its environment and using that information to become ever more responsive and effective. Evidence is not something cranked out only when needed to keep an accreditor happy. It is a habit, a way of life.

Jargon Alert!

Closing the Loop, Continuous Improvement, and Continuous Quality Improvement

Closing the loop flows from the work of W. Edwards Deming (2000), who promoted an ongoing four-step quality improvement cycle that is often referred to as *continuous improvement, continuous quality*

(Continued)

(*Continued*)

improvement, or *total quality management.* The cycle can be applied to a college as follows:

1. Set goals and plan strategies to achieve them.
2. Implement programs, services, or initiatives to achieve those goals.
3. Collect evidence on how well those programs, services, or initiatives are achieving those goals.
4. Use that evidence to identify ways to improve the steps of the cycle . . . which closes the cycle or loop.

Recognize and Celebrate Successes

Not every piece of evidence demands improvement. When your college achieves its goals and meets its targets, celebrate these successes! (I have joked that accreditors should require that the "use" of such evidence be a mandatory pizza party.) Then focus on sharing these successes more effectively with your stakeholders.

But if your college's culture is one of ongoing betterment, questions may be considered, even when results look great. Should your standards be raised? Can you achieve your goals or assess your results more efficiently? Should you turn your attention to enhancing relevance to your audiences? The answers may be no, not now, but the questions are still considered.

Use Evidence to Advance Quality and Effectiveness

The most common uses of evidence that I see are minor tweaks. Faculty who are dissatisfied with their students' skills in citing research literature, for example, may agree to spend more time explaining this in their classes, to provide more examples and homework, and perhaps to address this skill in more courses in their program. This kind of fine-tuning is low-cost and requires the consensus of a relatively small number of faculty, but it does not lead to substantive advancements in your college's overall quality and effectiveness.

Using evidence to make broader or more substantive changes is harder, but it can be done. The Education Trust has shared the stories of eight U.S. universities that used analyses of systematic evidence to implement changes that improved their student success rates dramatically (Yeado, Haycock, Johnstone, & Chaplot, 2014). Here are additional examples:

- After examining the retention rates of first-year, second-year, and transfer students, as well as those of students of color, along with results from the National Survey of Student Engagement (NSSE) (http://nsse.iub.edu) and the Faculty Survey of Student Engagement (FSSE) (http://fsse.iub.edu), the University of Wisconsin–Oshkosh redesigned its general education curriculum to foster earlier and more pervasive use of strategies that promote student learning and success (Kuh & O'Donnell, 2013).

- After assessing student learning in its writing-intensive, capstone, and service-learning courses, Daemen College hired a writing coordinator and writing-in-the-disciplines specialist, added an information literacy component to its first-year writing course, increased the proportion of first-year writing courses taught by full-time faculty from 35 to 90 percent, and offered workshops for faculty teaching writing-intensive courses (Morace & Hibschweiler, n.d.).

- After reviewing a variety of measures on its academic advisement programs, including NSSE results, student/advisor ratios, and a program review, the University of Tennessee–Knoxville increased the number of full-time advisors, restructured orientation advising for new first-time students, and implemented a new advising policy targeting at-risk students (NSSE, 2012).

Use Evidence to Deploy Resources Prudently

There is a common theme among these examples: *meaningful advancements in quality and effectiveness require resource investments.* One of the characteristics of good stewardship is that evidence is used to inform resource deployment decisions, and you can see that in these examples. An important way to link evidence to resource decisions is to require "business plans" for any initiative that is proposed or under review, as discussed in Chapter 20. Here are some other suggestions for linking evidence to resource decisions.

Include student learning evidence in the mix of evidence, as shown in the above examples. If you find this difficult, the problem may be that:

- Your college is not yet assessing truly important learning outcomes.
- Your college has not yet clearly defined what successful learning outcomes look like (see Chapter 15).
- Faculty do not see value in identifying areas for improvement in teaching and learning (see Chapter 18).

Use external as well as internal evidence. Enrollment management decisions may be informed more by market analysis than by evidence of student learning, for example.

Prepare for a time lag. I have joked that colleges need a one-month hiatus between the end of one fiscal year and the start of the next, to examine evidence from the previous year and use it to set or refine goals, plans, and resources for the next. The reality is that, at many colleges, next year's annual budget must be put in place before evidence from the current year is in hand. For colleges whose fiscal year runs from July 1 to June 30, for example, budgets for the following year are often put together in the spring, whereas evidence of student learning is often collected at the end of the spring semester, and other evidence, such as final financial figures, may not be available until after the current fiscal year ends.

There are a few ways to deal with this, although none is entirely satisfactory. One is to acknowledge a lag, allowing decision-makers time to "make meaning of and to reflect on assessment results" (Baker, Jankowski, Provezis, & Kinzie, 2012, p. 7). Student learning evidence collected at the end of the 2017–2018 academic year, for example, might be analyzed after the 2018–2019 academic year begins and used to inform the 2019–2020 budget. Another option is to build into each annual budget a reserve for funding any pressing needs identified through evidence. If you find that your students' writing skills are miserable, for example, you will want to fund immediate measures to improve them, rather than wait for the following fiscal year.

Use Evidence to Refine Goals and Targets

Sometimes, what needs attention is not your programs, services, and activities but your goals and targets. Suppose, for example, that your college aimed to raise $5 million this year toward a $20 million five-year target, but it brought in only $3 million. Yes, perhaps fundraising efforts could be improved, but perhaps the $20 million target was overly ambitious, especially if you raised only $1 million last year (in which case $3 million this year would be a terrific accomplishment). On the other hand, if you raised $8 million this year, you might want to consider stretching your $20 million five-year target to something more ambitious.

Before you cut back on what seems to be an overly ambitious goal, consider this: often the reason for falling short is not that your goal is too ambitious but that you have too many goals, causing your college and its faculty and staff to lose focus and diffuse energies. What can you scale back on or put on hold, freeing up time and resources to focus more on your critical goals?

This applies to goals for student learning as well. If your students are not writing as well as you would like, for example, look at all your other goals for them. Are you expecting them to learn too many things? Can time spent on a less-critical goal be scaled back, freeing faculty and student time to work on writing?

Use Evidence Fairly, Ethically, and Responsibly

A few principles (Suskie, 2009) are worth highlighting here.

Evidence should not make decisions for you; it should only advise you as you use your professional judgment to make suitable decisions.

Do not base a major decision on only one piece of evidence, such as the results of a single assessment of student learning.

Do not use evidence punitively. Past use of evidence—good or bad—affects people's willingness to participate in gathering and using evidence now (Petrides & Nodine, 2005). Do not react to disappointing evidence by immediately eliminating a program or denying promotion or tenure to the faculty involved. Instead, provide an opportunity to address the problems identified through the evidence.

Be careful how you recognize and honor evidence of success. It is tempting to reward successful results with, say, merit pay increases, but this can backfire, tempting individuals to distort, if not outright falsify, evidence in order to look as good as possible. This kind of practice can also force faculty and staff to compete against one another for a limited pool of pay increase funds, which can destroy the culture of collaboration that is an essential component of quality. Yes, evidence of success should be celebrated, but so should efforts to understand and improve quality, especially collaborative efforts, even if those efforts initially fail or yield disappointing results.

For More Information

Many of the reports cited in this chapter offer more great examples of using evidence to inform improvements. Chapter 10 of *Effective Grading: A Tool for Learning and Assessment in College* (Walvoord & Anderson, 2010) and Chapter 18 of *Assessing Student Learning: A Common Sense Guide* (Suskie, 2009) both address using student learning assessment results.

SUSTAINING A CULTURE OF BETTERMENT

As I note at several points throughout this book, while a lot of colleges today have accrued a good deal of evidence, many are not yet using it to inform decisions and advance quality. Why not? Chapter 4 discusses the obstacles I see most frequently to a pervasive, enduring culture of betterment. Beyond the prerequisite of setting clear, justifiable targets defining success, discussed in Chapter 15, I do not have a magic answer to getting evidence off the shelf and using it for betterment. Too much depends on your college's culture and history. But this chapter will offer you some ideas to consider.

Foster a Culture of Community

All five cultures of quality require your college community to work together to take your college on its journey. Nowhere is this more important than with the culture of betterment. Chapter 7 offers many suggestions on ways to foster a culture of community, including building cultures of respect, communication, collaboration, growth and development, and shared collegial governance. Chapter 7 also suggests offering support such as guidance, professional development, and constructive feedback.

One particularly important strategy is to empower faculty oversight of student learning assessment. Juniata College found, for example, that turning assessment from "a very top-down process that has political overtones" to one controlled by faculty makes it "really rooted and faculty-centered" (Jankowski, 2011, p. 3). The greater the role that faculty have in developing and implementing student learning assessments, the more ownership they have of the process and results, and the more likely that they will take the results seriously and use them to identify and implement advancements in quality and effectiveness. "Perhaps the surest way to ensure that [assessment measures] will be used is to involve the individuals who ought to use them in their initial selection and development" (Banta & Borden, 1994, p. 103) and have them specify "the kinds of data they will consider credible and helpful" (p. 98).

Value Efforts to Change, Improve, and Innovate

Some colleges have a thriving culture of innovation. Carnegie Mellon University's vision, for example, is to "meet the changing needs of society by building on its traditions of innovation, problem solving, and interdisciplinarity" (n.d., para. 1). One of Excelsior College's values is "innovation as a source of improvement" (2013, "Values," para. 3). But many colleges do not yet have cultures valuing innovation and improvement. Concrete, tangible incentives, recognition, and rewards can help nurture such a culture (Kuh, Jankowski, Ikenberry, & Kinzie, 2014).

Incorporate college priorities into criteria for performance review, including merit pay and faculty promotion and tenure (P&T). Review criteria should value and reward work to advance your college's quality agenda. Some examples:

- If your college is focusing on advancing its culture of evidence, establish performance evaluation criteria for vice presidents and deans that value their effectiveness in building a culture of evidence within their units, and ensure that faculty P&T criteria value substantive faculty work on assessing student learning.

- If your college is focusing on advancing its culture of community, establish performance evaluation and P&T criteria that value collaborative work, especially to provide a cohesive education experience.

- If your college is focusing on advancing its culture of betterment, allow faculty and staff to stumble occasionally as they try their best to improve what they do. Establish performance evaluation and P&T criteria that reward innovation, even if those efforts are not at first successful. Encourage teaching innovation by offering faculty a semester or year of grace from student evaluations of teaching when they try implementing research-informed teaching methods.

Offer stipends, fellowships, or merit pay for extraordinary work that helps to advance your college's quality agenda. Assessing student learning in courses and programs is simply part of teaching, of course, but above-and-beyond work, such as coordinating the assessment of the general education curriculum, deserves special recognition. "Next to disciplinary accreditation, funding from an external source may be the second most powerful incentive for turning faculty angst and even anger about assessment to acceptance, and even appreciation" (Banta, 2010, p. 3).

A great strategy to promote cultures of evidence and betterment is to offer mini-grants *only* to faculty who have assessed student learning and are disappointed with the results. Faculty can use the mini-grants to research, plan, and implement improvements and changes that have been suggested by evidence. Business and communication faculty at LaGuardia Community College, for example, used mini-grants to address business students' underachievement in oral communication by incorporating new activities into introductory business courses (Provezis, 2012). Special mini-grants available only to address disappointing evidence are a wonderful counterpoint to any rumors that such evidence will be treated punitively.

Offer other recognition, such as letters of commendation or awards from college leaders, provided that these are based on fair, consistent criteria. A luncheon, a wine and cheese party, a barbecue, an event akin to a conference poster session, or another celebratory event may also be appreciated, depending on your college's culture.

Offer other incentives. Some provosts have told me, for example, that they have told their departments, "If you haven't submitted your assessment report, don't give me a budget request."

The Perfect Is the Enemy of the Good

The most frequent "use" of evidence that I see is refining the tool or process used to collect the evidence. Rubrics are tweaked to make them clearer; survey administration procedures are revised to achieve a better response rate. On one hand, this makes sense. People at colleges are very good at research, and good research often includes refining the methodology after a pilot study.

On the other hand, it is a lot easier to change rubric criteria than to use rubric results to make substantive changes to curricula and teaching methods. Research protocols do not call for endless pilot studies, and neither should colleges in their pursuit of quality. Repeated refinements of evidence-collection tools and processes are stalling tactics, putting off the day when the evidence is used to make meaningful improvements (Blaich & Wise, 2011).

There is no perfect measure of quality. Every kind of evidence—and every approach to collecting, sharing, and using evidence—has inherent imperfections and limitations, and any one measure alone provides an incomplete and possibly distorted picture of quality. Some examples:

- Some important goals cannot be measured meaningfully with single performance indicators. There is no single quantitative metric, for example, that will tell you how well your college is achieving its goals of improving the cultural climate of the region, linking budget decisions to institutional plans, giving students an appreciation of the arts, or graduating students with a commitment to civic engagement (Suskie, 2006).

- While some published tests of college-level skills and competencies are promising, at this point many remain works in progress regarding their validity, as discussed in Chapter 14.

- Retention and graduation rates alone do not tell you *why* students are leaving before graduating, information that is critical in determining whether the rates are adequate.

Because there is no perfect assessment measure, try to look at more than one source of evidence. If one of your goals is to strengthen your college's financial health, for example, keep an eye on a number of financial measures and ratios.

Keep things simple and cost-effective. Imagine an accreditation review team dropping in unannounced on your college three years after your formal accreditation review. What would it find? Would the processes and evidence of quality in place at the time of the last formal review persist?

The answer lies in the cost and complexity of your college's quality processes. Simple, cost-effective structures and processes are far more likely to be sustained, while overly complex or ambitious structures or processes, such as an unwieldy governance structure or requests for 20-page annual assessment reports, quickly collapse under their own weight.

Efforts to implement a culture of quality should yield value that justifies the time and expense put into them. Assessments of student learning should not take so much time that they detract from teaching. Independent "blind" scoring of student work is a good research practice, for example, but it is costly in terms of time and perhaps money as well as morale. Is this where your college should be deploying scarce resources? Is the added confidence in the results worth the extra cost?

Start at the end and work backward. Begin by looking at your students shortly before they graduate. If you are satisfied with their achievement of a learning outcome—say, they are writing beautifully—there is no need to drill down into their achievement of that outcome in earlier courses.

Look for the biggest return on investment. Capstone experiences are great opportunities to assess several key program learning outcomes at once. And, no matter how many general education courses your college offers, there are probably no more than 15 or 20 courses that the vast majority of students take to complete general education requirements. Start your assessment of general education learning outcomes by assessing student learning in just those 15 or 20 courses. Your evidence from this initial assessment can have a broad impact on the great majority of your students, with far less work than assessing learning in every general education course.

Do not collect more evidence than you can handle. A ten-page alumni survey will yield ten pages of results that faculty and administrators must tabulate, analyze, and discuss. A two-page survey, while not yielding the same breadth of information, will take far less time to implement, summarize, share, and use.

Minimize the reporting burden. Do all you can to keep reports on evidence, betterment, and the other dimensions of quality to a bare-bones minimum, and streamline and simplify the process of preparing them. The next section offers some specific ideas to consider.

Document Evidence

If evidence is not recorded, it cannot be shared; if it is not shared, it cannot be discussed and used (Bresciani, 2006). If records of evidence and the decisions flowing from them are not maintained, progress cannot be tracked and memory is lost. So a certain amount of recording and preparation of summaries and analyses of evidence is an unavoidable part of developing and sustaining a culture of quality.

In the beginning, templates can help everyone understand good practices. If your college is launching an effort to build a culture of evidence and betterment, templates for documenting assessment processes and for recording and sharing evidence can be useful teaching tools. At this early stage, a detailed template like the one in Exhibit 18.1 may be helpful *if* it is shared when people *begin to plan* the collection of evidence, just like a rubric helps students learn *if* it is shared with them when they receive an assignment. Assessment committees and coordinators, charged with ensuring and advancing cultures of evidence and betterment, can then use the completed templates to offer collegial feedback and support to faculty and administrators on their efforts.

As your college develops a culture of evidence and betterment and people across campus increasingly engage in good practices to collect and use evidence, scale back reports on assessment processes and focus on what is far more important: reports that share evidence and document how evidence is used for betterment. The assessment committee and coordinator can move from reviewing processes to reviewing the shared evidence and records of decisions to confirm that cultures of evidence and betterment continue to be advanced.

Consider assessment information management systems to record and manage evidence. They can simplify the analysis of evidence and preserve evidence through inevitable personnel transitions, but they can also frustrate those whose evidence does not fit with the system's structure or who find the system's reports less than transparent. The key is to choose a technology that will meet your college's needs, not one that will require your practices to conform to its design and structure (Suskie, 2009). Beware of a system designed primarily to get you through accreditation; aim for one that focuses on helping you ensure and improve quality and effectiveness, with accreditation evidence as a by-product. Unless your accreditor requires that evidence be recorded in a certain way, be flexible: offer the system as a tool, but also offer the option of recording and storing evidence in alternative ways.

EXHIBIT 18.1. Sample Template for Documenting Nascent Student Learning Assessment Processes

Student Learning Outcome	Create organized, effective visual presentations of information and ideas	Write effectively within the discipline
How do students learn this? In what course(s) and/or co-curricular experience(s)?	*In required courses ABC 105, ABC 310, and the capstone course*	*In every course in the curriculum*
How and in what course do they demonstrate that they've achieved this outcome?	*In the capstone course, in which they develop a visual presentation of the results of their research project*	*In the capstone course, in which they prepare a written report on the results of their research project*
How and when do you assess the achievement of all students in your program before they graduate and record the results of your assessment?*	*In the capstone course, a rubric to evaluate their visual presentation*	*In the capstone course, a rubric to evaluate the written report*
What do you consider satisfactory achievement of this outcome? WHY?	*See attached rubric. We expect all students to score at least "satisfactory" on documenting sources of information, because respect for intellectual property is a key value of our program. We expect 85% to score at least "satisfactory" on all other criteria because employers have advised us that, while they are collectively important, none alone is absolutely vital for employee success.*	*See attached rubric. We expect all students to score at least "satisfactory" on all criteria. We expect at least 50% to score "exceptional," because we consider effective writing a distinctive hallmark of our program, compared to peer programs at other universities.*

What are the recent results of your assessment? How many students were assessed?	See attached rubric with results. At least 85% of students scored at least satisfactory on all criteria except documenting sources of information, where 28% of students scored "needs improvement."	See attached rubric with results. All students scored at least satisfactory on all criteria for effective writing except in integrating ideas, where 10% of students scored "need improvement." No more than 40% of students scored "exceptional" on any criterion.
How do the results compare with your expectations for satisfactory learning? Are you satisfied with the results?	We are dissatisfied with how well our students are documenting sources of information. Achievement in all other areas meets our standards.	We are dissatisfied with how well our students are integrating ideas and with the proportion of students with "exceptional" writing skill. Achievement in all other respects meets our standards.
If you are NOT satisfied with the results, what do you plan to do to improve student learning? When will you implement changes?	We have identified assignments in three other required courses that we will modify for Spring 20__ so that they include documenting sources of information.	We have identified assignments in three other required courses that we will modify for Spring 20__ so that they require integrating ideas. By Fall 20__ we will complete a proposal for an honors track in our program that emphasizes outstanding writing.
Do you plan to modify your assessment of student achievement of this objective? If so, how?	No	The relatively low proportion of students with "exceptional" writing may be related to the complexity of the research project. In the coming academic year, we will also evaluate writing skills in a shorter, simpler assignment in ABC465, another required senior-level course.

*If it is not possible or practical to assess all students in your program before they graduate, explain why and provide the number/proportion of students assessed.

Should you keep student work on file? A few specialized accreditors do require colleges or programs to keep actual student work (exams, papers, portfolios, projects, and so on) on file, but otherwise keep only what will be useful to you. It often makes sense to keep a few examples on file—a mix of top-rated, mediocre-but-acceptable, and unacceptable work—to track any shifts in your standards over time. The mediocre-but-acceptable and unacceptable examples can be nice examples of your college's rigor, should anyone ask.

Periodically Regroup and Reflect

Implementing a culture of quality is a perpetual work in progress. Your college changes; its students change; society and its needs change. I sometimes advise colleges whose communities have been working hard for a few years on some of the cultures of quality, especially the culture of evidence, to take a breather for a semester, regroup, and reflect on what has been accomplished.

- What is going well?
- Where have you seen the most progress?
- What has been a struggle?
- What has been helpful but has taken too much time, effort, or money?
- Where has progress been slower than you anticipated?

Rubrics evaluating the status of your college's cultures of quality can be helpful here (Fulcher, Swain, & Orem, 2012; Penn, 2012). Exhibit 18.2 is an example of one for evaluating the culture of evidence. Consider asking a sample of faculty, administrators, and board members to complete such a rubric, based on their perceptions of what is happening throughout your college. Then repeat the review annually to gauge and document your progress in advancing the cultures of quality.

EXHIBIT 18.2. Rubric to Appraise a College's Culture of Evidence and Betterment

No plans = No documented evidence that we have plans to do this.

No evidence = Our college appears to be aware that we should do this, but there is no documented evidence that this is happening.

Nascent = We have documented evidence that this is happening in just a few areas.

Some = We have documented evidence—not just assurances—that this is happening in some but not most areas.

Most = We have documented evidence—not just assurances—that this is happening in most but not all areas.

Pervasive = We have documented evidence—not just assurances—that this is happening everywhere: all units, programs, services, and initiatives, no matter where located or how delivered.

	No plans	No evidence	Nascent	Some	Most	Pervasive
Expected college-wide (strategic), unit, program, and curricular goals are clearly articulated and relevant to students and other stakeholders.						
Targets for determining whether goals are achieved are clear, appropriate, and justifiable.						
Evidence of goal achievement is of sufficient quality that it can be used with confidence to make meaningful, appropriate decisions.						
Evidence is clearly linked to goals.						
Evidence is shared in useful, understandable, accessible forms with relevant stakeholders.						
Evidence is used to inform meaningful decisions, including resource deployment decisions, teaching and learning improvement, and goals and plans.						
Evidence is used to assure relevant public stakeholders of the effectiveness of the college, programs, services, and curricula in meeting stakeholder needs.						
Processes to collect and use evidence have sufficient engagement, momentum, and simplicity to assure that the cultures of evidence and betterment will remain sustained and pervasive.						

This rubric uses ideas in the "Rubric for Evaluating Institutional Student Learning Assessment Processes" published by the Middle States Commission on Higher Education (2008).

For More Information

The National Institute for Learning Outcomes Assessment (NILOA) has published a number of reports on advancing cultures of evidence and betterment. Three important ones are *Using Assessment Results: Promising Practices of Institutions That Do It Well* (Baker, Jankowski, Provezis, & Kinzie, 2012), *Valuing Assessment: Cost-Benefit Considerations* (Swing & Coogan, 2010), and *From Gathering to Using Assessment Results: Lessons from the Wabash National Study* (Blaich & Wise, 2011).

Assessment Update (www.assessmentupdate.com) has frequent articles sharing practical experience and advice on advancing a culture of evidence. Chapter 2 of *Assessment Clear and Simple: A Practical Guide for Institutions, Departments, and General Education* (Walvoord, 2010) and Chapters 5 through 7 of *Assessing Student Learning: A Common Sense Guide* (Suskie, 2009) offer a lot of suggestions. Examples of dashboards are in *Institutional Dashboards: Navigational Tool for Colleges and Universities* (Terkla, Sharkness, Cohen, Roscoe, & Wiseman, 2012). Chapter 6 of *Assessing Student Learning* includes a list of questions to ask as you investigate assessment information management systems.

CONCLUSION:
Integrating and Advancing the Five Dimensions of Quality

CHAPTER 19

DEMONSTRATING QUALITY TO ACCREDITORS

E very accreditor has its own requirements, and this book
and this chapter do not serve as substitutes for them. As
explained in the Preface, the purposes of this book are to help
you understand *why* accreditors require what they do and to give
you practical advice on meeting those requirements. But if any
of my advice contradicts what your accreditor says, go with your
accreditor!

Jargon Alert!

Accreditation Standards, Criteria, and Requirements

Accreditors use different language to describe their expectations.
What the Middle States Commission on Higher Education (MSCHE)
(www.msche.org) calls *standards*, for example, the Higher Learning
Commission (HLC) of the North Central Association (www.ncahlc
.org/) calls *criteria*. I use the generic term *requirements*, but use
whatever term your accreditor uses.

Use Accreditation Processes as a Tool and Lever

Believe it or not, accreditation is good for you (Mark Curchack, personal communication, July 11, 2013). Accreditation actions force colleges to address problems that have been swept under the rug too long, like an outdated curriculum or a dysfunctional governance system. Accreditation is both a carrot and stick. The carrot is that no one likes being rebuked or "dinged" by an accreditor or the burden of extra reporting that follows; as Rose Mary Healy has explained, "It's just easier to be good" (personal communication, September 5, 2013). The stick is getting that ding and being asked for that additional report; while no one likes it, virtually every college I have worked with has eventually admitted that it was the kick in the pants the college community needed to improve quality and effectiveness.

Even if your college has no major issues, accreditation processes are a great opportunity to advance a quality agenda and bring about needed change. With the right mindset—that you are implementing the cultures of quality for yourselves, not for your accreditor—no matter how good your college is now, it will be even better after an accreditation review.

Understand What Your Accreditor Is Looking For . . . and Why

Whether I am asked what accreditors are looking for or what good practices in higher education are, I give the same answers, because *accreditation requirements are intended to be principles of good practice*.

The key to meeting accreditation requirements, especially those of regional accreditors, is thus not to comply blindly with specific requests or requirements but to understand *why* accreditors are asking for those things. Every accreditation requirement is there for a reason. The better you understand the reason—the principles of good practice underlying each requirement—the better your chances of doing what your accreditor wants you to do and of undergoing a successful review.

Read the directions and ask questions. The most important resources for preparing an accreditation report are the information and guidelines provided by your accreditor. Yes, its requirements can be a long, slow read, but read them carefully nonetheless, at least those that are applicable to the report you are preparing. Read equally carefully your accreditor's guidelines for the report you are preparing, along with any other materials from the accreditor that provide context. Many accreditors offer training sessions or other venues for addressing specific questions not answered through their materials.

Understand your accreditor's underlying concerns with your college. All reports to accreditors have the same fundamental purpose: to verify that your college meets all or some of the accreditor's requirements. No matter what the accreditor requests, even something straightforward such as an audited financial statement, the accreditor's fundamental concern is with compliance with one or more of its requirements. Make sure you understand which requirements are the subject of your current review. If you are asked for a report on your enrollment management plan, for example, is the accreditor concerned with student retention or with tuition revenues and your college's financial health? Read the accreditor's request for the report carefully. Review prior reports and correspondence between your college and your accreditor to gain a sense of the history of the issue at hand.

Start Early, with an Honest Appraisal
of Where You Are

The success of your accreditation review will depend largely on your capacity to be honest with yourself, recognize quality and compliance shortcomings, and grasp what you need to do to address them before the review is conducted. Colleges that fail to acknowledge that they are out of compliance with a requirement until their accreditor points this out often waste time in anger and denial before getting down to the business of making needed changes by stipulated deadlines.

The following continuum of quality may help you determine where your college is regarding accreditation compliance.

Level 1: A pervasive, enduring culture of quality, actively embracing all five dimensions. Your college not only has thorough documentation of compliance on hand but uses that documentation on a regular basis to inform decisions. This is the best possible scenario; preparation for accreditation review consists simply of conducting an overall analysis of existing documentation. Faculty who assess student learning regularly, for example, have on hand a good body of evidence plus documentation of resulting actions that they need merely summarize and analyze for the accreditation review.

Level 2: A culture of quality, but one that is informal, without systematic documentation. As some people have told me, "We're doing this; we just need to organize and document it better." Developing and implementing documentation processes and systems can take some time. To make matters worse, without systematic documentation, what was done for the last review may have been lost or forgotten, so extra time is spent reinventing the quality wheel.

A word of caution: undocumented perceptions can be wrong. For example, during my first year of full-time freelance consulting on assessment and accreditation, I could have sworn that the advice I gave colleges most frequently was to clarify their goals. Then I did a qualitative analysis of my consulting reports. To my surprise, my most frequent advice was to invest in faculty professional development (Suskie, 2013). I have seen enough other examples of undocumented perceptions not matching the reality of systematic evidence to conclude that *assessment without documentation is not assessment*, and many colleges that think they are at Level 2 are really at Level 3. By the time they come to realize this, they are often so close to the accreditation review that they do not have enough time to make necessary changes.

Level 3: Not yet a pervasive culture of quality, so not yet doing everything your accreditor requires. Preparing for an accreditation review when you are at this level is a major undertaking. If an academic program has not yet begun work on assessing student learning, for example, the faculty must articulate key program learning outcomes, then identify where in the curriculum they are addressed, then identify or develop assessment opportunities, then collect evidence, then review it, then use it to identify and implement improvements. This cannot be done in one semester.

I often suggest that colleges make a chart listing every line of text in their accreditor's requirements: every sentence, phrase, or clause. Next to each line, list the college's source(s) of documented evidence of compliance with that aspect of the accreditor's requirements, and annotate how well the evidence demonstrates compliance. This can help everyone grasp where your college is in terms of compliance.

You may conclude that your college is at varying levels of compliance; some areas are at Level 1, while others are at Level 2 or perhaps even Level 3. I discuss how thorough your college's compliance should be later in this chapter.

Understand Your Accreditor's Emphasis on the Five Cultures of Quality

Of all the stakeholders who want to see evidence of your college's quality and effectiveness, none expects more than your accreditors. Many stakeholders are interested in only some aspects of your college's quality, but accreditors' interests encompass all five cultures of quality. Your accreditor may emphasize some of the cultures of quality more than others, however. Stay up-to-date with your accreditor's emphases by reading its correspondence and attending its meetings and workshops.

Focus on the culture of evidence. When the regional accreditors revised their requirements around the turn of the century to focus on evidence of achievement of goals (outcomes assessment), they knew they could not snap their fingers and immediately have all colleges in compliance with these heightened expectations. So they initially expected assessment plans and then gradually scaled up expectations of compliance, moving to expecting implementation of those plans, to expecting assessment results: evidence of achievement of key goals. As discussed in Chapter 20, specialized accreditors also require attention to the culture of evidence, although their emphasis on it varies.

Focus on the culture of betterment. As colleges are increasingly amassing evidence, regional accreditors and some other accreditors are now looking for evidence of the culture of betterment: the pervasive use of systematic evidence to ensure and advance quality, including informing goals, plans, and resource deployment.

Watch for increasing emphasis on the culture of relevance, including stewardship, accountability and transparency, integrity, and meeting stakeholder needs and the public good, especially by regional and national accreditors.

Demonstrate a pervasive, consistent, enduring culture of quality. Accreditors have a responsibility to ensure, for example, that all your students, no matter where or how they are learning, achieve your learning outcomes at appropriate levels of rigor. Accreditors also have a responsibility to ensure that your college can sustain compliance into the future. An accreditor would be concerned, for example, that a one-time gift is balancing your annual operating budget or that your assessment program is currently funded by a grant with no concrete, viable plans to sustain it after the gift or grant ends.

Organize Your Report and Supporting Documentation

Accreditors can be quite prescriptive in how they want your report and supporting documentation organized, so my fundamental advice here is to attend your accreditor's meetings, webinars, and workshops and read and follow its guidelines. That said, consider the following approaches to organizing your report if they fit with your accreditor's directives.

Organize information on your activities and evidence around your purpose and key goals. Regional accreditors in particular begin their reviews with your college's mission and strategic goals literally in hand, continually comparing your evidence against the promises made in those statements. Evidence that is not clearly connected to key goals may not have much meaning to them. I see so many accreditation reports organized with one section on goals, another on programs and activities, another on assessments (with perhaps one subsection on rubric results and another on the results of a published test or survey), and yet another on improvements. Accreditation reviewers look at all this and think, "Well, we're glad that you're doing all those things and that you've collected all that evidence and made all those improvements, but what we really want to know is how they connect. What are those rubric and test results telling you about your achievement of your goals? How did those improvements flow from that evidence?"

These questions call for organizing and presenting evidence and improvements by goal, rather than separately. A college that has been asked by its accreditor to report on its assessment of its general education curriculum, for example, might organize its report as shown below if it has the flexibility to do so.

Organization of an Accreditation Report on General Education Assessment

- Introduction, with an overview of the college, a description of its general education curriculum, and the context for the accreditor's request
- A brief history of how and why the college arrived at the curriculum's structure and learning outcomes, showing that they reflect research and good practices

- Separate sections or subsections for each learning outcome of the general education curriculum, each providing:
  - The learning outcome
  - A description of how student achievement of this learning outcome is assessed, with documentation, such as copies of rubrics, in an appendix
  - A summary of the assessment results for this learning outcome, such as scores for each rubric criterion, presented in a simple table
  - Analysis of the assessment results, comparing them to the college's definitions of successful results, with defensible justifications of those definitions
  - Overall conclusions regarding student achievement of this outcome (tying together, perhaps, rubric scores, results of relevant survey questions, and relevant test sub-scores)
- Overall conclusions from the assessments and next steps
  - Identification of outcomes for which student learning is satisfactory
  - For less than satisfactory outcomes, steps that have been or are being taken to improve student learning
  - Plans for improvements in general education assessment processes, as appropriate

View the report as a cousin of reports to your college leaders. Accreditors should see what your college's board and leadership team should be asking to see: evidence, not assurances, of the five cultures of quality, presented concisely, with more thorough documentation available if needed. Indeed, if your college truly embraces the five cultures of quality, your accreditation report may consist largely of the reports of evidence that college decision-makers see and records of the decisions they have made based on those reports, such as minutes or e-mail streams. If so, the only thing that needs to be added is an overall analysis.

View the report as a cousin of a scholarly research paper. The structure suggested in the list above is similar to the structure of scholarly research reports familiar to many faculty. Table 19.1 compares the two.

TABLE 19.1. Comparison of Research Reports and Accreditation Reports

Elements Common to Both	In a Research Report	In an Accreditation Report
Begin with an introduction or overview.	Overview of the study	Overview of your college and the accreditation requirements under review
Address clearly articulated goals.	Purpose of the study	College and program/unit-level goals that are germane to the accreditation requirements under review
Articulate targets for those goals.	Hypothesis	Justifiable targets for key measures
Describe how evidence was collected, to provide assurance of the quality of the evidence and to replicate the work if warranted.	Methodology	Summary of how evidence was collected
Provide summaries of evidence related to goals and targets, often in simple tables.	Results	Documentation in supporting appendices, sufficient to demonstrate achievement of goals and to track the impact of subsequent improvements
Analyze evidence.	Analysis	Analysis
Present conclusions.	Conclusions	Conclusions
Identify further action based on the evidence.	Recommendations for further study	Implemented improvements based on the presented evidence

Should you use other reports as models? Chapter 16 talks about the importance of telling the story of your college's effectiveness and quality in its own voice, and this is important to regional accreditors, who evaluate your college's quality and effectiveness within the context of its purpose and goals. Combine this with the increasing rigor with which accreditors are enforcing their requirements, and it is not hard to see that the report written last year by a college down the road (or that you wrote five years ago) may not be a good model for what you need to write today.

I often compare accreditation reports to the writing assignments that faculty give to students. Some writing assignments, such as lab reports, expect all students to say pretty much the same thing in the same way. Likewise, some accreditors expect all their colleges to follow a consistent report format and structure. In these cases, using other recent reports as models may be helpful. But some writing assignments expect students to speak in their own voices, identifying their own topics and theses and organizing the assignment in whatever way best conveys their points. If your accreditor expects this approach, models of other reports will not be as helpful. In fact, following the model of someone else's report may adversely impact the integrity of your story.

Provide Good Quality Documented Evidence for Everything You Say

Accreditors are obliged by their quality assurance responsibilities to require documented evidence and to verify that evidence. Platitudes and unsubstantiated assertions such as "We are in compliance with this standard" have no place in an accreditation report; *answers without documentation are not answers* (George Kuh, personal communication, August 26, 2013). Assertions like those in Table 19.2 need to be supported with solid evidence or removed.

Beware of phrases such as, "we believe," "we hope," "we anticipate," or "we are confident that." It is better to say, "we project, based on this evidence . . ." or "our plans, based on the evidence in Appendix A, are to. . . ."

No matter what kind of evidence you provide, it should meet the characteristics of good evidence that were discussed in

TABLE 19.2. Examples of Assertions with Suitable Evidence in Accreditation Reports

Examples of Assertions	Examples of Suitable Evidence
The strategic plan guides decision making.	Meeting minutes and/or annual reports documenting decisions and how the plan supported them
Funding is expected to continue.	Letters of commitment from funding sources
The board is composed of well-respected, qualified experts in their respective fields.	List of board members and the key qualifications of each. ("Well-respected" would be difficult to document and should probably be deleted.)
Faculty and staff are appropriate in size, preparation, and experience to fulfill their responsibilities and to support the college in fulfilling its mission.	Tables summarizing the credentials of faculty and staff and comparing those credentials against their responsibilities and the college's mission
The Board self-evaluates the overall functioning of the Board of Trustees.	Board reports on its self-evaluation process, results, and actions based on those results

Chapter 14. Evidence should be useful, current, and consistent, flow from goals, and have justifiable targets for success. Your report should document not just the existence of evidence but an ongoing, pervasive culture of evidence.

Provide evidence of outcomes, not just efforts. Many accreditors, including regional accreditors, focus more on outcomes than on the structures or processes used to arrive at those outcomes. Instead of requiring a specific governance structure, for example, your accreditor may want evidence that your governance structure is fulfilling its stated responsibilities and is a support, not a hindrance, to achieving your college's purpose and goals. Similarly, accreditors do not want mere descriptions of assessment processes (or, worse yet, only plans to develop and implement them). Their interest is in whether those processes are generating systematic evidence that is used to advance the quality and effectiveness of teaching, learning, and your college's programs and services.

How much evidence is enough? One of the most frequent questions I am asked is, "What does the accreditor want to see?" Actually, though, people know the answer to this: accreditors want to see evidence that your college is meeting accreditation requirements. Their real question is, "How much evidence is enough to satisfy the accreditor?"

Two very different questions are being asked here. One is how thorough your college's *documentation* should be. Does your accreditor need to see all faculty résumés or a summary of faculty credentials? Does your accreditor want to see every course syllabus and assessment reports from every academic program, or will samples suffice? The answer is, of course, to ask your accreditor. A word of caution, however: if you provide a sample, you need to convince your accreditor that your sample is truly representative of what is happening across your college. If you share, say, student learning evidence for just three academic programs, your accreditor may naturally wonder whether those three are truly a representative sample of what is happening across your college, or your college's best efforts, or the only three programs where assessment is happening. Your accreditor may also be skeptical if your largest programs are omitted or if your examples of student learning evidence are largely from professional programs with specialized accreditation, with little or nothing from your liberal arts programs or your general education curriculum.

The other question asked here is how thorough your college's *compliance* with your accreditor's requirements should be. Will your accreditor be satisfied, for example, if only half of your college's academic programs have systematic evidence of student achievement of their key learning outcomes? If only three of your college's eight general education learning outcomes are being assessed? If dashboard indicators have been identified for four of your strategic goals but not the other two? If most programs and units have collected at least some evidence of their effectiveness, but most have not yet acted on that evidence? If each program has examined ten student portfolios? The answer to these questions is, again, to ask your accreditor.

But all these questions are the wrong questions. They imply that you are collecting evidence merely to satisfy an accreditor, not to advance a pervasive, enduring culture of quality, including cultures of evidence and betterment. If you are only collecting evidence of student learning in some programs, in some general education requirements, or at some locations, for example, your college is essentially saying that you care about some students more than others (Lynn Priddy, personal communication, July 9, 2013).

So my answer to these questions is, "How much is enough for *you* to understand and improve quality throughout your college and ensure an enduring, pervasive culture of quality?" While there are formulas and algorithms for calculating appropriate sample sizes of student work, for example (Suskie, 2009), I find that many faculty and administrators have a good sense of how many student papers or survey responses they need to see in order to draw meaningful conclusions and make appropriate decisions.

If your evidence is time-consuming to collect and analyze— things like student papers, portfolios, or interviews—try a qualitative approach to deciding how much evidence is enough (Suskie, 2009). Use a sample of ten papers or portfolios to draw tentative conclusions about your students' performance. Then take another sample of ten, and see whether it modifies your initial conclusions. If it confirms your initial conclusions, you are done. But if you gain new insight from the second sample, look at a third sample of ten. Keep doing this until you look at a sample of ten that does not change your conclusions.

Put Shortcomings in Context . . . with Integrity

Nowhere is a culture of candor and honesty more important than with accreditors. In fact, if you misrepresent your college to your Title IV gatekeeper (Chapter 2), you expose your college to possible charges of Title IV fraud and abuse, with fines that can run into millions of dollars.

An accreditation report is, of course, an opportunity to celebrate achievements. If your college is like the vast majority of colleges, you have a great deal to be proud of, and your accreditation reports should reflect that. But nothing raises a red flag faster with accreditors than a completely positive report, painting a picture of a college in which everything is great and there are no areas for improvement other than staying the course. No such college exists, so painting this distorted picture raises questions about your college's integrity. When your college glosses over or omits information on a key issue from an accreditation report, accreditors cannot help but wonder, "What else are they hiding?" That suspicion is hard to eradicate.

As I noted at the beginning of this chapter, it is just easier to be good. Frame your report to provide full and balanced information, share your college's story ethically and responsibly, and present an appropriate balance between strengths and accomplishments and areas that need attention.

What if your college is not yet doing everything your accreditor requires? Simply stating intentions to comply with requirements at some point in the future is insufficient. Instead, as suggested in Chapter 16, place shortcomings in context, explaining why progress has been slow, then focus on what you are doing to rectify those shortcomings, with detailed information on how and when solutions will be implemented. If, for example, some of your academic programs are not yet assessing student achievement of their key learning outcomes, explain why and provide concrete, detailed action plans and prompt timelines describing exactly how and when the programs will articulate learning outcomes, identify assessment strategies, implement the assessments, collect the results, discuss them, and identify and implement any modifications. Such thorough action plans assure the accreditor that you understand what needs to be done and that things will be taken care of as soon as possible.

Respect the Reviewers' Time

If you have flexibility in preparing your accreditation report, possibly your biggest challenge will be balancing the needs for thoroughness and conciseness. On one hand, you must include in the report everything that the accreditor expects, clearly documenting compliance with every requirement under review, with pervasive rather than spotty documentation. On the other hand, accreditation reviewers are typically volunteers with day jobs. While they want to give your report the careful attention that it deserves, there is a limit to how much time they can spend. Your task is to craft a report that is simultaneously thorough and concise, comprehensive yet succinct.

Use a brief introduction to orient the reviewers. The reviewers may never have heard of your college or may have only a passing familiarity with it. Give the reviewers an overview of characteristics of your college that they need to know in order to appreciate the accreditation story you are sharing. Share things like your college's size, scope of program offerings, and locale. Include here a brief summary of any practices that might be considered outside the higher education mainstream, such as a non-traditional governance structure or faculty reward system, and any recent developments, such as leadership turnover, new programs or campuses, and financial challenges. Keep this section brief; use links or cross-references to later sections of the report to provide more thorough information.

Cull irrelevant information. I have seen reviewers visibly annoyed at having to wade through useless information. You do not want annoyed reviewers! Include only those documents or evidence that are essential to demonstrating your college's compliance with the requirements at hand. Avoid "data dumps" of everything that seems remotely applicable, limit appendices to germane evidence, and cull out all irrelevant documentation. As discussed earlier in this chapter, report only those improvements that clearly flow from evidence that, in turn, flows from key goals. In some cases, excerpts, summaries, or representative samples—but not isolated examples—of evidence may suffice. Documentation of board actions, for example, might consist of the text and dates of relevant actions, rather than the full minutes of the meetings at which those actions were taken.

Make the case for compliance up front. Do not simply say "Appendices 1 through 25 demonstrate our compliance with the assessment requirement," making the reviewers pore through your supporting materials to figure out on their own whether you have sufficient evidence to demonstrate compliance. Present your own analysis of the appendices; the reviewers should need to refer to the appendices only to verify your analysis.

Connect the dots. The cultures of quality are not discrete, and neither are accreditation requirements nor the many things your college is doing. Accreditation reports, therefore, rarely fall into simple linear narratives and can thus be a challenge to organize. A successful first-year-experience program, for example, may provide evidence of compliance with accreditation requirements on an integrated curriculum, student support services, assessment of student learning outcomes, and retention. Make sure the reviewers can easily see appropriate interconnections and interrelationships among the cultures of quality. Build in plenty of cross-references among sections of the report to remind the reviewer that Issue X was discussed more thoroughly back on page 4 and that Initiative Y will be discussed more thoroughly on page 11.

Keep your report an easy read, following the suggestions in Chapter 16. Here are some additional suggestions:

- Find a writer or editor whose strengths are organization and business or technical writing. You want a report that is "tight and right," not a flowery exposition.

- Help reviewers easily find the supporting documents they are seeking either by using hyperlinks or by giving supporting documents intuitive, self-explanatory names and a clear numbering system.

- Watch out for jargon and acronyms that the reviewers might not understand.

- Ask willing board members and someone at another college to read your draft report and advise you on how easily they digest it.

For More Information

Again, your accreditor is your key resource for deciding how to demonstrate quality, effectiveness, and compliance. My earlier advice bears repeating: read your accreditor's publications and website and attend its events. Salina Diiorio's "Preparing for Accreditation: Sowing the Seeds of Long-Term Change" (2006) offers many practical suggestions. (Today the document room she describes preparing for the team visit is typically replaced by online resources available to the team before and during its visit.)

CHAPTER 20

PROGRAM REVIEWS
Drilling Down into Programs and Services

Program reviews are comprehensive reviews of individual programs. They often include the same three elements as accreditation processes: a self-study conducted by the program's faculty and staff, a visit by one or more external reviewers, and recommendations for improvement based on the conclusions of the self-study and the reviewer.

Program reviews are critical to ensuring, advancing, and demonstrating quality because college-wide quality efforts can go only so far. Regional accreditation teams, for example, cannot possibly have the expertise to look into the quality and effectiveness of every program and service a college offers. Several regional accreditors therefore now require regular systems of program review.

While many colleges focus on program reviews of academic programs, program reviews can be valuable for everything a college does, including student development programs, student support programs, and administrative operations.

What Is a Quality Program?

I use two frameworks for defining a quality program, service, or operation and thereby organizing a program review—pick whichever

one you like better. The one that I used for many years has three
fundamental criteria for reviewing academic programs (Shirley &
Volkwein, 1978):

1. *Quality:* the quality of
   - *Inputs:* faculty credentials, student qualifications, facilities,
     library holdings, and so on
   - *Processes:* curriculum design, teaching methods, academic
     advisement, and so on
   - *Outcomes:* student learning outcomes, research and
     community impact, and so on

   Of these, the most important are outcomes, specifically student
   learning outcomes.

2. *Need and demand:* the number of potential students interested
   in the program and demand for graduates by employers, graduate programs, and the like

3. *Cost and cost-effectiveness:* how much the program costs and
   how efficiently and effectively it uses its resources

The second framework reorganizes these criteria into the five
cultures of quality.

A *culture of relevance.* A quality program provides honest,
balanced information and treats students and other stakeholders
fairly and consistently. Its resources—such as facilities, technology infrastructure, library collection, administrative oversight,
and faculty and staff with appropriate experience and expertise—
are sufficient to ensure the program's health and well-being, and
it deploys those resources effectively, prudently, and efficiently. It
meets stakeholder needs, especially those of its students, and there
is enough demand and need for the program by students, employers, and others, now and continuing into the future, to ensure its
viability. It is also effective in serving the public good, achieving
its purpose and goals, and demonstrating that it is meeting its
responsibilities.

A *culture of community*. A quality program's culture is one of respect, communication, collaboration, growth and development, shared collegial governance, and documentation.

A *culture of focus and aspiration*. A quality program has a clear sense of purpose that supports the college's mission. It has clear goals, along with programs and services designed to meet the needs of its students and other key stakeholders and to help the college achieve its overall purpose and goals.

A *culture of evidence*. A quality program regularly collects useful, good-quality evidence of its effectiveness, especially evidence of what its students have learned and how successful they are in later pursuits. It has clear, justifiable definitions of what successful students look like.

A *culture of betterment*. A quality program uses systematic evidence to advance its quality and effectiveness. Indeed, some accreditors now require that evidence from program reviews be incorporated in college planning and resource allocation decisions.

Specialized Accreditation as a Form of Program Review

Specialized accreditation can be the epitome of program review. Because specialized accreditation reviews are overseen by external organizations using consistent criteria and trained reviewers, specialized accreditation has a credibility that internally driven program reviews cannot achieve.

Specialized accreditors vary greatly in their purposes and requirements. Some specialized accreditations, especially those in medical disciplines, are mandatory if graduates are to be eligible for licensure or employment, while others are completely optional. Some specialized accreditors are Title IV gatekeepers (Chapter 2) recognized by the U.S. Department of Education (ED), while dozens more are recognized by the Council on Higher Education Accreditation (CHEA). Some are recognized by both bodies, and some are not recognized by either.

Specialized accreditors also vary considerably in their attention to the five cultures of quality. While all recognized accreditors now expect a culture of evidence, for example, some specialized accreditors place more emphasis on this than others do. Some still place considerable weight on inputs into the learning process, such as faculty credentials and facilities, even though the connection of those inputs to quality and effectiveness is not well established, as discussed in Chapter 4. As a result, the value of specialized accreditation in ensuring quality is inconsistent.

Unless specialized accreditation is required for licensure, for Title IV funds, or by your regional accreditor, consider the costs and benefits. Maintaining some specialized accreditations can cost tens of thousands of dollars or more every year. What are the benefits, and how do they weigh against those costs? What systematic evidence do you have that your key stakeholders demand specialized accreditation? How much does specialized accreditation affect enrollment and revenue? Are the benefits worth the investment in specialized accreditation, or could those resources be deployed in other ways that might more effectively advance the program's quality and effectiveness? Consider developing business plans (discussed later in this chapter) for specialized accreditation that examines these questions.

Integrate multiple accreditations. If your college has more than one accreditation (for example, regional accreditation and several specialized accreditations), look for ways to integrate your accreditation work. While requirements understandably vary across accreditors (specialized accreditors, for example, require evidence of competencies specific to their professions), most share requirements related to the five dimensions of quality.

Many colleges prepare charts or "crosswalks" that align regional and specialized accreditation requirements; check with peer colleges that have recently undergone review to see whether they have one to share, or prepare your own. In many cases, the material prepared for a specialized accreditation review can be used for a regional accreditation review; it may simply need some updating and perhaps expansion.

View Program Reviews as Cousins of Grant Proposals and Business Plans

Effective program reviews have much in common with grant proposals and the business plans that entrepreneurs take to potential investors when seeking start-up funding. All three make an evidence-informed case for investment through systematic evidence and by showing that the nuts and bolts for getting things done have been thought through. Proposals for new initiatives at your college, such as adding a new program, introducing a new curricular requirement, offering a program online, or seeking specialized accreditation, should have a similar design and intent as well. Table 20.1 lists questions that might be addressed in program reviews and proposals for new initiatives.

TABLE 20.1. Questions to Consider in Proposals for New Initiatives and in Academic Program Reviews

Proposals for New Initiatives	Program Reviews for Existing Academic Programs
Relevance	
Why is this initiative a good idea? What problem or need will it address? Who will benefit from this initiative? Who are its stakeholders? Whom will it serve?	Whom does this program serve? What kinds of students?
What is the demand for this initiative? Is demand anticipated to grow, diminish, or remain stable? Is there enough demand for the initiative to be worthwhile? How will the initiative be promoted to its intended stakeholders?	What is the student and employer demand for this program? Is demand anticipated to grow, diminish, or remain stable? Is there enough demand for this program to remain viable?
What are the start-up and ongoing costs for this initiative, including faculty and staff, time, technology infrastructure, facilities, and professional development?	What are the ongoing costs for the program, including faculty and staff, time, technology infrastructure, facilities, and professional development?
How will this initiative demonstrate that it is deploying resources effectively, prudently, and efficiently?	What is the evidence that this program is deploying resources (faculty, facilities, library resources, etc.) effectively, prudently, and efficiently?

(Continued)

TABLE 20.1. Continued

Proposals for New Initiatives	Program Reviews for Existing Academic Programs
What are the projected revenues, if any?	What are current and projected revenues, if any?
What is the return on investment? If not an income stream, what are the tangible benefits of the college's investment in this initiative? How will those benefits be measured and tracked?	What is the return on investment? If not an income stream, what are the tangible benefits of the college's investment in this program?
How will this initiative demonstrate that it is meeting its responsibilities?	How does this program demonstrate that it is meeting its responsibilities?

Community

How will the initiative be administered or overseen?	How effectively is the program administered or overseen?

Focus and Aspiration

What is the purpose of this initiative? What exactly will it do?	What is the purpose of this program?
How does this initiative help the college achieve its purpose and goals?	How does this program help the college achieve its purpose and goals? How might the college be different if this program did not exist?
Are there any competitors for this initiative? If so, how is this initiative distinctive? Why should people participate in this initiative and not other existing ones?	Are there any competitors for this program? If so, how is this program distinctive? How does it compare against peer and competing programs? Why should students enroll in this program and not others?

Evidence

What is the evidence that this initiative will be successful in achieving its purpose and goals and meeting stakeholder needs?	What is the evidence that students are achieving this program's intended learning outcomes? That they are successful in their later pursuits? That this program's activities are effective in achieving its other goals, such as for research or community service? That it is meeting student needs?

Proposals for New Initiatives	Program Reviews for Existing Academic Programs
How do you define and justify what you mean by success?	How do you ensure that your standards for student learning are of appropriate rigor?
Betterment	
How do you plan to ensure the ongoing quality of the program: its cultures of responsiveness, community and support, focus and aspirations, and evidence?	How do you plan to ensure the ongoing quality of the program: its cultures of responsiveness, community and support, focus and aspirations, and evidence?

Note: Some of the questions in this table are adapted from the "Create Your Business Plan" guide from the U.S. Small Business Administration (n.d.).

The questions in Table 20.1 are not easy to answer! They suggest a team approach to program review, with information and evidence developed not just by the faculty and administrators in the program, but by others as well, including your college's institutional research, budget, and marketing offices.

Ensure Program Review Integrity and Value

In good times, program reviews can become undisciplined wish lists, concluding that nothing is wrong that an infusion of resources would not cure. In difficult times, when program cutbacks and closures may be contemplated, they can become defenses of the status quo, full of assurances that everything is the best possible quality. And, in both good and bad times, some program reviews simply end up on a shelf. None of these outcomes helps a college or program advance its quality agenda.

Require a usable program review . . . and use it. Effective program reviews are used by college leaders as well as members of the program to inform decisions regarding the program's vision, plans, and support. In order to accomplish this:

- Conclude program reviews with proposed action steps and timelines to advance the program's quality and effectiveness that flow from and are supported by the systematic evidence provided in the program review.

- Require the program chair/director, dean, and vice president to review and jointly sign off on the completed program review, endorsing the proposed action steps and agreeing to provide needed support. These endorsements keep the proposed actions from turning into an unrealistic wish list that will never go anywhere.

- Make a college-level commitment that any final decisions to cut back or terminate a program will be preceded, if at all possible, by reasonable opportunities and resources to address shortcomings.

- Ask the program for annual updates on its progress in implementing the action steps, to ensure that follow-through is indeed happening.

Use an external reviewer to help ensure the program review's integrity, quality, and value. Some disciplinary associations offer review processes or clearinghouses of screened reviewers. The American Chemical Society (ACS), for example, offers an approval program for bachelor's degree programs, and the American Sociological Association (ASA) offers a Department Resource Group of consultants who can assist with program review.

But how is an external reviewer chosen when these kinds of resources are not available? Program faculty might argue that anyone outside their discipline, such as a dean, does not understand their discipline well enough to select an appropriate reviewer. But if the faculty select their own reviewer, they might be tempted to choose a colleague who will simply reinforce their own conclusions and not bring an independent perspective. Then there are truly one-of-a-kind programs, often interdisciplinary, that have no peers and, thus, few potential reviewers. Options for addressing all these challenges include the following:

- Ask program faculty to identify two or three potential reviewers and let the dean or provost make the final selection.

- Insist that prospective reviewers have credentials demonstrating their broad experience engaging with an array of comparable programs.
- Provide the reviewer with clear expectations for objectivity and evidence-supported conclusions. These expectations can be conveyed through a meeting with the dean, written guidelines, or a template for the reviewer's report.

For More Information

Two of my favorite readings on program review are old classics: "Establishing Academic Program Priorities" (Shirley & Volkwein, 1978) and "20 questions that deans should ask their mathematics departments (or, that a sharp department will ask itself)" (Steen, 1992). (Many of Steen's questions apply to any academic department, not just mathematics.)

More recent readings include *Outcomes-Based Academic and Co-Curricular Program Review: A Compilation of Institutional Good Practices* (Bresciani, 2006), *Prioritizing Academic Programs and Services: Reallocating Resources to Achieve Strategic Balance* (Dickeson, 2010), and "Program Review as a Model of Vision-Based Continuous Renewal" (Pollack, 2006). Chapter 9 of *Designing Effective Assessment: Principles and Profiles of Good Practice* (Banta, Jones, & Black, 2009) offers a variety of real-life examples of program reviews.

The *CAS Professional Standards for Higher Education* (Council for the Advancement of Standards in Higher Education, 2012) offer standards for more than forty non-academic areas, such as academic advisement, campus police, registrar, and veterans programs.

Break Down Silos

Silos are among the most pervasive obstacles I see to implementing the five cultures of quality. Address them by advancing a culture of community (see Chapters 7 and 8).

Tell Meaningful Stories of Your Successes

A quality college has distinctive traits, and each group of stakeholders has its own interests and needs regarding evidence and information. Make sure that the information you provide reflects your college's voice and is truly relevant and meaningful to your students and other stakeholders.

How Can Higher Education Leaders and Others Help?

Several years ago, I noted: "There are increasing calls both within and outside the academy to do all we can to ensure that students graduate with the knowledge, skills, and competencies they need for successful careers and rich, fulfilling lives. We in higher education are responding by embarking on nothing less than a radical transformation of what and how we teach our students" (Suskie, 2008, p. 6).

This is even truer today. The kind of transformation that U.S. higher education needs—one that embraces all five cultures of quality—can happen only with the active involvement of higher education leaders, including college presidents, higher education associations, and accreditors. Foundations, government policymakers, employers, and current and prospective students have critical roles as well. In Chapter 1, I listed a few of the ways that many of these groups have been stepping up to the plate. But higher education leaders and others can do more to continue to ensure and advance quality in U.S. higher education by focusing on the six big ideas that I have just put forth.

1. *Know higher education's stakeholders, and make higher education relevant and responsive to them.* Accreditors can increase their

focus on expecting colleges to meet stakeholder needs and serve the public good (Ralph Wolff, personal communication, July 17, 2013). Foundations and higher education associations can:

- Continue to sponsor research on the needs and interests of higher education's key stakeholders, including current and prospective students and their families, employers, and government policymakers.

- Continue to facilitate meaningful conversations on how colleges can respond most effectively to concerns about economic development, return on investment, and the changing college student.

- Educate public stakeholders about the benefits of higher education beyond starting salary, such as lifetime earnings, better opportunities for advancement, and the public good.

- With employers, address incongruities of pay and job requirements, ensuring that jobs that do not need college-level skills do not require a college degree and that jobs requiring a college degree pay fairly and appropriately.

- Encourage colleges to identify distinctive goals and relevant measures when it is appropriate to deviate from the norm, while recognizing that standard goals and measures can have value in some circumstances.

2. *Encourage and support great teaching and learning.* Government policymakers and think tanks can move their focus from assessment and completion to great teaching and learning. Accreditors can require the use of research-informed teaching practices. Disciplinary associations can endorse the scholarship of teaching as a valued form of research. And, when looking at colleges, prospective students can ask for concrete evidence of the use of research-based teaching practices, not just general student satisfaction ratings or unsubstantiated platitudes. Students who "swirl" through multiple colleges and programs can ask about

capstone experiences that help make their degrees more than a collection of courses.

3. *Put your money where your mouth is.* Foundations and donors can all do more to address the five cultures of quality, especially supporting research on and adoption of effective teaching strategies.

4. *Fight complacency.* Foundations and higher education associations can continue to develop alternatives to the model of quality based on reputation, perhaps building on the work of the New Leadership Alliance for Student Learning and Accountability (NLASLA) (2012a). Foundations can continue to provide incentives for evidence-informed innovation. Accreditors can make clear that "closing the loop"—using assessment results for betterment—incorporates external evidence along with the results of assessments of current endeavors.

5. *Break down silos.* Higher education associations and foundations can foster increased collaboration among higher education sectors and cohorts. College leaders can attend one of the Lilly Conferences on College and University Teaching (http://lillyconferences.com/), for example. Blue-ribbon panels, commissions, and other national conversations on higher education reform, now often limited to what David Longanecker has called "a bunch of important people listening to a bunch of somewhat more important people" (Lederman, 2011) can include teaching faculty, student development professionals, and college assessment directors.

Accreditors can incorporate into their requirements more explicit expectations for college communities to work collaboratively. Regional accreditors can continue to break down accreditation silos by creating a common base of requirements and expanding common language (ACE, 2012; Council of Regional Accrediting Commissions, 2014; National Advisory Committee on Institutional Quality and Integrity [NACIQI], 2012; Ralph Wolff, personal communication, July 17, 2013). I am not suggesting a merger of the regionals, although a bit of consolidation might have some merit. Having several regional accreditors allows them to operate as think tanks (American Council on Education [ACE], 2012), with each exploring new accreditation processes, others learning from those experiences, and all consequently improving their effectiveness.

6. *Tell meaningful stories of higher education's successes.* Higher education associations, foundations, and government policymakers can work together to:

- Continue to explore ways to share information on college quality that are succinct, relevant to students and other key college stakeholders, and respectful of colleges' distinctive traits.

- Help higher education stakeholders easily find information they want or need to see (Jankowski, Ikenberry, Kinzie, Kuh, Shenoy, & Baker, 2012), perhaps scaling back the current mind-numbing array of information sources.

- Design data systems that collect information on students' goals upon enrolling in college (for example, do they want to earn a degree, transfer before graduating, or simply bone up on some work-related skills?), update their goals as appropriate, and compare college outcomes against their goals.

- Develop dashboards of quality that go beyond graduation rates, placement rates, and starting salaries to address the full array of stakeholder needs and the five cultures of quality.

Accreditors can also do more to get out the stories of higher education's successes. They can continue to work toward providing transparent public information on accreditation concerns and actions. The report of the ACE National Task Force on Institutional Accreditation (American Council on Education [ACE], 2012) offers a number of thoughtful suggestions concerning this.

Accreditors can also work with higher education associations to put accreditation's success stories into the hands of government policymakers and other stakeholders. Accreditation usually receives media attention under one of two circumstances: when it threatens the removal of a college's accreditation (or removes it) or when it does not appear to act sufficiently promptly and forcefully on a college that public stakeholders perceive to be of poor quality. These actions are both relatively rare, because most colleges move swiftly and aggressively to address accreditation shortcomings and the vast majority of accreditation actions are sound and appropriate. The actions receiving media attention thus do not provide a balanced picture of what accreditors do. Largely untold are accreditation's success stories: the hundreds of colleges undergoing review each year whose accreditations are never in jeopardy, but who nonetheless improve their quality and effectiveness through the review process in substantive ways. As Judith Eaton has noted, "The evidence is there, but not adequately marshaled or deployed" (2013, "Reauthorization Options," para. 3).

Finally, accreditors can communicate the cost of accreditation and its alternatives. U.S. accreditation is not cheap, but any alternative would be far more expensive, because accreditation reviews are now largely conducted by volunteer peer reviewers: dedicated individuals who derive a great deal of satisfaction from working with colleagues at peer colleges to verify and improve quality. Accreditors are, in a sense, low-cost consultants who can offer excellent collegial advice.

If accreditation processes are forced to become more regulatory or complex, however, this model cannot continue. Only the rare volunteers will want to take time from their day jobs to, say, pore through course syllabi to verify that stated learning outcomes are addressed. Take away the rewarding aspects of accreditation review and add in tedious fact-checking, and volunteers will need to be replaced with paid staff at a far higher cost. Accreditors and the higher education community must communicate to government policymakers the costs of more exacting review.

Three More Ideas for Accreditation

I have spent nearly forty years in higher education, and I have never seen a group of people who took their responsibilities more seriously or deliberately than accreditors—and remember that accreditation commissioners and peer reviewers are largely volunteers. Their dedication convinces me that no other system can be more effective in ensuring—and assuring—the quality and effectiveness of U.S. higher education.

That said, some of the concerns about accreditation summarized in Chapter 2 are legitimate. This chapter has already suggested ways that accreditors can help the rest of the higher education community ensure and advance quality and effectiveness, but I have three more ideas that I think are worth exploring.

Take more steps to ensure that peer reviewers are dependably prepared to interpret and apply requirements consistently and appropriately. I do not have a ready answer on how to make this happen, because peer reviewers are largely volunteers with day jobs, and few would have the time for more comprehensive training than accreditors now offer. But a consistent combination of a common core of principles or expectations among the regional accreditors, as suggested earlier, online modules followed by brief learning assessments, and a well-trained assistant chair for each team might go a long way.

Build the reputation of national accreditation as an alternative to regional accreditation. The age and longstanding reputation of many regional accreditors' member colleges have pushed some colleges to seek regional accreditation when it is not a good fit for them. Not every student needs or wants a liberal arts education, for example. Accreditors and the higher education community can convey more clearly the value of nationally accredited colleges and schools for some students, depending on their interests and needs.

Create a competitive environment for regional accreditation. Schools and colleges of business can choose from among three potential accreditors: the Association to Advance Collegiate

Schools of Business (AACSB), the Accreditation Council for Business Schools and Programs (ACBSP), and the International Assembly for Collegiate Business Education (IACBE). Each has different requirements and attracts different kinds of business programs. AACSB, for example, attracts business schools that emphasize research and scholarship, while IACBE attracts business programs that focus on demonstrating student achievement of learning outcomes.

Regional accreditors might function the same way, with each accrediting any college in the country—or perhaps the world—that meets its requirements. Eventually, there would be a sorting out as colleges chose the accreditor that seemed to be the best fit for them. I would not want to see sector-specific accreditors, but one regional might eventually attract colleges that want a very structured accreditation process, one might attract colleges with non-traditional delivery modes, one might attract colleges that focus on traditional, residential, liberal arts experiences, and so on. Perhaps the time will come when this is an idea worth considering.

Can We Do This?

Absolutely! This book points you to many colleges that are already embracing key components of the five cultures of quality. You, your colleagues, and those throughout higher education can do this. There is no choice; the future of your college, your students, and the higher education enterprise—as well the public good—depend on it.

● REFERENCES

Accrediting Commission of Career Schools and Colleges (ACCSC). (n.d.). Overview of ACCSC. Retrieved from www.accsc.org/About-Us/Over view.aspx

Adelman, C. (2006, February). *The toolbox revisited: Paths to degree completion from high school through college.* Washington, DC: U.S. Department of Education.

Adelman, C., Ewell, P., Gaston, P., & Schneider, C. G. (2011, January). *The degree qualifications profile.* Indianapolis, IN: Lumina Foundation.

AFT Higher Education. (2010, March). *American academic, Volume 2: A national survey of part-time/adjunct faculty.* Washington, DC: Author.

Alexander, J. S., & Gardner, J. N. (2009, May/June). Beyond retention: A comprehensive approach to the first college year. *About Campus,* pp. 18–26.

Allen, C., Bacow, L. S., & Trombley, L. S. (2011). Making metrics matter: How to use indicators to govern effectively. *Trusteeship, 19*(1), 9–14.

Allen, I. E., & Seaman, J. (2013, January). *Changing course: Ten years of tracking online education in the United States.* Boston, MA: Babson Survey Research Group and Quahog Research Group.

Alter, J. (2009, October 23). The PDQ presidency. *Newsweek.* Retrieved from www.thedailybeast.com/newsweek/2009/10/24/the-pdq-presidency .html

Ambrose, S. A., Bridges, M. W., DiPietro, M., Lovett, M. C., & Norman, M. K. (2010). *How learning works: 7 research-based principles for smart teaching.* San Francisco, CA: Jossey-Bass.

American Association of University Professors (AAUP). (1940). *Statement of principles on academic freedom and tenure.* Washington, DC: Author.

American Council on Education (ACE). (2012). *Assuring academic quality in the 21st century: Self-regulation in a new era: A report of the ACE National Task Force on Institutional Accreditation.* Washington, DC: Author.

Anderson, L. W., Krathwohl, D. R., Airasian, P. W., & Cruikshank, K. A. (2000). *A taxonomy for learning, teaching, and assessing: A revision of Bloom's taxonomy of educational objectives.* London, England: Pearson.

Angelo, T. A., & Cross, K. P. (1993). *Classroom assessment techniques: A handbook for college teachers* (2nd ed.). San Francisco, CA: Jossey-Bass.

Associated Press. (2013, June 24). 4 ways in which higher education has changed in the wake of the Great Recession. *Washington Post.* Retrieved from www.washingtonpost.com/business/4-ways-in-which-higher-education-has-changed-in-the-wake-of-the-great-recession/2013/06/24/aee1830e-dce5–11e2-a484–7b7f79cd66a1_story.html

Association of American Colleges & Universities (AAC&U). (2002). *Greater expectations: A new vision for learning as a nation goes to college.* Retrieved from www.greaterexpectations.org

Association of American Colleges & Universities (AAC&U). (2011). *The LEAP vision for learning: Outcomes, practices, impact, and employers' views.* Washington, DC: Author.

Association of Governing Boards of Universities and Colleges and the Council for Higher Education Accreditation (AGB and CHEA). (2009). *AGB-CHEA joint advisory statement on accreditation & governing boards.* Washington, DC: Authors.

Bain, K. (2004). *What the best college teachers do.* Cambridge, MA: Harvard University Press.

Baker, G. R., Jankowski, N., Provezis, S., & Kinzie, J. (2012). *Using assessment results: Promising practices of institutions that do it well.* Urbana, IL: University of Illinois and Indiana University, National Institute for Learning Outcomes Assessment (NILOA).

Baker, V. L., Baldwin, R. G., & Makker, S. (2012, Summer). Where are they now? Revisiting Breneman's study of liberal arts colleges. *Liberal Education, 98*(3). Retrieved from www.aacu.org/liberaleducation/le-su12/baker_baldwin_makker.cfm

Banta, T. W. (2010, September/October). Editor's notes: A little extra funding goes a long way. *Assessment Update, 22*(5), 3–4.

Banta, T. W., & Borden, V.M.H. (1994). Performance indicators for accountability and improvement. In V.M.H. Borden & T. W. Banta

(Eds.), *Using performance indicators to guide strategic decision making.* (New Directions for Institutional Research, No. 82, pp. 96–97). San Francisco, CA: Jossey-Bass.

Banta, T. W., Jones, E. A., & Black, K. E. (2009). *Designing effective assessment: Principles and profiles of good practice.* San Francisco, CA: Jossey-Bass.

Banta, T. W., & Palomba, C. A. (2014). *Assessment essentials: Planning, implementing, and improving assessing in higher education* (2nd ed.). San Francisco, CA: Jossey-Bass.

Barr, R. B., & Tagg, J. (1995). From teaching to learning: A new paradigm for undergraduate education. *Change, 27*(6), 12–25.

Baum, S., & McPherson, M. (2011, January 18). Is education a public good or a private good? *Chronicle of Higher Education.* Retrieved from http://chronicle.com/blogs/innovations/is-education-a-public-good-or-a-private-good/28329

Berger, N., & Fisher, P. (2013, August 22). *A well-educated workforce is key to state prosperity.* Washington, DC: Economic Analysis and Research Network.

Blaich, C. F., & Wise, K. S. (2011, January). *From gathering to using assessment results: Lessons from the Wabash National Study* (NILOA Occasional Paper No. 8). Urbana, IL: University of Illinois and Indiana University, National Institute for Learning Outcomes Assessment.

Block, G. D. (2013, March 14). College is more than a "return on investment." *Washington Post.* Retrieved from www.washingtonpost.com/opinions/higher-education-is-more-than-a-return-on-investment/2013/03/14/2bae3660-8a94-11e2-8d72-dc76641cb8d4_story.html

Bloom, B. S. (Ed.) (1956). *Taxonomy of educational objectives, handbook 1: Cognitive domain.* New York, NY: Longman.

Bok, D. (2006, March/April). Seizing the initiative for quality education. *Trusteeship,* pp. 9–13.

Bowen, H. R. (1997). *Investment in learning: The individual and social value of American higher education.* Baltimore, MD: Johns Hopkins University Press.

Boyer, E. L. (1997). *Scholarship reconsidered: Priorities of the professoriate.* Stanford, CA: Carnegie Foundation for the Advancement of Teaching.

Bresciani, M. J. (2006). *Outcomes-based academic and co-curricular program review: A compilation of institutional good practices.* Sterling, VA: Stylus.

Brown, M., & Caldwell, S. (2013, April 17). Young student loan borrowers retreat from housing and auto markets. New York, NY: Federal Reserve Bank of New York. Retrieved from http://libertystreeteconomics

.newyorkfed.org/2013/04/young-student-loan-borrowers-retreat-from-housing-and-auto-markets.html

Buckles, K., Hagemann, A., Malamud, O., Morrill, M. S., & Wozniak, A. K. (2013, July). *The effect of college education on health* (NBER Working Paper No. 19222). Cambridge, MA: National Bureau of Economic Research.

Business-Higher Education Forum. (2004). *Public accountability for student learning in higher education: Issues and options.* Washington, DC: American Council for Education.

Busteed, B. (2013, August 27). Is college worth it? *Gallup Business Journal.* Retrieved from http://businessjournal.gallup.com/content/164108/college-worth.aspx#2

California State University East Bay. (2012, June 19). *Changes to mission and transition from mandates to shared strategic commitments.* Retrieved from http://www20.csueastbay.edu/about/strategic-planning/files/pdf/CSUEB%20Mission,%20Commitments%20and%20ILOs,%20 2012%20June%2019.pdf

Carnegie Mellon University. (2008). *Carnegie Mellon 2008 strategic plan.* Retrieved from www.cmu.edu/strategic-plan/2008-strategic-plan/2008-strategic-plan.pdf

Carnegie Mellon University. (n.d.). *Vision & mission.* Retrieved from www.cmu.edu/about/mission.shtml

Carnevale, A. P., Smith, N., & Strohl, J. (2013, June). *Recovery: Job growth and education requirements through 2020.* Washington, DC: Georgetown University, Georgetown Public Policy Institute, Center on Education and the Workforce.

Carroll, L. (1865/1997). *Alice's adventures in wonderland.* Mineola, NY: Dover Publications.

Center for Community College Student Engagement. (2014). *Contingent commitments: Bringing part-time faculty into focus (A special report from the Center for Community College Student Engagement).* Austin, TX: The University of Texas at Austin, Program in Higher Education Leadership.

Central Penn College. (2011–2013). *Mission, vision & core values: The principles that guide Central Penn.* Retrieved from www.centralpenn.edu/about-central-penn/mission,-vision-core-values/

Central Penn College. (n.d.). *2014 Catalog, Vol. 91.* Summerdale, PA: Author.

Community College of Baltimore County. (2013). *General education requirements.* Retrieved from http://catalog.ccbcmd.edu/content.php?catoid=16&navoid=978

Complete College America. (2011). *Time is the enemy.* Washington, DC: Author.

Connor, R. (2011, June). Navigating a perfect storm. *NILOA Newsletter.* Urbana, IL: University of Illinois and Indiana University, National Institute for Learning Outcomes Assessment. Retrieved from www .learningoutcomesassessment.org/NILOApieces.html#Connor2011

Cordero de Noriega, D. (2006). Institutional vision, values, and mission: Foundational filters for inquiry. In A. Driscoll & D. Cordero de Noriega (Eds.), *Taking ownership of accreditation: Assessment processes that promote institutional improvement and faculty engagement* (pp. 37–51). Sterling, VA: Stylus.

Council for the Advancement of Standards in Higher Education. (2012). *CAS professional standards for higher education* (8th ed.). Washington, DC: Author.

Council of Regional Accrediting Commissions (C-RAC). (2011). *Interregional guidelines for the evaluation of distance education programs (online learning).* Philadelphia, PA: Middle States Commission on Higher Education.

Council of Regional Accrediting Commissions (C-RAC). (2014, April 9). Regional accreditors announce efforts to improve public understanding of commission actions. Retrieved from www.msche.org/documents/ CRACCommonTermsRelease.pdf

Council on Foreign Relations. (2013). *Renewing American progress report and scorecard: Remedial education federal education policy.* New York, NY: Author.

Creswell, J. W. (2012). *Qualitative inquiry and research design: Choosing among five approaches* (3rd ed.). Thousand Oaks, CA: Sage.

Damiano, A., & Dodson, D. (2014, March 28). *Lessons learned: Insights from the road to redemption.* Presentation at Institutional Follow-Up Reports and Visits event of the Middle States Commission on Higher Education, Philadelphia, PA. Retrieved from www.msche.org/documents/ LessonsLearned.pdf

Delprino, R. P. (2013). *The human side of the strategic planning process in higher education.* Ann Arbor, MI: Society for College and University Planning.

Deming, W. E. (2000). *Out of the crisis.* Cambridge, MA: MIT Press.

Diamond, R. M. (2008). *Designing and assessing courses and curricula: A practical guide* (3rd ed.). San Francisco, CA: Jossey-Bass.

Dickeson, R. C. (2010). *Prioritizing academic programs and services: Reallocating resources to achieve strategic balance.* San Francisco, CA: Jossey-Bass.

Dickey, J. (2014, March 17). Hey, sports fans, it's time for math class. *Time*, pp. 56–61.

Diiorio, S. (2006). Preparing for accreditation: Sowing the seeds of long-term change. In A. Driscoll & D. Cordero de Noriega (Eds.), *Taking ownership of accreditation: Assessment processes that promote institutional improvement and faculty engagement* (pp. 53–71). Sterling, VA: Stylus.

Duncan, A. (2013, July 9). *The coming crossroads in higher education*. Remarks to the State Higher Education Executive Officers Association Annual Meeting. Retrieved from www.ed.gov/news/speeches/coming-crossroads-higher-education?utm_source=dlvr.it&utm_medium=twitter

Dunn, D. S., McCarthy, M. A., Baker, S. G., & Halonen, J. S. (2011). *Using quality benchmarks for assessing and developing undergraduate programs*. San Francisco, CA: Jossey-Bass.

Dutchess Community College. (2013). *Our mission*. Retrieved from www.sunydutchess.edu/aboutdcc/ourmission.html

Eagan, K., Lozano, J. B., Hurtado, S., & Case, M. H. (2014). *The American freshman: National norms 2013*. Los Angeles, CA: Higher Education Research Institute (HERI), UCLA.

Eaton, J. S. (2013, June 3). Accreditation and the next reauthorization of the Higher Education Act. *Inside Accreditation with the President of CHEA, 9*(3). Retrieved from http://chea.org/ia/IA_2013.05.31.html

Enterprise asks what customer's thinking and acts. (2006, May 22). *USA Today*, p. 6B.

Evans, J. (2013, February 11). The rising cost of tuition surpasses the rate of inflation. *Diverse Issues in Higher Education*. Retrieved from http://diverseeducation.com/article/51243/#

Ewell, P. (2005). Can assessment serve accountability? It depends on the question. In J. C. Burke & Associates (Eds.), *Achieving accountability in higher education: Balancing public, academic, and market demands* (pp. 104–124). San Francisco, CA: Jossey-Bass.

Ewell, P. T. (2012, July/August). From the states: Learning and accreditation: The elites push back. *Assessment Update, 24*(4), 10–11.

Ewell, P. T. (2013). *Making the grade: How boards can ensure academic quality* (2nd ed.). Washington, DC: Association of Governing Boards.

Excelsior College. (2013). About Excelsior College. Retrieved from www.excelsior.edu/about

Fain, P. (2013, April 17). Big disruption, big questions. *Inside Higher Ed*. Retrieved from www.insidehighered.com/news/2013/04/17/competency-based-education-heats-new-entrants

Fink, L. D. (2003). *Creating significant learning experiences: An integrated approach to designing college courses*. San Francisco, CA: Jossey-Bass.

Frye, N. E. (2012). From dancing alone to line dancing: Coordinating the assessment of the core curriculum. *Impact: The Newsletter of the Assessment Network of New York, 2*(2), 5–6.

Fulcher, K. H., Swain, M. S., & Orem, C. D. (2012, January/February). Expectations for assessment reports: A descriptive analysis. *Assessment Update, 24*(1), 1–2, 14–16.

Gallaudet University. (2013). Mission & vision statements. Retrieved from www.gallaudet.edu/about_gallaudet/mission_and_goals.html

Gallup, Inc. (2014, February 25). *The 2013 Lumina study of the American public's opinion on higher education and U.S. business leaders poll on higher education: What America needs to know about higher education redesign.* Omaha, NE: Author.

Gaston, P. L. (2013). *Higher education accreditation: How it's changing, why it must.* Stirling, VA: Stylus.

Gold, L., Rhoades, G., Smith, M., & Kuh, G. (2011, May). *What faculty unions say about student learning outcomes assessment* (NILOA Occasional Paper No. 9). Urbana, IL: University of Illinois and Indiana University, National Institute for Learning Outcomes Assessment.

Gonick, L. S. (2013, January 3). The year ahead in IT, 2013. *Inside Higher Ed.* Retrieved from www.insidehighered.com/views/2013/01/03/predictions-about-higher-ed-technology-2013-essay

Greenfield, G. M., Keup, J. R., & Gardner, J. N. (2013). *Developing and sustaining successful first-year programs: A guide for practitioners.* San Francisco, CA: Jossey-Bass.

Hackman, J. D. (1989, Winter). The psychological context: Seven maxims for institutional researchers. In P. Ewell (Ed.), *New directions for institutional research: Vol. 64* (pp. 35–48).

Hagelskamp, C., Schleifer, D., & DiStasi, C. (2013). *Is college worth it for me? How adults without degrees think about going (back) to school.* New York, NY: Public Agenda.

Halpern, D. F. (2004). Outcomes assessment 101. In D. S. Dunn, C. M. Mehrotra, & J. S. Halonen (Eds.), *Measuring up: Educational assessment challenges and practices for psychology* (pp. 11–26). Washington, DC: American Psychological Association.

Hamilton College. (2013). College purposes and goals. Retrieved from www.hamilton.edu/catalogue/college-purposes-and-goals

Harris, E., & Muchin, S. (2002). Using information architecture to improve communication. *Evaluation Exchange, 8*(3). Retrieved from www.hfrp.org/evaluation/the-evaluation-exchange/issue-archive/public-communications-campaigns-and-evaluation/using-information-architecture-to-improve-communication

Hart Research Associates. (2013, April 10). *It takes more than a major: Employer priorities for college learning and student success.* Retrieved from www.aacu.org/leap/documents/2013_EmployerSurvey.pdf

Hawthorne, J., & Kelsch, A. (2012, July/August). Closing the loop: How an assessment project paved the way for GE reform. *Assessment Update,* 24(4), 1–2, 15–16.

Hendrickson, R. M., Lane, J. E., Harris, J. T., & Dorman, R. H. (2013). *Academic leadership and governance of higher education: A guide for trustees, leaders, and aspiring leaders of two- and four-year institutions.* Sterling, VA: Stylus.

Higher Learning Commission of the North Central Association (HLC). (2013, January). *Criteria for accreditation* (Policy No. CRRT.B.10.010). Chicago, IL: Author.

Hinton, K. E. (2012). *A practical guide to strategic planning in higher education.* Ann Arbor, MI: Society for College and University Planning.

Humphreys, D. (2013, Spring). Success after college: What students, parents, and educators need to know and do. *Liberal Education,* 99(2). Retrieved from www.aacu.org/liberaleducation/le-sp13/humphreys.cfm

Humphreys, D., & Kelly, P. (2014). *How liberal arts and sciences majors fare in employment.* Washington, DC: Association of American Colleges & Universities and National Center for Higher Education Management Systems.

Jankowski, N. (2011, July). *Juniata College: Faculty led assessment* (NILOA Examples of Good Assessment Practice). Urbana, IL: University of Illinois and Indiana University, National Institute for Learning Outcomes Assessment (NILOA).

Jankowski, N. A., Ikenberry, S. O., Kinzie, J., Kuh, G. D., Shenoy, G. F., & Baker, G. R. (2012, March). *Transparency & accountability: An evaluation of the VSA College Portrait pilot.* Urbana, IL: University of Illinois and Indiana University, National Institute for Learning Outcomes Assessment (NILOA).

Jankowski, N., & Provezis, S. (2011). *Making student learning evidence transparent: The state of the art.* Urbana, IL: University of Illinois and Indiana University, National Institute for Learning Outcomes Assessment (NILOA).

Jaschik, S. (2013, July 19). Jobs mismatch. *Inside Higher Ed.* Retrieved from www.insidehighered.com/news/2013/07/19/do-faculty-members-share-students-and-parents-focus-jobs

Jenson, J. D., & Treuer, P. (2014, March/April). Defining the e-portfolio: What it is and why it matters. *Change.*

John N. Gardner Institute for Excellence in Undergraduate Education. (2005a). *First year focus—foundational dimensions (Four-year college version).* Retrieved from www.jngi.org/foe-program/foundational-dimensions/four-year-first-year-focus/

John N. Gardner Institute for Excellence in Undergraduate Education. (2005b). *First year focus—foundational dimensions (Two-year college version).* Retrieved from www.jngi.org/foe-program/foundational-dimensions/first-year-focus-two-year/

Johnstone, S. M., & Soares, L. (2014, March/April). Principles for developing competency-based education programs. *Change.* Retrieved from www.changemag.org/Archives/Back%20Issues/2014/March-April%202014/Principles_full.html

Kamlet, M. S. (2010). *Criteria for university-level strategic international engagements.* Pittsburgh, PA: Carnegie Mellon University. Retrieved from www.cmu.edu/leadership/assets/intl-strategic-criteria.pdf

Kelly, A. P., & Hess, F. M. (2013). *Beyond retrofitting: Innovation in higher education.* Washington, DC: Hudson Institute.

Krupnick, M. (2013, December 26). College accreditors under pressure to crack down. *The Hechinger Report.* Retrieved from http://hechinger report.org/content/college-accreditors-under-pressure-to-crack-down_14300/

Kuh, G. D., Jankowski, N., Ikenberry, S. O., & Kinzie, J. (2014, January). *Knowing what students know and can do: The current state of student learning outcomes assessment in U.S. colleges and universities.* Urbana, IL: National Institute for Student Learning Outcomes Assessment (NILOA).

Kuh, G., Kinzie, J., Schuh, J. H., Whitt, E. J., & Associates. (2010, June). *Student success in college: Creating conditions that matter.* San Francisco, CA: Jossey-Bass.

Kuh, G. D., & O'Donnell, K., with Reed, S. (2013). *Ensuring quality & taking high-impact practices to scale.* Washington, DC: Association of American Colleges & Universities.

Kuh, G. D., & Pascarella, E. T. (2004, September/October). What does institutional selectivity tell us about educational quality? *Change, 36*(5), 52–58.

LeBlanc, P. J. (2013, January 31). Accreditation in a rapidly changing world. *Inside Higher Ed.* Retrieved from www.insidehighered.com/views/2013/01/31/competency-based-education-and-regional-accreditation

Lebanon Valley College. (1995–2003). General education. Retrieved from www.lvc.edu/general-education/

Lederman, D. (2011, October 7). An unusual conference. *Inside Higher Ed*. Retrieved from www.insidehighered.com/news/2011/10/07/future_of_state_universities_conference_promotes_online_learning

Lederman, D. (2012, January 23). State support slumps again. *Inside Higher Ed*. Retrieved from www.insidehighered.com/news/2012/01/23/state-funds-higher-education-fell-76–2011–12

Lederman, D. (2013, July 17). Turning big ships. *Inside Higher Ed*. Retrieved from www.insidehighered.com/news/2013/07/17/even-healthy-universities-make-big-changes-free-funds-priorities

Light, T. P., Chen, H. L., & Ittelson, J. C. (2011). *Documenting learning with eportfolios: A guide for college instructors*. San Francisco, CA: Jossey-Bass.

Looney, A., & Greenstone, M. (2012, October). *Regardless of the cost, college still matters*. The Hamilton Project. Retrieved from www.hamiltonproject.org/papers/regardless_of_the_cost_college_still_matters/

Marcus, J. (2013, October 1). Who's running U.S. higher ed.? Increasingly, foundations. *The Hechinger Report*. Retrieved from http://hechingerreport.org/content/whos-running-u-s-higher-ed-increasingly-foundations_13221/

Marcus, J. (2014, January 25). The new college exam: A test to graduate. *Time*. Retrieved from http://nation.time.com/2014/01/25/the-new-college-exam-a-test-to-graduate/

Maxwell, D. (2013, February 4). Time to play offense. *Inside Higher Ed*. Retrieved from www.insidehighered.com/views/2013/02/04/college-leaders-need-reframe-discussion-value-essay

McClenney, K., Marti, C. N., & Adkins, C. (n.d.). *Student engagement and student outcomes: Key findings from CCSSE validation research*. Austin, TX: The University of Texas at Austin Community College Leadership Program.

McCormick, A. C., Gonyea, R. M., & Kinzie, J. (2013, May/June). Refreshing engagement: NSSE at 13. *Change*. Retrieved from www.changemag.org/Archives/Back%20Issues/2013/May-June%202013/refreshing-engagement-full.html

McKendree University. (2013). Student learning outcomes. Retrieved from www.mckendree.edu/offices/provost/assessment/student-learning-outcomes.php

Middle States Commission on Higher Education (MSCHE). (2006). *Characteristics of excellence in higher education: Requirements of affiliation and standards for accreditation*. Philadelphia, PA: Author.

Middle States Commission on Higher Education (MSCHE). (2008). Rubric for evaluating institutional student learning assessment processes. Retrieved from https://www.msche.org/publications_view.asp?idPubl icationType=5&txtPublicationType=Guidelines+for+Institutional+ Improvement

Middle States Commission on Higher Education (MSCHE). (2009). *Highlights from the Commission's first 90 years.* Philadelphia, PA: Author.

Middle States Commission on Higher Education (MSCHE). (2010). *Governing boards: Understanding the expectations of the Middle States Commission on Higher Education.* Philadelphia, PA: Author.

Midwestern Higher Education Compact. (2014). *Transparent pathways, clear outcomes: Using disciplinary tuning to improve teaching, learning, and student success.* Minneapolis, MN: Author.

Miller, M. A. (2013, March/April). Editorial: Benefit/cost=value. *Change.* Retrieved from www.changemag.org/Archives/Back%20Issues/2013/ March-April%202013/editorial_full.html

Mintz, S. (2013, July 22). The future is now: 15 innovations to watch for. *Chronicle of Higher Education.* Retrieved from http://chronicle.com/ article/The-Future-Is-Now-15/140479/

Moore, C. A., & Whittaker, B. (2013, December 2). A four-step plan to "right-size" the curriculum. *New England Journal of Higher Education.* Retrieved from www.nebhe.org/thejournal/a-four-step-plan-to-right-size-the-curriculum/

Morace, R., & Hibschweiler, I. (n.d.). *Daemen College and the use of VALUE rubrics.* Retrieved from www.aacu.org/value/casestudies/ daemen.pdf

Morrill, R. (2013, Winter). Collaborative strategic leadership and planning in an era of structural change: Highlighting the role of the governing board. *Peer Review, 15*(1).

Morse, R. (2012, September 11). How *U. S. News* calculates its best colleges rankings. Retrieved from www.usnews.com/education/best-colleges/ articles/2012/09/11/how-us-news-calculates-its-best-colleges-rankings

Morse, R. (2013, September 3). Preview: Methodology changes for 2014 best colleges rankings [Blog]. Retrieved from www.usnews.com/ education/blogs/college-rankings-blog/2013/09/03/preview-methodology-changes-for-2014-best-colleges-rankings

Mortenson, T. G. (2012, Winter). State funding: A race to the bottom. *The Presidency.* Retrieved from www.acenet.edu/the-presidency/columns-and-features/Pages/state-funding-a-race-to-the-bottom.aspx

National Advisory Committee on Institutional Quality and Integrity (NACIQI). (2012, April). *Report to the U.S. Secretary of Education: Higher Education Act reauthorization accreditation policy recommendations.* Washington, DC: U.S. Department of Education.

National Center for Education Statistics (NCES). (2012). *Digest of Education Statistics 2011, Table 200: Total fall enrollment in degree-granting institutions, by attendance status, sex, and age: Selected years, 1970 through 2020.* Washington, DC: Author.

National Survey of Student Engagement (NSSE). (2012). *Moving from data to action: Lessons from the field—volume 2.* Bloomington, IN: Indiana Center for Postsecondary Research.

Nelson, L. A. (2013, May 29). Too much information. *Inside Higher Ed.* Retrieved from www.insidehighered.com/news/2013/05/29/audit-monroe-community-college-finds-officials-were-over-communicating-students

New England Association of Schools and Colleges Commission on Institutions of Higher Education (NEASC). (2011, July 1). *Standards for accreditation.* Retrieved from http://cihe.neasc.org/standards_policies/standards/standards_html_version

New Leadership Alliance for Student Learning and Accountability (NLASLA). (2012a). *Assuring quality: An institutional self-assessment tool for excellent practice in student learning outcomes assessment.* Retrieved from https://kry224-site0001.maxesp.net/alliance_publications/assuring%20quality-pdf%20version.pdf

New Leadership Alliance for Student Learning and Accountability (NLASLA). (2012b). *Committing to quality: Guidelines for assessment and accountability in higher education.* Retrieved from www.chea.org/pdf/Committing%20to%20Quality.pdf#search="alliance"

Newell, M. (2012a, July). The pursuit of credibility. *Career College Central,* pp. 55–56.

Newell, M. (2012b, September). The pursuit of credibility: Part two. *Career College Central,* pp. 28–29.

Newell, M. (2021c, November). The pursuit of credibility: Part three. *Career College Central,* pp. 34–36.

1998 Amendment to the Higher Education Act of 1965, Pub. L. No. 105–244, Title IV, Part H, Sec. 492(b)(4)(E)

Oakton Community College. (1998, October 20). *Our vision, mission, & values.* Retrieved from www.oakton.edu/about/mission/index.php

Organisation for Economic Co-operation and Development (OECD). (2013). *Education at a Glance 2013: OECD Indicators.* Retrieved from http://dx.doi.org/10.1787/eag-2013-en

Pace University. (2010, January 1). *Opportunitas in the 21st century: Seizing the moment: Strategic plan 2010–2015*. New York, NY: Author.

Pascarella, E. T., & Blaich, C. (2013, March/April). Lessons from the Wabash National Study of Liberal Arts Education. *Change*. Retrieved from www.changemag.org/Archives/Back%20Issues/2013/March-April%202013/wabash_full.html

Pascarella, E. T., & Terenzini, P.T. (2005). *How college affects students: A third decade of research*. San Francisco, CA: Jossey-Bass.

Patel, V. (2014, April 14). Educators point to a "crisis of mediocre teaching." *Chronicle of Higher Education*. Retrieved from http://chronicle.com/article/Educators-Point-to-a-Crisis/145901/

Pearce, E. (2013, July 30). The burning question: Why has college enrollment dropped? *MSN News*. Retrieved from http://news.msn.com/us/the-burning-question-why-has-college-enrollment-dropped?goback=.gde_82991_member_262133198

Penn, J. D. (2012, November/December). Assessing assessment: Strategies for providing feedback on assessment practices. *Assessment Update*, 24(6), 8–9, 13.

Petrides, L., & Nodine, T. (2005, Spring). Accountability and information practices in California community colleges: Toward effective use of information in decision making. *iJournal: Insight into Student Services*, 10. Retrieved from www.ijournal.us/issue_10/print_version/ij_issue10_prt_07.htm

Pierce, S. R. (2014). *Governance reconsidered: How boards, presidents, administrators, and faculty can help their colleges thrive*. San Francisco: Jossey-Bass.

Pike, G. (2012, January/February). Assessment measures: Criteria for evaluating campus surveys. *Assessment Update*, 24(1), 10–12.

Pollack, S. (2006). Program review as a model of vision-based continuous renewal. In A. Driscoll & D. Cordero de Noriega (Eds.), *Taking ownership of accreditation: Assessment processes that promote institutional improvement and faculty engagement* (pp. 73–94). Sterling, VA: Stylus.

Provezis, S. (2012, June). *LaGuardia Community College: Weaving assessment into the institutional fabric* (NILOA Examples of Good Assessment Practice). Urbana, IL: University of Illinois and Indiana University, National Institute for Learning Outcomes Assessment.

Pryor, J. H., Hurtado, S., Saenz, V. B., Santos, J. L., & Korn, W. S. (2007, April). *The American freshman: Forty year trends*. Los Angeles, CA: Higher Education Research Institute (HERI), UCLA.

Quality Matters Program. (2011). *Quality Matters rubric workbook for higher education*. Annapolis, MD: MarylandOnline, Inc.

Regnier, P. (2013, August 2). Does college still pay off? *Money*. Retrieved from http://money.cnn.com/2013/08/01/pf/college/college-education.moneymag/index.html?iid=EL

Rhodes, T. L., & Finley, A. (2013). *Using the VALUE rubrics for improvement of learning and authentic assessment*. Washington, DC: Association of American Colleges and Universities.

Rooney, J. J., & Vanden Heuvel, L. N. (2004, July). Root cause analysis for beginners. *Quality Progress, 37*(7), 45–53.

Salluzzo, R., & Tahey, P. (2010). *Strategic financial analysis for higher education* (7th ed.). Washington, DC: National Association of College and University Business Officers (NACUBO).

Sams, A., & Bergmann, J. (2012). *Flip your classroom: Reach every student in every class every day*. Washington, DC: International Society for Technology in Education (ISTE).

Sanders, L., & Filkins, J. (2009). *Effective reporting* (2nd ed.). Tallahassee, FL: Association for Institutional Research (AIR).

Saunders, K. (n.d.). *Using VALUE rubrics to have an impact on learning*. Retrieved from www.aacu.org/value/casestudies/drake.pdf

Schramm, J. B., Aldeman, C., Rotherham, A., Brown, R., & Cross, J. (2013, November). *Smart shoppers: The end of the "college for all" debate?* Washington, DC: College Summit.

Selingo, J. J. (2013). *College (un)bound: The future of higher education and what it means for students*. Boston, MA: Houghton Mifflin Harcourt.

Sharp, M. D., Komives, S. R., & Fincher, J. (2011). Learning outcomes in academic disciplines: Identifying common ground. *Journal of Student Affairs Research and Practice, 48*(4), 481–504.

Shirley, R. C., & Volkwein, J. F. (1978). Establishing academic program priorities. *Journal of Higher Education, 49*(5), 472–488.

Shugart, S. (2013, January/March). The challenge to deep change: A brief cultural history of higher education. *Planning for Higher Education, 41*(2), 7–17.

Shulman, L. S. (2007). Counting and recounting: Assessment and the quest for accountability. *Change, 39*(1), 20–25.

Slippery Rock University. (2013). Academic catalog: Academic life. Retrieved from http://catalog.sru.edu/content.php?catoid=22&navoid=434#libe_stud

Southern Association of Colleges and Schools Commission on Colleges (SACS-COC). (2012). *The principles of accreditation: Foundations for quality enhancement*. Decatur, GA: Author.

Steen, L. A. (1992, May). 20 questions that deans should ask their mathematics departments (or, that a sharp department will ask itself). *AAHE Bulletin, 44*(9), 3–6.

Stengel, R. (2012, May 28). Bibi's choice. *Time*. Retrieved from www.time
.com/time/subscriber/article/0,33009,2115042,00.html

Steve Jobs. (2011, October 6). *The Economist*. Retrieved from www
.economist.com/blogs/babbage/2011/10/obituary

Stevenson University. (2013). *Our mission*. Retrieved from http://stevenson
.edu/academics/mission.asp

Sullivan, E. (2013, June 18). New report makes a strong case for higher
education [blog entry]. Retrieved from www.cofinteract.org/
rephilanthropy/?p=6793

SUNY College of Environmental Science & Forestry. (n.d.). *Vision 2020*.
Retrieved from www.esf.edu/vision2020/vision2020.pdf

Suskie, L. (2000). Fair assessment practices: Giving students equitable
opportunities to demonstrate learning. *AAHE Bulletin, 52*(9), 7–9.

Suskie, L. (2006). Accountability and quality improvement. In P. Hernon,
R. E.. Dugan, & C. Schwartz (Eds.), *Revisiting outcomes assessment in
higher education* (pp. 13–38). Westport, CT: Libraries Unlimited.

Suskie, L. (2008). Understanding the nature and purpose of assessment. In
J. E. Spurlin, S. A. Rajala, & J. P. Lavelle (Eds.), *Designing better engineering education through assessment* (pp. 3–22). Sterling, VA: Stylus.

Suskie, L. (2009). *Assessing student learning: A common sense guide* (2nd
ed.). San Francisco, CA: Jossey-Bass.

Suskie, L. (2010, October 26). Why are we assessing? *Inside Higher Ed.*
Retrieved from www.insidehighered.com/views/2010/10/26/Suskie

Suskie, L. (2013, March/April). Editor's notes: Helping faculty members
learn. *Assessment Update, 25*(2), 3–4, 13.

Swing, R. L., & Coogan, C. S. (2010, May). *Valuing assessment: Cost-
benefit considerations* (NILOA Occasional Paper No. 5). Urbana, IL:
University of Illinois and Indiana University, National Institute for
Learning Outcomes Assessment.

Terkla, D. G., Sharkness, J., Cohen, M., Roscoe, H. S., & Wiseman, M.
(2012, Winter). *Institutional dashboards: Navigational tool for colleges and
universities* (AIR Professional File #123). Tallahassee, FL: Association
for Institutional Research.

Tinto, V. (2012). *Completing college: Rethinking institutional action*. Chicago,
IL: University of Chicago Press.

Tufte, E. R. (1997). *Visual explanations: Images and quantities, evidence and
narrative*. Cheshire, CT: Graphics Press.

U.S. Census Bureau. (n.d.). *Survey of income and program participation
Table 2B: Mean monthly earnings by selected characteristics: Fourth
quarter (October, November, and December) 2011*. Washington, DC:
Author.

U.S. Department of Education (ED). (2006). *A test of leadership: Charting the future of U.S. higher education*. Washington, DC: Author.

U.S. Small Business Administration. (n.d.). *Create your business plan*. Retrieved from www.sba.gov/category/navigation-structure/starting-managing-business/starting-business/how-write-business-plan

Walvoord, B. E. (2010). *Assessment clear and simple: A practical guide for institutions, departments, and general education* (2nd ed.). San Francisco, CA: Jossey-Bass.

Walvoord, B. E. (2014). *Assessing and improving student writing in college: A guide for institutions, general education, departments, and classrooms*. San Francisco, CA: Jossey-Bass.

Walvoord, B. E., & Anderson, V. J. (2010). *Effective grading: A tool for learning and assessment in college* (2nd ed.). San Francisco, CA: Jossey-Bass.

Webley, K. (2012, October 18). Can an online degree really help you get a job? *Time*. Retrieved from http://nation.time.com/2012/10/18/can-an-online-degree-really-help-you-get-a-job/

Western Association of Schools and Colleges Accrediting Commission for Senior Colleges and Universities (WASC Senior). (2013, July 1). *2013 handbook of accreditation*. Alameda, CA: Author.

Wilmington University. (n.d.). Wilmington University mission, vision, and values. Retrieved from www.wilmu.edu/mission.aspx

Winkelmes, M. (2013, Spring). Transparency in teaching: Faculty share data and improve students' learning. *Liberal Education, 99*(2). Retrieved from www.aacu.org/liberaleducation/le-sp13/winkelmes.cfm

Wiseman, P. (2013, June 24). Seeking soft skills: Employers want graduates who can communicate, think fast, work in teams. *Star Tribune*. Retrieved from www.startribune.com/business/212770791.html

Yeado, J., Haycock, K., Johnstone, R., & Chaplot, P. (2014, January). *Top 10 analyses to provoke discussion and action on college completion: Learning from high-performing and fast-gaining institutions*. Washington, DC: The Education Trust.

● INDEX

Page references followed by *fig* indicate an illustrated figure; followed by *t* indicate a table.

A

ABET (formerly the Accreditation Board for Engineering and Technology), 12

Academic freedom, 44

Academic Leadership and Governance of Higher Education: A Guide for Trustees, Leaders, and Aspiring Leaders of Two- and Four-Year Institutions (Hendrickson, Lane, Harris, & Dorman), 96

Academic program reviews. *See* Program reviews

Accountability: college responsibility for quality and, 52, 57–58; definition of, 58; New Leadership Alliance for Student Learning and Accountability (NLASLA) support of, 243; rising movement and demand for, 9; University and College Accountability Network (U-CAN), 184; Voluntary Framework for Accountability (VFA), 184; Voluntary System of Accountability (VSA), 172, 184

Accreditation: additional information and resources on, 227; examining and assessing the process of, 21–23; functioning as a tool and lever for improvement, 212; Higher Education Opportunity Act (HEOA) provisions on, 12; legitimate concerns over, 18–21, 246; national, 12–13, 246; as process of collegial peer review, 15–16; program reviews that integrate multiple, 232; as shared responsibility of "triad" of

entities, 11–12; specialized, 12, 231–232; standards, criteria, and requirements of, 211; starting with honest appraisal of your college at present, 213–215; state agencies role in, 11. *See also* Quality assurance; Regional accreditation; U.S. Department of Education (USED)

Accreditation Council for Business Schools and Programs (ACBSP), 247

Accreditation reform movement, 10

Accreditation reports: additional information and resources on, 227; comparison of research reports and, 219t; examples of assertions and suitable evidence in, 220–221t; including shortcomings in context with integrity, 223–224; organize supporting documentation for your, 216–220; provide good quality documented evidence for your, 220–223. *See also* Program reviews; Reviewers

Accrediting Commission of Career Schools and Colleges (ACCSC), 12–13, 17

Accreditors: additional information and resources on, 227; criticisms of accreditation and, 18–21; description and types of, 12–13; Higher Education Act (HEA) Title IV gatekeeper status of, 16, 17, 18, 221; national, 12–13; providing an honest appraisal of where your college is now to, 213–215; on serving the "public good," 19; specialized or disciplinary, 12, 231–232;

standards, criteria, and requirements of, 211; understanding emphasis on the five culture of quality by, 215–216; understanding what they are looking for and why, 212–213; U.S. Department of Education (ED) recognition of, 16, 21–22. *See also* Regional accreditors; Reviewers

ACE National Task Force on Institutional Accreditation report (ACE), 244

Action steps, 113

Additional information resources. *See* Information resources

Adelman, C., 9, 120, 172

Aldeman, C., 7, 83

Adjunct faculty support, 84–85

Adkins, C., 129

Administrators: marginalization of, 43; meeting the needs of internal stakeholders as, 56; ongoing venues for discussions on quality by, 83; providing constructive feedback to, 85; six-point agenda for advancing quality by, 241–245. *See also* Human capital; Presidential leadership

AFT Higher Education, 84

Airasian, P. W., 122

Aldeman, C., 7, 56

Alexander, J. S., 83

Alice's Adventures in Wonderland (Carroll), 45

Allen, I. E., 140

Alter, J., 162

Alumni: board members who are also, 91–92; meeting the needs of employers of your, 55. *See also* Students

Ambrose, S. A., 129, 131

American Association of Community Colleges (AACC), 96, 184

American Association of State Colleges and Universities (AASCU), 172, 184

American Association of University Professors (AAUP): resources on faculty role in shared governance from the, 88; "Statement of Principles on Academic Freedom and Tenure" (1940) of the, 44

American Chemical Society (ACS), 236

American Council of Teachers of Foreign Languages (ACTFL) proficiency guidelines, 154

American Council on Education (ACE): ACE National Task Force on Institutional Accreditation report by, 244; on college closures by regional accreditors, 22; on creating common accreditation requirements and language, 243; on criticisms of

U.S. accreditation and accreditors, 18, 19; on increasing costs of higher education, 7; National Task Force on Institutional Accreditation on peer review, 15; on regional accreditors operated as think tanks, 244; on weaker preparation for success in college by students, 8

American Sociological Association (ASA), 236

America's Top Colleges (*Forbes* magazine), 184

Andersen, C., 134

Anderson, L. W., 122

Anderson, V. J., 127, 142, 152, 156, 158, 196

Angelo, T. A., 156

"The Art, Science, and Craft of Administrative Support" (Dunn, McCarthy, Baker, & Halonen), 88

Arts and sciences education, 137–139

Assessing and Improving Student Writing in College: A Guide for Institutions, General Education, Departments, and Classrooms (Walvoord), 159

Assessing Student Learning: A Common Sense Guide (Suskie): on accreditation integrity, 58; on advancing a culture of evidence, 208; on assessing student learning, 158; on evidence used to inform improvements, 196; on good practices in testing and measurement in, 165; on learning outcomes, 127; on setting targets for success, 176; on sharing evidence, 188; on sources of resistance to student learning assessment, 48

Assessment. *See* Institutional assessment; Student learning assessment

Assessment Clear and Simple: A Practical Guide for Institutions, Departments, and General Education (Walvoord), 208

Assessment Essentials: Planning, Implementing, and Improving Assessing in Higher Education (Banta & Palomba), 158–159

Assessment information management systems, 203

Assessment Update, 208

Associated Press (2013), 14

Association for Assessment of Learning in Higher Education (AALHE), 159

Association for Authentic, Experiential, and Evidence-Based Learning (AAEEBL), 159

Association for Institutional Research (AIR), 159

Association of American Colleges and Universities (AAC&U): concerns over higher education by, 4; Essential Outcomes initiative of the, 120; general education and liberal arts resources by the, 143, 152; "Give Students a Compass" initiative of the, 139; on isolation of higher education evidence from the, 38; liberal education advocated by the, 138; on strategies to help students learn, 129–130t; VALUE rubrics developed by, 124, 153, 154, 172, 176

Association of Catholic Colleges and Universities, 96

Association of Governing Boards (AGB), 88, 96

Association of Governing Boards of Universities and Colleges (AGB), 57, 58

Association of Public Land Grant Universities (APLU), 172, 184

Association of Theological Schools (ATS), 12

Association to Advance Collegiate Schools of Business (AACSB), 247

Attribution: definition of, 133; strategies to help student, 132–134

Auden, W. H., 100

B

Backwards curriculum design, 136

Bain, K., 129, 136

Baker, G. R., 155, 156, 172, 180, 185, 186, 194, 208

Baker, S. G., 35, 88

Baker, V. L., 22

Balanced scorecards, 181

Baldwin, R. G., 22

Banta, T. W., 158, 159, 198, 199, 237

Barr, R. B., 132

Baum, S., 56

Berger, N., 7, 57

Bergmann, J., 140

Betterment: accreditation functioning as a tool and lever for, 212; description of, 30. *See also* Change; Culture of betterment; Improvement

Black, K. E., 158, 237

Blaich, C., 39, 41, 200, 208

Blake, L. P., 7

Block, G. D., 57

Bloom, B. S., 122

Bloom's taxonomy, 122

Board leadership: additional information and resources on, 96; capacity and commitment of, 90–91; collaborative approach of, 93–94; description of, 89; empowered, 91; engagement by the, 94; getting the right people for, 94–95; independent, 91–92;

oversight entity of, 92–93; providing ongoing education and development to, 95; responsibilities of the, 89; six-point agenda for advancing quality by, 241–245. *See also* Institutional governance

Bok, D., 94, 96

Borden, V.M.H., 198

Bowen, H. R., 56

Boyer, E. L., 67, 68

Bresciani, M. J., 202, 237

Bridges, M. W., 129, 131

Brightline, 183

Brown, M., 8

Brown, R., 7, 56

Bryn Mawr College, 14

Buckles, K., 57

Budgets: ensuring your college's financial health through, 59, 60–63; how underlying values impact decision for, 103–104; quality six-point agenda by providing sufficient, 240, 243; supporting your strategic plan, 114. *See also* Financial issues

Bulleted lists, 180

Bullying, 44

Business-Higher Education Forum, 181

"Business plans," 194

Busteed, B., 55, 121, 138

C

Caldwell, S., 8

California State University East Bay, 100

Callout boxes, 180

Capella University, 188

Capital investment. *See* Financial issues

Capstone experiences: curriculum that includes synthesizing, 137; definition of, 131; program learning outcomes opportunities through, 202

Carnegie Classification of Institutions of Higher Education, 171

Carnegie Mellon University (CMU), 115, 198

Carnevale, A. P., 6, 120

Carroll, L., 45

CAS *Professional Standards for Higher Education* (CAS), 237

Case, M. H., 7

Catalyst for Learning: ePortfolio Resources and Research website, 159

Center for Community College Student Engagement, 85

Central Penn College, 100, 104, 125

Certificate program curriculum map, 135e

"The Challenge to Deep Change: A Brief Cultural History of Higher Education" (Shugart), 48

Chamber of Commerce, 55

Change: barriers to college adoption of, 39–41; "business plans" required for proposed initiative or, 194; creating incentive to, 40–41; flexibilty and adaptability to, 122. See also Betterment; Improvement

Chaplot, P., 193

Checklists, 165

Chen, H. L., 155

Chief executive officers (CEOs), 90. See also Presidential leadership

Chief operating officers (COOs), 90

The Chronicle of Higher Education, 10

Churchack, M., 23, 212

Classrooms: flipped, 109, 140; learning-centered, 132

Closing the loop, 191–192

Cohen, M., 159, 181, 208

Collaboration: additional resources on meaningful learning outcomes, 127; quality through culture of, 81–82; as soft skill valued by employers, 122; strategic planning as process of, 110; student learning outcomes facilitated through, 124

"Collaborative Strategic Leadership" (2013), 100

College appraisal: level 1: culture of quality, 214; level 2: culture of quality, 214; level 3: culture of quality, 215; start accreditation process with your honest, 213–215

College Board's College Search, 184

College Compass (U.S. News & World Report), 184

College cultures: introduction to betterment, 29–33; introduction to community, 26–27, 32, 33, 42; introduction to disrespect, 43–44, 78–80; introduction to evidence, 28–29, 31–33, 39; introduction to excellence, 25–26, 32; introduction to focus and aspiration, 27, 31–32; introduction to relevance, 26, 31–32; introduction to respect, 78–80; introduction to reticence, 38–39; introduction to silos, 41–42, 241, 243–244. See also specific culture

College Guide (Washington Monthly), 184

College Navigator (U.S. Department of Education), 184

College Portrait of Undergraduate Education, 184

College Rankings (Kiplinger's), 184

College responsibilities: as central to deployment of resources, 64–65; demonstrate that you are ensuring quality and meeting, 52, 57–58; evidence using ethically, fairly, and in keeping with, 195–196; keep your promise, 52, 56; know your key stakeholders and meet their needs, 52, 54–56; listed, 52; put your students first, 52, 53–54; serve the public good, 52, 56–57, 186. See also Stewardship

College Results Online (Education Trust), 184

College Search (College Board), 184

College transfers, 141–142

College (Un)Bound: The Future of Higher Education and What It Means for Students (Selingo), 10

"College wage premium" (1970s to 2012), 7

Colleges: accreditation report prepared by, 216–227; Carnegie Classification of Institutions of Higher Education and, 171; cost, access, quality, productivity, and relevance problems of, 5; description of, 4; distinctive traits that set apart your, 102–103; duty to be transparent, 58; Education Trust's stories on changes implemented by, 193; facilitating transferred course credits between different, 141–142; financial health of your, 59, 60–63, 201–202; five fundamental responsibilities of, 52–58; gauging responsiveness to student diversity, 149; institutional effectiveness of, 52; "Is it good for the kids?" principle guiding priorities of, 162; lack of money supporting assessment at, 37; overview of the five cultures required for excellence at, 25–33; pockets of mediocrity found in all, 47–48; public information resources on U.S. higher education and, 183–184; recent criticisms of, 4–5; silos within, 41–42, 241, 243–244; student-centered, 133; telling the story of your, 183–186; traditional vs. swirl pathway through, 9. See also Students; U.S. higher education

Collegial peer review, 15–16

Collegiate Learning Assessment (CLA), 154, 172

Collier, A., 71

Commission on Higher Education Accreditation (CHEA), 16, 21, 23

Commission on the Future of Higher Education, 18. See also Spellings Commission report (2006)

Communication: creating culture of respect through honest, 80–81; honest and balanced, 186–188, 213–215, 223–224; regarding appraisal of your college, 213–215; regarding college shortcomings in context, 223–224; for sharing evidence, 177–188

Community College of Baltimore County, 125

Community College Survey of Student Engagement (CCSSE), 55

Community (local), 56. See also Culture of community

Competency-based programs: cautions regarding implementation of, 72, 73; description of, 71, 72

Complacency barrier, 240, 243

Complete College America, 9

Computer skills, 123

Connect to Learning project, 159

Connor, R., 129

Continuous improvement, 191–192

Continuous quality improvement, 191–192

Coogan, C. S., 208

Cooperative Institutional Research Program (CIRP) Freshman Survey, 55

Cordero de Noriega, D., 105

Council for Higher Education Accreditation (CHEA), 57, 231

Council for the Advancement of Standards in Higher Education (CAS), 237

Council of Regional Accrediting Commissions (C-RAC), 142, 243

Council on Foreign Relations, 5, 6

Council on Occupational Education, 13

Council on Social Work Education (CSWE), 12

Course syllabi: periodically reviewing, 137; template for a curriculum map for, 136e

Courses: adjunct faculty teaching, 84–85; capstone experiences included in a, 131, 137, 202; curriculum map for a hypothetical certificate requiring four, 135e; ensuring appropriate consistency across sections of a, 137; facilitating transfer of credits from another college, 141–142; streamlining offerings of co-curricular activities and, 65–66; template for a curriculum map for a syllabus for, 136e. See also Curricula; Online courses/programs

Creativity, 122

Creditworthiness score, 61–62

Creswell, J. W., 156, 158

Critical thinking: as a fuzzy term, 126; strengths and weaknesses perspective when assessing, 170; valued by employers, 122; various definitions of, 126

Cross, J., 7, 56

Cross, K. P., 156

Cruikshank, K. A., 122

Culture of betterment: accreditor's focus on the, 216; additional information and resources on, 208; defining program and teaching excellence through, 32, 33; documenting evidence to support, 202–206; fostering a culture of community to sustain a, 197–198; helping its students to persist and succeed through, 133; interrelationship with other cultures, 31–32; periodically regroup and reflect to sustain, 206; program review framework criteria of, 231; providing evidence of shortcomings to fill demands of, 187–188; questions on new initiatives proposals and academic program reviews on, 235t; questions raised about successes to promote, 192; road trip analogy of, 29–31; rubrics to appraise college's, 206–207e; strategies to strengthen your college's financial health within, 201–202; value efforts to change, improve, and innovate, 198–200. See also Betterment; Improvement

Culture of community: breaking down silos by fostering, 42, 241, 243–244; building respect to create, 78–80; collaboration to build, 81–82; defining program and teaching excellence through, 32, 33; documentation component of, 87–88; fostering a, 197–198; growth and development through, 82–85; helping its students to persist and succeed through, 133; honest communication to build, 80–81; importance of creating a, 26–27; interrelationship with other cultures, 31–32; program review framework criteria of, 231; questions on new initiatives proposals and academic program reviews on, 234t; shared collegial governance component of, 85–87. See also Community (local)

Culture of disrespect: characteristics and root causes of, 43–44; difficulty of turning around a, 78; strategies for transforming a, 78–80

Culture of evidence: accreditor's focus on the, 215–216; additional information and resources on, 208; defining program and teaching excellence through, 32–33; fostering culture of betterment through, 197–208; for gauging success, 147–159; helping its students to persist and succeed through, 133; interrelationship with other cultures, 31–32; need to use data collected by colleges, 39; program review framework criteria of, 231; questions on new initiatives proposals and academic program reviews on, 234t–235t; road trip analogy of, 28–29; uses of good evidence, 161–165. *See also* Evidence

Culture of excellence: commitment to pervasive and enduring, 25–26; defining program and teaching excellence through, 32; quality defined as, 32–33, 51–52. *See also* Excellence; Teaching excellence

Culture of focus and aspiration: defining college purpose to build, 99–105; defining program and teaching excellence through, 32; helping its students to persist and succeed through, 133; helping students learn and succeed component of, 129–143; identifying what makes students become successful component of, 119–127; interrelationship with other cultures, 31–32; program review framework criteria of, 231; questions on new initiatives proposals and academic program reviews on, 234t; road trip analogy of, 27; setting goals and making plans component of, 107–117

Culture of quality: accreditor's focus on the, 216; level 1: a pervasive and enduring, 214; level 2: informal and without systematic documentation, 214; level 3: not yet a pervasive culture of quality, 215. *See also* Five cultures of quality; Quality

Culture of relevance: accreditor's focus on the, 216; defining program and teaching excellence through, 32; helping its students to persist and succeed through, 133; interrelationship with other cultures, 31–32; program review framework criteria of, 230; providing evidence of quality to fill demands of, 187–188; questions on new initiatives proposals and academic program reviews on, 233t–234t; road trip analogy of, 26

Culture of reticence, 38–39

Culture of silos, 41–42, 241, 243–244

Curricula: additional information and resources on, 142–143; backwards design for, 136; designed to support student learning and success, 134–137; general education, 137–139, 143; including integrative, synthesizing capstone experiences in, 131, 137, 202; role of liberal arts and sciences, 137–139. *See also* Courses

Curriculum alignment, 135

Curriculum maps: definition of, 135; for a hypothetical four-course certificate, 135e; template for a course syllabus, 136e

D

Damiano, A., 23

Dashboard indicators: additional information and resources on, 159; definition of, 147; examples for hypothetical college goals, 151t; for hypothetical college strategic goal, 182e–183; sharing evidence through, 181. *See also* Measurement

Data: assessment information management systems for, 203; brightline used to highlight shared, 183; dashboards used to display, 147, 151t, 159, 181, 182e–183; definition of, 180; infographics used to convey, 181; make clear and meaningful points using your, 179–183

"Data dumps," 225

Debt-to-income ratio. *See* Financial assistance programs

Decisions: documentation of, 87; fair, ethical, and responsible use of evidence for, 195–196; shared evidence used to make, 177–179; underlying values serving as rationales for, 103–104

Degree Qualifications Profile (DQP) rubrics, 120, 124, 176

Delprino, R., 77

Deming, W. E., 191

Designing and Assessing Courses and Curricula: A Practical Guide (Diamond), 142

Designing Effective Assessment: Principles and Profiles of Good Practices (Banta, Jones, & Black), 158

Diamond, R. M., 142

Dickeson, R. C., 237

Dickey, J., 45

Diiorio, S., 227

DiPietro, M., 129, 131

Direct evidence of student learning, 157

Disciplinary (or specialized) accreditors, 12, 231–232

Display material. *See* Visuals

Disrespect: difficulty of turning around a culture of, 78; roots causes of, 43–44; strategies for transforming a culture of, 78–80

Distinctive traits, 102–103

Distrust, 43

Diversity: gauging responsiveness to student, 149; as historic strength of U.S. higher

education, 102–103; intercultural knowledge and skills related to, 123
Documentation: of evidence that supports culture of betterment, 202–206; keeping student work on file as part of, 206; organizing your report to accreditor and supporting, 216–220; of policies, evidence, and decisions, 87; on responsibilities and integration into organization, 87; sharing organizational, 88; supporting your report by providing good quality evidence, 220–223; templates used for, 203, 204e–205e
Dodson, D., 23
Dorman, R. H., 96
Drake University, 170
Drexel University, 188
Duncan, A., 5
Dunn, D. S., 35, 88
Dutchess Community College, 111

E

Eagan, K., 7
"Early warning systems," 114
Eaton, J. S., 20, 245
Economic development: gauging college contributions to, 149–150; higher education role in, 5–6; human capital as important driver of, 5; initiatives to address issues of, 9–10
Eder, D., 185
Education models: cautions regarding alternative, 73; competency-based programs, 71, 72; online courses and programs, 71, 72; problem-based learning, 71
Education Trust, 184, 193
Effective Grading: A Tool for Learning and Assessment in College (Walvoord & Anderson), 127, 142, 158, 196
Effective Reporting (Sanders & Filkins), 188
Effectiveness. *See* Institutional effectiveness
Eggleston, T., 71
Employer advisory councils, 55
Employers: employer perceptions of online and face-to-face degrees by Drexel University, 188; "hard" skills wanted by, 120–121; meeting the needs of future, 55, 124; "soft" skills wanted by, 121–122
Empowered college leadership, 91
Enterprise Rent-a-Car, 8
Equity ratio, 61
Essential activities: description of, 101; identify your college's, 101–102; mission creep expansion of, 102

Essential Outcomes, 120
"Establishing Academic Program Priorities" (Shirley & Volkwein), 237
Ethical judgment, 123, 158
Evans, J., 7
Evergreen College, 139
Evidence: additional information and resources on gathering, 165, 196; aim for reasonably accurate and truthful, 163–165; culture of betterment sustained through, 197–208; direct and indirect, 157; documentation of, 87–88, 202–206; to ensure and advance quality and effectiveness, 192–193; examples of accreditation report assertions and suitable, 220–221t; external and internal, 194; fair, ethical, and responsible use of, 195–196; "genuine inquiry" driver of good, 162; identifying and implementing improvements using, 167–176; "ineffables" form of, 157–158; make it accessible and easy to find, 186; numbers have meaning only when they are compared against other numbers, 169; preparing for time lag when examining, 194–195; prudent deployment of resources using, 193–195; refining goals and targets using, 195; stakeholder interest in specific types of student success, 148–149, 161–162; strategic planning used external and internal, 109; supporting your report to accreditors with documented, 220–223; SWOT analysis using, 110; tied to key goals, 162–163; transparency and sharing, 177–188; uses of good, 161–165; using the most current, 165; validity and reliability issues of, 163–164. *See also* Culture of evidence; Gauging success; Instruments; Measurement
Ewell, P., 37, 39, 96, 120, 172
Excellence. *See* Culture of excellence
Excelsior College, 198
External evidence, 194
External reviewers, 236–237

F

Faculty: advancing quality and effectiveness by, 192; assessment movement (1980s) involvement of, 46–47; challenge to become change agent, 39–40; common misunderstandings about academic freedom by, 44; creating culture of respect by tapping expertise of, 79; linchpin role of full-time, 63; marginalization of, 43; meeting the needs of internal stakeholders as, 56; monitoring how time is spent by, 67; offering stipends, fellowships, or merit pay for extraordinary work, 199–200; ongoing venues for discussions on quality by, 83; peer review by and of, 15–16; resistance to assessment by mediocre, 47; shared responsibility for student learning by students and, 132; supporting adjunct, 84–85; teaching-learning center (TLC) providing support ot, 83; watching for both turnover and stagnation of, 68. *See also* Human capital

Faculty promotion and tenure (P&T): benefits of assessment focus on, 47; documenting decisions on, 87; incorporating college priorities into criteria for, 198–199

Fain, P., 142

"Fair Assessment Practices: Giving Students Equitable Opportunities to Demonstrate Learning" (Suskie), 58

Fairness: building culture of respect through, 78; documenting "the rules of the game" and applying with, 87; evidence using ethically, responsibly, and with, 195–196

Federal financial responsibility composite scores, 62

Federal Occupational Outlook Handbook, 55

Feedback (professional development), 85

Fighting complacency barrier, 240, 243

Filkins, J., 188

Financial assistance programs: college's financial health required to support, 61; Higher Education Act (HEA) Title IV establishment of, 16, 61, 232; monitoring debt-to-income ratio of student loans from, 69–70, 149

Financial health: ensuring your college's, 59, 60–63; strategies to strengthen your college's, 201–202

Financial issues: creditworthiness score, 61–62; federal financial responsibility composite scores, 62; monitoring debt-to-income ratio of student loans, 69–70, 149; monitoring the impact of financial investment, 59, 68–69; stewardship related to, 59, 63–66. *See also* Budgets

Financial ratio analysis: creditworthiness score, 61–63; description of, 61

Fincher, J., 120

Finger Lakes Community College, 159

Fink, L. D., 120, 122, 136

Finley, A., 124

Fisher, P., 7, 57

Fitch, 62

Five cultures of quality: for defining program excellence, 32; as framework for program review, 230–231; interrelations of the, 31–32; overview of the, 25–33; when there is lack of financial support of, 37. *See also* Culture of quality; Quality; *specific culture*

Flipped classrooms, 109, 140

Focus and aspiration. *See* Culture of focus and aspiration

Forbes magazine list of America's Top Colleges, 184

"A Four-Step Plan to 'Right-Size' the Curriculum" (Moore and Whittaker), 73

Freshman Survey, 55

From Gathering to Using Assessment Results: Lessons from the Wabash National Study (Blaich & Wise), 208

Frye, N. E., 80

Fulcher, K. H., 206

"Fuzzy" terminology: as barrier to quality, 45; critical thinking as, 126; student learning outcomes and strategic goals, 112–113, 126–127

G

Gallaudet University, 134

Gallup, Inc., 120

Gardner, J. N., 83, 132

Gaston, P., 23, 120, 172

Gauging success: achievement of college purpose and goals component of, 150, 151t; contributions to the public good component of, 150; economic development contributions component of, 149–150; information used for, 148–149; measurements used for, 147; responsiveness to the changing college student component of, 149; student learning component of, 150–157. *See also* Evidence

General education: accreditation report on assessment of, 217–220; additional information and AAC&U resources on, 143, 152; definition of, 138; educational role of, 137–139; ensuring that requirement benefits outweigh barriers to graduation, 142; NEASC requirement for, 142; recommendations to fulfill potential of, 139

Georgetown University, 14

"Give Students a Compass" initiative (AAC&U), 139

Goals. *See* Strategic goals
Gold, L., 44
Gonick, L. S., 140
Gonyea, R. M., 129, 156
Governance. *See* Institutional governance
Government policymakers, 55–56
Grades, 156–157
Graduation rates (University of Alaska
　Anchorage), 188
Graphs, 180
Great Recession (2008–2009), 63
Greenfield, G. M., 132
Greenstone, M., 7

H
Hackman, J. D., 188
Hagemann, A., 57
Halonen, J. S., 35, 88
Halpern, D. F., 45
Hamilton College, 100, 125, 186
Hancock College, 84
"Hard" skills, 120–121
Harris, E., 180
Harris, J. T., 96
Hart Research Associates, 120, 121
Harvard Institute for Higher Education, 96
Hawthorne, J., 162
Haycock, K., 193
Healy, R. M., 212
The Hechinger Report, 4
Hendrickson, R. M., 96
Hess, F. M., 9
Hibschweiler, I., 193
Higher Ed News, 10
Higher education. *See* U.S. higher education
*Higher Education Accreditation: How It's
　Changing, Why It Must* (Gaston), 23
Higher Education Act (HEA): focus on
　evidence of outcomes in, 17–18; overview
　of the, 16–17; Title IV establishing
　financial assistance programs, 16, 61, 232;
　Title IV gatekeepers, 16, 17, 18, 221; U.S.
　Department of Education regulations for, 17
Higher Education Act (HEA) Amendments
　[1998], 18
Higher Education Opportunity Act (HEOA),
　12, 18
Higher Education Research Institute (HERI), 38
Higher Learning Commission (HLC) of the
　North Central Association of Colleges and
　Schools, 13, 19, 211
Hinton, K. E., 41, 105, 116

Historical perspective, 170
Honest communication: regarding appraisal
　of your college, 213–215; regarding college
　shortcomings in context, 223–224; sharing
　evidence with balanced and, 186–188. *See
　also* Integrity; Trust
Human capital: as economic development
　driver, 5; as one of the greatest college
　resources, 60; questions to ask about invest-
　ing in, 64. *See also* Administrators; Faculty
Humphreys, D., 81, 138
Hurtado, S., 7

I
Ikenberry, S. O., 37, 83, 94, 153, 155, 156,
　172, 180, 185, 186, 198
Improvement: accreditation functioning as a
　tool and lever for, 212; description of, 30;
　evidence used to identify and implement,
　167–176; failure to financially support,
　45; lack of active support for teaching, 37;
　value efforts to change, innovate, and seek,
　198–200. *See also* Betterment; Change;
　Culture of betterment
Independent college leadership, 91–92
Indianapolis Assessment Institute, 159
Indirect evidence of student learning, 157
Industry groups, 55
"Ineffables" measurements, 157–158
Infographics, 180, 181
Information: assessment information
　management systems for, 203; brightline
　used to highlight shared, 183; dashboards
　used to display, 147, 151t, 159, 181,
　182e–183; definition of, 180; infographics
　used to convey, 181; make clear and
　meaningful points using your, 179–183
Information literacy, 123
Information resources: on accreditors and
　accreditation reports, 227; on advancing
　cultures of evidence and betterment,
　208; on curricula, 142–143; on dashboard
　indicators, 159; on gathering evidence,
　165; on general education, 143, 152;
　on institutional governance, 88; on
　instruments, 158–159; on measurement,
　165; on presidential and board leadership,
　96; on program reviews, 237; on purpose,
　105; on sharing evidence, 188; on student
　learning assessment, 158–159; on student
　learning outcomes, 127; on student success,
　127; on student success targets, 176; on

tests and examinations, 165; on U.S. colleges, 183–184. *See also* Resources

Innovation: employer value of soft skill of, 122; value efforts to change, improve, and promote, 198–200

Inside Higher Ed, 10

Institution, 4

Institutional assessment: definition of, 148; gauging student success component of, 148–149; portfolios, 155; reflective writing, 155–156. *See also* Student learning assessment

Institutional Dashboards: Navigational Tool for Colleges and Universities (Terkla, Sharkness, Cohen, Roscoe, & Wiseman), 159, 208

Institutional effectiveness: definition of, 52, 148; evidence used to advance quality and, 192–193

Institutional governance: benefits of a collaborative and shared, 93–94; board leadership of, 89–96; as community of culture component, 85–87; definition of, 86; documentation of, 87–88; keep the structure lean and focused, 71; resources for additional information on, 88. *See also* Board leadership; Presidential leadership

"Institutional Vision, Values, and Mission: Foundational Filters for Inquiry" (Cordero de Noriega), 105

Instruments: additional information and resources on, 158–159; grades, 156–157; local tests and examinations, 156; rubrics, 120, 124, 142, 152–155, 167, 168e–169, 172, 176, 206–207e; subject-specific tests and examinations, 154; surveys and self-ratings, 55, 154, 156, 169, 170, 171, 173; tests to assess intellectual skills and competencies, 154; validity and reliability issues of, 163–165. *See also* Evidence; Measurement; Student learning assessment

Integrity: of college meeting its responsibilities, 52–58; as component of quality, 52; ensuring program review value and, 235–237. *See also* Honest communication

Intercultural knowledge and skills, 123

Internal evidence, 194

International Assembly for Collegiate Business Education (IACBE), 347

Inter/National Coalition for Electronic Portfolio Research, 159

International Journal of ePortfolio, 159

"Is it good for the kids?" principle, 162

Ittelson, J. C., 155

J

Jankowski, N., 37, 83, 94, 153, 155, 156, 172, 180, 185, 186, 188, 194, 198, 208

Jaschik, S., 38

Jobs, S., 138

John N. Gardner Institute for Excellence in Undergraduate Education, 132, 133, 143

Johnstone, R., 193

Johnstone, S. M., 73

Jones, E. A., 158, 237

Juniata College, 198

Justifiable success targets, 173–175

K

Kamlet, M. S., 115

Keeping promises, 52, 56

Kelly, A. P., 9

Kelly, P., 138

Kelsch, A., 162

Keup, J. R., 132

Key performance indicators, 147

Kinzie, J., 37, 83, 94, 129, 153, 155, 156, 172, 180, 185, 186, 194, 198, 208

Kiplinger's College Rankings, 184

Komives, S. R., 120

Korn, W. S., 7

Krathwohl, D. R., 122

Krupnick, M., 22

Kuh, G. D., 37, 44, 83, 94, 102, 129, 132, 139, 153, 155, 156, 172, 180, 185, 186, 193, 198, 220

L

LaGuardia Community College, 159, 199

Lane, J. E., 96

Leadership. *See* Administrators; Board leadership; Presidential leadership

LEAP (Liberal Education and America's Promise), 120, 124

Learning. *See* Student learning

Learning-centered classrooms, 132

Learning competencies, 123

Learning goals, 123

Learning objectives, 123

Learning outcomes. *See* Student learning outcomes

Lebanon Valley College, 23, 82, 125

LeBlanc, P., 5

Lederman, D., 7, 65, 243

Lehigh University, 14

Liberal arts education, 137–139

Liberal Education and America's Promise (LEAP), 120, 124
Light, T. P., 155
Lilly Conferences on College & University Teaching, 142, 243
Local community, 56
Local tests and examinations, 156
Long Island University (LIU), 84
Longanecker, D., 243
Looney, A., 7
Lovett, M. C., 129, 131
Lozano, J. B., 7, 36
Lumina Foundation, 10, 120

M

Magna Publications' Teaching Professor imprint, 142
Major Field Tests (MFTs), 154
Making Connections National Resource Center (LaGuardia Community College), 159
Making Student Learning Evidence Transparent: The State of the Art (Jankowski & Provezis), 188
Making the Grade: How Boards Can Ensure Academic Quality (Ewell), 96
Makker, S., 22
Malamud, O., 57
Marcus, J., 37
Marginalization, 43
Marti, C. N., 129
Massive open online courses (MOOCs), 72
Maxwell, D., 139
McCarthy, M. A., 35, 88
McClenney, K., 129
McCormick, A. C., 129, 156
McKendree University, 71, 124
McPherson, M., 56
Meaningful goals, 109
Measurement: additional information and resources on, 165; adopting common, 172; choose an appropriate perspective for comparison, 169–173; definition and various terminology used to describe, 147; different perspectives of, 170–173; numbers have meaning only when they are compared against other, 169; for tracking progress toward goals, 164–165; understanding that there is no perfect way to approach quality, 200–201; validity and reliability issues of, 163–165. *See also* Dashboard indicators; Evidence; Instruments
Measurement perspectives: historical, 170; peer, 171–173; remember that no

perspective is perfect, 173; strengths and weaknesses, 170–171; value-added, 171
Mediocrity problem, 47–48
Metrics, 147
Middle States Commission on Higher Education (MSCHE): accreditation standards, criteria, and requirements of, 211; description of, 13, 14; on identifying essential goals, 108
Midwestern Higher Education Compact, 127
Miller, M., 37, 39
Mintz, S., 57
"Minute paper," 156
Mission: description of, 101; McKendree University's learning outcomes tied to its, 124
Mission creep, 102
Mission statements: Carnegie Mellon University's, 115; definition of, 101; purpose communicated through, 100, 105; taking actions that support your, 45
Monetary support. *See* Budgets
Monitoring: are you bringing in the right people?, 67; how is time spent by faculty and staff, 67; impact of college investments, 68–69; watch for both high turnover and stagnation, 68; what proportion of revenues go toward meeting student needs, 66–67; what proportion of revenues go toward priorities, 66
MOOCs (massive open online courses), 72
Moody's, 62
Moore, C. A., 73
Morace, R., 193
Morrill, M. S., 57
Morrill, R., 40, 71, 80, 86, 110
Mortenson, T. G., 57
Muchin, S., 180

N

Narrow-mindedness, 43
NASDAQ, 92
National accreditation: as alternative to regional accreditation, 246; description of, 12–13
National accreditors, 12–13
National Advisory Committee on Institutional Quality and Integrity (NACIQI), 11, 18, 20, 21, 243
National Association of College and University Business Officers (NACUBO), 73
National Association of Independent Colleges and Universities (NAICU), 184

National Center for Education Statistics (NCES), 8

National Council Licensure Examination (NCLEX), 154

National Institute of Learning Outcomes Assessment (NILOA), 4, 152, 155, 172, 185, 186, 208

National Institute of Learning Outcomes Assessment (NILOA) Transparency Framework, 188

National Resource Center for the First-Year Experience and Students in Transition, 143

National Survey of Student Engagement (NSSE), 55, 154, 169, 170, 171, 173, 193

National Task Force on Institutional Accreditation, 15

Net income ratio, 62

New England Association of Schools and Colleges (NEASC): Commission on Institutions of Higher Education of, 13; general education requirements of, 142; on interrelationship of accreditation requirements, 31

New initiatives proposals, 233t–235t

New Leadership Alliance for Student Learning and Accountability (NLASLA), 243

New York Stock Exchange, 92

New York University, 14

Newell, M., 23

NILOA Transparency Framework, 188

Nodine, T., 196

Norman, M. K., 129, 131

North Central Association of Colleges and Schools, 13

Northwest Commission on Colleges and Universities (NWCCU), 13

Numbers. See Measurement

O

Oakton Community College, 100

Obama, B., 162

Objectives: definition of, 113; learning, 123. See also Strategic goals

O'Brien, P., 40

Observable action verbs, 113

O'Donnell, K., 102, 129, 132, 139, 193

Ohio State University, 71

Online courses/programs: cautions regarding implementing, 71, 73; Council of Regional Accrediting Commissions (C-RAC) guidelines for reviewing, 142; MOOCs (massive open online courses), 72; rubric of eight standards for, 142; student learning through, 140. See also Courses

Operational plans, 113–114

Orem, C. D., 206

Organisation for Economic Co-operation and Development (OECD), 6

Outcomes-Based Academic and Co-Curricular Program Review: A Compilation of Institutional Good Practices (Bresciani), 237

P

Pace University, 111

Palomba, C. A., 158, 159

Pascarella, E. T., 129, 1323

Patel, V., 240

Pearce, E., 103

Peer perspective, 171–173

Peer review, 15–16, 245

Penn, J. D., 206

Performance indicators, 147

Performance measures, 147

Persistence: definition of, 133; go-to resources on, 143; strategies to help student, 132–134; student-centered colleges' active focus on, 133

Petrides, L., 196

Pierce, S. R., 88

Pike, G., 163

Planning. See Strategic planning

Pockets of mediocrity, 47–48

Policies, documenting, 87

Portfolios, 155

"Preparing for Accreditation: Sowing the Seeds of Long-Term Change" (Diiorio), 227

Presidential leadership: additional information and resources on, 96; capacity and commitment of, 90–91; collaborative approach of, 93–94; description of, 89; empowered, 91; independent, 91–92; oversight entity of, 92–93; providing ongoing education and development to, 95; responsibilities of the, 89; six-point agenda for advancing quality by, 241–245. See also Administrators; Chief executive officers (CEOs); Institutional governance

President's Innovation Fund (Lebanon Valley College), 82

Priddy, L., 223

Primary reserve ratio, 61

"Principles for Developing Competency-Based Education Programs" (Johnstone and Soares), 73

Prioritizing Academic Programs and Services: Reallocating Resources to Achieve Strategic Balance (Dickeson), 237

Problem-based learning: caution regarding implementation of, 73; description of, 71; real-world problem solving skill and, 122

Professional development programs: for adjunct faculty, 84–85; constructive feedback to support, 85; focusing on college's priorities, 83–84; providing education on student learning assessment, 84; teaching-learning center (TLC) for, 83

Proficiency Profile (PP), 154, 172

"Program Review as a Model of Vision-Based Continuous Assessment: Principles and Profiles of Good Practice" (Banta, Jones, & Black), 237

Program reviews: additional information and resources on, 237; ensure integrity and value of, 235–237; five cultures of quality framework used for, 230–231; questions to consider for new initiative proposals and academic, 233t–235t; specialized accreditation as a form of, 231–232; three fundamental criteria framework for, 230. *See also* Accreditation reports

Promise keeping, 52, 56

Promotion. *See* Faculty promotion and tenure (P&T)

Provezis, S., 188, 194, 199, 208

Pryor, J. H., 7

Public good: accreditor service to the, 19; attitudes, values, and dispositions that contribute to the, 121; college responsibility to serve the, 52, 56–57, 186; gauging contributions to the, 150; liberal arts education serving the, 138; strategic goal focus on the, 108

Published instruments: rubrics, 124, 142, 152–155; subject-specific tests and examinations, 154; surveys of student experiences, 55, 154, 156; tests to assess intellectual skills and competencies, 154

Purpose: additional information on delineating your, 105; articulating your, 105; creating a distinctive sense of, 102–103; gauging achievement of goals and, 150; identifying essential activities to drive your, 101–102; mission statements that identify college, 45, 100, 101, 105; questions to ask to clearly delineate your, 99–100; students as your target clientele, 104; underlying values for decisions that drive, 103–104

"The Pursuit of Credibility" (Newell), 23

Q

Quality: continually defined by reputation and not effectiveness, 35–37; cost-effective measures of, 201–202; defined as component of the five cultures of quality, 26–31; evidence used to advance effectiveness and, 192–193; integrity component of, 52–58; interrelations among the five cultures for, 31–32; lack of money supporting five cultures of, 37; making a commitment to culture of excellence and, 25–26; as more important than quantity, 108; understanding there is no perfect measure of, 200–201; *U.S. News & World Report* college ranking list on, 35–36. *See also* Culture of quality; Five cultures of quality

Quality assurance: accreditation as relatively low-cost system of, 23; accreditation as source of information on, 21; college responsibility for, 52, 57–58; description of, 11; evidence used to advance quality and, 192–193. *See also* Accreditation

Quality barriers: culture relying on antecedents and anecdotes as, 45–46; emphasizing assessment over learning as, 46–47; failure to financially support improvement as, 45; fuzzy focus and aspirations as, 45; misunderstandings about academic freedom as, 44; pockets of mediocrity as, 47–48; silos as, 41–42, 241, 243–244

Quality Matters Program, 142

Quality of life, 121

Quality programs: five cultures of quality framework for reviewing, 230–231; three fundamental criteria framework for reviewing, 230; writing program review of, 231–237

Quality six-point agenda: break down silos, 41–42, 241, 243–244; encourage and support great teaching and learning, 240, 242–243; fight complacency, 240, 243; on how higher education leaders and others can help, 241245; know your stakeholders and be relevant and responsive to, 239–240, 241–242; put your money where your mouth is, 240, 243; tell meaningful stories of your successes, 241

Quantitative skills, 123

R

Real-world problem solving skills, 122

Reflect and regroup, 206

Reflective writing, 155–156

Regional accreditation: building reputation of national accreditation alternative to, 246; creating a competitive environment for, 246–247; description of, 12. *See also* Accreditation

Regional accreditors: college closures by, 22; commitment to traditional higher education values by, 14–15; description of, 12; internal discipline by, 15; labeled as "private clubs," 14, 15; list of the seven, 13; operating as think tanks, 244; organizational model followed by, 14. *See also* Accreditors

Regnier, P., 7

Relevance. *See* Culture of relevance

Reliability: accurate and truthful evidence, 163–164; definition of, 164

Reporting. *See* Sharing evidence

Research reports, 219t

Resource deployment monitoring: are you bringing in the right people?, 67; how is time spent by faculty and staff, 67; of the impact of your investments, 68–69; watch for both high turnover and stagnation, 68; what proportion of revenues go toward meeting student needs, 66–67; what proportion of revenues go toward priorities, 66

Resource deployment strategies: consider streamlining course and co-curricular offerings, 65–66; don't let efficiency adversely affect effectiveness, 70; evidence used to guide prudent, 193–195; fold evidence of efficiency into reviews and decisions, 70; keep the governance structure lean and focused, 71; monitor efficiency as well as effectiveness, 70; monitor the impact of your investments, 68–69; monitor where the money is going, 66–68; proceed carefully with alternative education models, 71–73; review low-enrollment courses, 65; scale back time spent on tangential activities, 65; stewardship practiced through efficient, 59

Resources: efficient deployment of college, 59, 69–73; on higher education developments, 10; key college responsibilities as central to deployment of, 64–65; recognize that people and their time are great, 60. *See also* Information resources; Stewardship

Responsibilities. *See* College responsibilities

Retention: definition of, 133; strategies to help student, 132–134

Return on investment: "college wage premium" (1970s to 2012), 7; of higher education, 5, 6–8

Reviewers: connect the dots for your, 226; cull irrelevant information for, 225; external, 236–237; keep your report an easy read, 226; make the case for compliance up front for your, 226; peer, 15–16, 245; provide a brief introduction to orient the, 225; respecting the time of your accreditation report, 224–226. *See also* Accreditation reports; Accreditors

Rhoades, G., 44

Rhodes, T. L., 124

Rivera, J. J., 175

Road trip analogy: on college cultures and quality, 26, 27–31; defining student success using the, 169

Robertson, J., 84

Rooney, J. J., 112

Root cause analysis: of culture of disrespect, 78; on life-long application of learning outcomes, 126

Roscoe, H. S., 159, 181, 208

Rotherham, A., 7, 56

Rubrics: American Council of Teachers of Foreign Languages (ACTFL) proficiency guidelines, 154; to appraise college's culture of betterment, 206–207e; Degree Qualifications Profile (DQP), 120, 124, 176; description and applications of, 152–154; of Quality Matters Programs for online courses, 142; results on a hypothetical written communication skills assessment, 167, 168e–169; VALUE, 124, 153, 154, 172, 176

S

Saenz, V. B., 7

Salluzzo, R., 73

Sams, A., 140

Sanders, L., 188

Santos, J. L., 7

Scaffolding, 131

Schneider, C. G., 120, 172

Scholarly research tradition: goals of, 39; process of change as foreign to the, 39–41

Scholarship of application: description of, 68; focus on solving real-world problems as, 102

Scholarship of discovery, 67

Scholarship of teaching, 68

Scholarship Reconsidered (Boyer), 68

Schramm, J. B., 7, 56

Sciences education, 137–139

Seaman, J., 140

Securities and Exchange Commission (SEC), 92

"Seizing the Initiative for Quality Education" (Bok), 96
Self-centeredness, 43
Self-ratings. *See* Surveys and self-ratings
Selingo, J., 10
"Seven Maxims for Institutional Researchers" (Hackman), 188
Sharing evidence: additional information and resources on, 188; designing structures and formats for, 177–179; dilemma of balancing quality and shortcomings when, 187–188; headings, subheadings, and hyperlinks used for, 183; honest and balanced approach to, 186–188; make clear and meaningful points when, 179–183; make the evidence easy to find when, 186; tell your story in your own voice when, 183–186; tools for drawing attention to key points when, 183. *See also* Stakeholders; Student learning assessment; Visuals
Sharkness, J., 159, 181, 208
Sharp, M. D., 120
Shenoy, G. F., 155, 156, 172, 180, 185, 186
Shirley, R. C., 230, 237
Shugart, S., 48
Shulman, L., 185
Sidebars, 180
Silos, 41–42, 241, 243–244
Six-point agenda. *See* Quality six-point agenda
Slippery Rock University, 125, 186
Smith, M., 44
Smith, N., 6, 7, 120
Soares, L., 73
Society for College and University Planning (SCUP), 105, 117, 159
"Soft" skills, 121–122
Southern Association of Colleges and Schools Commission on Colleges (SACS-COC), 13, 17
Specialized (or disciplinary) accreditors, 12, 231–232
Spellings Commission report (2006), 18, 183. *See also* Commission on the Future of Higher Education
St. Olaf College, 186
Staff: monitoring how time is spent by, 67; watching for both turnover and stagnation of, 68
Stagnation problem, 68
Stakeholders: accreditation perceived as not putting enough emphasis on needs of, 19–20; be relevant and responsive to your, 239–240, 241–242; college responsibility to know and meet needs of, 52, 54–56; concerns over student loans vs. ability to pay, 69–70; definition of, 51; honest and balanced communication with, 186–188; strategic goal focus on the needs of, 108; student success evidence wanted by, 148–149, 161–162. *See also* Sharing evidence
Standard & Poor's, 62
"Statement of Principles on Academic Freedom and Tenure" (AAUP), 44
Steen, L. A., 237
Stengel, R., 191
Stevenson University, 111
Stewardship: to deploy resources efficiently, 59, 69–73; to ensure your college's health and well-being, 59, 60–63; to monitor the impact of your investments, 59, 68–69; to monitor where your money is going, 59, 66–68; overview of the responsibilities of, 59; to put your money where your mouth is, 59, 63–66. *See also* College responsibilities; Resources
Storytelling: by Education Trust on changes implemented for successes, 193; of your successes, 241
Strategic aims, definition of, 107
Strategic directions, definition of, 107
Strategic Financial Analysis for Higher Education (Salluzzo and Tahey), 73
Strategic goals: articulating the destination in your, 111–113; be prepared to attune and adjust your, 116–117; dashboard for hypothetical college, 182e–183; definition of, 107; establishing key or, 107; evidence tied to key, 162–163; evidence used to refine, 195; "fuzzy," 45, 112–113, 126; gauging achievement of purpose of, 150; integrating your strategic plans and, 115–116; "LEAP goals" on student learning outcomes, 120, 124; meaningful, 109; measures used to tracking progress toward, 164–165; observable action verbs used to describe, 113; SUNY college of Environmental Science & Forestry's *Vision 2020* on, 108; 3-to-6 rule for, 115. *See also* Objectives; Student success targets
Strategic planning: collaborative deliberations as the heart of, 110; external and internal evidence used in, 109; identifying destinations in your, 108–110; Society for College and University Planning resource for, 105, 117

Strategic plans: be prepared to attune and adjust your, 116–117; budget support of your, 114; description of, 113; how to write and support a, 113–115; integrating your strategic goals and, 115–116; operational, 113–114; prioritizing activities of your, 115; when assessment is not included in, 45

Strengths and weaknesses perspective, 170–171

Strohl, J., 6, 7, 120

Student-centered college, 133

Student learning: advancements in the assessment of, 10; capstones used to facilitate, 131, 137, 202; deploying resources using evidence on, 194; designing curricula that supports, 134–137; direct and indirect evidence of, 157; emphasizing assessment over, 46–47; establishing goals and objectives for, 123; gauging student success and, 150–157; identifying strategies to help, 129–130t; non-traditional venues and modalities for, 139–140; problem-based, 71, 73; quality six-point agenda on encouraging and supporting, 240, 242–243; research and ventures on improving, 9; scaffolding used to facilitate, 131; sharing faculty and student responsibility for, 132; strategic goal focus on the, 108–109; student-centered colleges' active focus on, 133; student engagement in their own, 131; what is required for, 120–123. See also Learning

Student learning assessment: additional information and resources on, 158–159; additional resources and information on, 127; benefits of faculty promotion and tenure (P&T) focus of, 47; C-RAC guidelines for reviewing online courses, 142; Capella University evidence on, 188; emphasized over learning, 46–47; gauging success and evidence terminology instead of, 152; "ineffables" used to measure, 157–158; learning lessons from mistakes made in, 80; offering rewards and incentives for, 199–200; pervasive language of, 152; rubric results on a hypothetical written communication skills, 167, 168e–169; template for documenting nascent, 203, 204e–205e. See also Accreditation reports; Instruments; Sharing evidence

Student learning outcomes: additional information and resources on, 127; articulating your college, 125–127; Bloom's taxonomy framework for viewing, 122; definition of, 123; "early warning systems" on, 114; HEA focus on evidence of, 17–18; identifying your college, 123–124; integrating throughout your college, 127; "LEAP goals" on, 120, 124; U.S. News & World Report college ranking dependence on, 35–36. See also Student success

Student needs: identifying and meeting, 55; monitoring what proportion of revenues goes toward meeting, 66–67

Student success: additional information and resources on, 127; characteristics that define, 119–120; designing curricula that supports, 134–137; Education Trust's stories on changes implemented to improve, 193; gauging, 147–159; go-to resources on, 143; monitoring, 69; recognize and celebrate, 192; road trip analogy of, 169; stakeholder interest in specific types of evidence on, 148–149; strategies that drive persistence and completion for, 132–134; student-centered colleges' active focus on, 133. See also Student learning outcomes

Student success targets: additional information and resources on, 176; choose an appropriate perspective for comparison, 169–173; establish clear goals and, 176; evidence used to refine, 195; set a range of minimal and aspirational, 175; set both milestone and destination, 176; set justifiably rigorous, 173–175. See also Strategic goals

Student work documentation, 206

Students: changing demographics of, 6, 8–9; college responsibility to put first your, 52, 53–54; as college target clientele, 104; creating culture of respect by involving, 79; debt-to-income ratio of student loans taken by, 69–70, 149; facilitating college transfers of, 141–142; gauging responsiveness to the changing, 149; helping them to become successful, 129–143; identifying successful, 119–127; increasing number taking online courses, 140; initiatives to address changing demographics of, 9–10; shared responsibility for student learning by faculty and, 132; strategies that drive persistence and completion by, 132–134; swirl college pathway of many, 9. See also Alumni; Colleges

Subject-specific tests, 154

Successful students. See Student success

SUNY college of Environmental Science & Forestry, 111

SUNY college of Environmental Science & Forestry's *Vision 2020*, 108

Surveys and self-ratings: Community College Survey of Student Engagement (CCSSE), 55; Cooperative Institutional Research Program (CIRP) Freshman Survey, 55; description of, 154, 156; National Survey of Student Engagement (NSSE), 55, 154, 169, 170, 171, 173, 193; Your First College Year (YFCY) survey, 154

Suskie, L., 48, 54, 58, 82, 84, 90, 123, 126, 127, 131, 153, 155, 156, 158, 165, 169, 171, 176, 180, 186, 188, 195, 196, 201, 203, 208, 214, 223, 240, 241

Swain, M. S., 206

Swing, R. L., 208

Swirl college pathway, 9

SWOT analysis, 110

Syllabi: periodically reviewing, 137; template for a curriculum map for, 136e

T

Tables, 180

Tactical plans, 113

Tagg, J., 132

Tahey, P., 73

Targets. *See* Student success targets

Taylor, B., 103

Teaching excellence: the five cultures for defining, 32–33; McKendree University's Student Learning, Assessment, and Teaching Effectiveness Committee for, 71; quality six-point agenda on encouraging and supporting, 240, 242–243; scholarship of teaching and, 68. *See also* Culture of excellence

Teaching-learning center (TLC), 83

Teaching Professor (Magna Publications), 142

Technological tools, 203

Templates: considering documentation, 203; for documenting nascent student learning assessment processes, 203, 204e–205fig

Tenure. *See* Faculty promotion and tenure (P&T)

Terenzini, P. T., 129, 132

Terkla, D. G., 159, 181, 208

Tests and examinations: additional information and resources on, 165; assessing intellectual skills and competencies, 154; locally developed, 156; subject-specific, 154

Thayne, L., 82

3-to-6 rule, 115

Time lag: strategies for handling evidence examination, 194–195; when examining new evidence, 194

Time resource: monitoring how faculty and staff spend time, 67; recognize the value of your, 60

Tinto, V., 132

Title IV financial assistance programs, 16, 61, 221, 232

Title IV gatekeepers, 16, 18, 221

Total quality management, 192

Transparency: college duty related to, 58; definition of, 58; sharing evidence component of, 177–188

Transparency Framework (NILOA), 188

Transparent Pathways, Clear Outcomes: Using Disciplinary Tuning to Improve Teaching, Learning, and Student Success (MHEC), 127

"Trends in Higher Education" newsletter (SCUP), 117

Trust, 78–79. *See also* Honest communication

Tufte, E. R., 188

Turnover problem, 68

"20 questions that deans should ask their mathematics departments (or, that a sharp department will ask itself)" [Steen], 237

U

University and College Accountability Network (U-CAN), 184

University of Alaska Anchorage graduation rates, 188

University of Pennsylvania, 14

University of Phoenix, 104

University of Tennessee–Knoxville, 193

University of Wisconsin–Oshkosh, 102

U.S. Census Bureau, 6

U.S. Department of Education (ED): accreditation role of, 12; accreditors recognized by the, 16, 21–22; College Navigator of the, 184; creditworthiness score as calculated by ratios of the, 61–62; HEA regulations developed by, 17; Spellings Commission report (2006) issued by the, 18, 183; Title IV gatekeepers recognized by the, 16, 18, 221. *See also* Accreditation

U.S. higher education: Carnegie Classification of Institutions of Higher Education, 171; the changing college student issue of, 5, 8–9; cost, access, quality, productivity, and relevance problems of, 5; culture of isolation and reticence issue of, 5; culture of isolation prevalent in, 37–38; culture of reticence prevalent in, 38–39; diversity as one of the historic strengths of the, 102–103; economic development role of, 5–6; Great Recession (2008–2009) impact on, 63; initiatives to address economic and demographic changes in, 9–10; Obama's "Is it good for the kids?" principle guiding priorities of, 162; perceived shortcomings and failures of, 3; public information resources on, 183–184; quality assurance of, 11; return on investment of, 5, 6–8; U.S. population by age with post-secondary education, 6. *See also* Colleges

U.S. News & World Report College Compass, 184

U.S. News & World Report college ranking list, 35–36

Using Assessment Results: Promising Practices of Institutions That Do It Well (Baker, Jankowski, Provezis, & Kinzie), 208

Using Quality Benchmarks for Assessing and Developing Undergraduate Programs (Dunn, McCarthy, Baker, & Halonen), 88

V

Validity: of accurate and truthful evidence, 163–164; definition of, 163

Value-added perspective, 171

VALUE (Valid Assessment of Learning in Undergraduate Education) rubrics, 124, 153, 154, 172, 176

Values: contributing to the public good and quality of life, 121; description and function of, 103; effort to change, improve, innovate, 198–200; serving as rationales for college decisions, 103–104

Valuing Assessment : Cost-Benefit Considerations (Swing & Coogan), 208

Vanden Heuvel, L. N., 112

Vision, 107

Vision statements, 108

Visual Explanations: Images and Quantities, Evidence and Narrative (Tufte), 188

Visuals: balanced scorecards, 181; callout boxes, 180; dashboards, 147, 151t, 159, 181, 182e–183; graphs, 180; infographics, 180, 181; sidebars, 180; tables, 180. *See also* Sharing evidence

Volkwein, J. F., 230, 237

Voluntary Framework for Accountability (VFA), 184

Voluntary System of Accountability (VSA), 172, 184

W

Walvoord, B. E., 127, 142, 152, 156, 158, 159, 196, 208

Washington Monthly College Guide, 184

Western Association of Schools and Colleges Accrediting Commission for Community and Junior Colleges (ACCJC), 13

Western Association of Schools and Colleges Accrediting Commission for Senior Colleges and Universities (WASC Senior), 13, 19

Whittaker, B., 73

Wilmington University, 100

Wise, K. S., 39, 41, 200, 208, 240

Wiseman, M., 159, 181, 208

Wiseman, P., 120, 122

Wolff, R., 22–23, 242, 243

Wozniak, A. K., 57

Wright, B., 163

Y

Yeado, J., 193

Your First College Year (YFCY) survey, 154

If you enjoyed this book, you may also like these:

Assessing Student Learning:
A Common Sense Guide
by Linda Suskie,
Trudy W. Banta
ISBN: 9780470289648

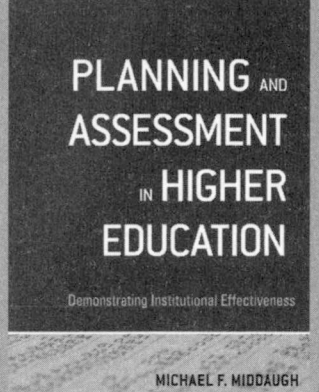

Planning and Assessment in
Higher Education: Demonstrating
Institutional Effectiveness
by Michael F. Middaugh
ISBN: 9780470400906

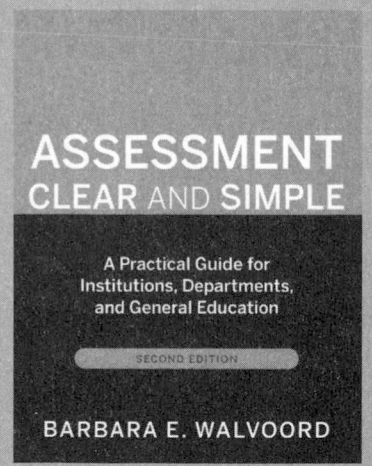

Assessment Clear and Simple:
A Practical Guide for Institutions,
Departments, and General
Education
by Barbara E. Walvoord
ISBN: 9780470541197

Using Quality Benchmarks for
Assessing and Developing
Undergraduate Programs
by Dana S. Dunn, Maureen A.
McCarthy, Suzanne C. Baker,
Jane S. Halonen, Peggy Maki
ISBN: 9780470405567

Want to connect?

Like us on Facebook
http://www.facebook.com/JBHigherEd

Subscribe to our newsletter
www.josseybass.com/go/higheredemail

Follow us on Twitter
http://twitter.com/JBHigherEd

Go to our Website
www.josseybass.com/highereducation